Making a Difference

As part of Houghton Mifflin's ongoing commitment to the environment, this text has been printed on recycled paper.

MAKING A DIFFERENCE

A Reader for Writers

Trudy Smoke
HUNTER COLLEGE

HOUGHTON MIFFLIN COMPANY   BOSTON   TORONTO
GENEVA, ILLINOIS   PALO ALTO   PRINCETON, NEW JERSEY

Sponsoring Editor: *Mary Jo Southern*
Managing Development Editor: *Melody Davies*
Associate Project Editor: *Danielle Carbonneau*
Senior Production/Design Coordinator: *Patricia Mahtani*
Senior Manufacturing Coordinator: *Priscilla Bailey*
Marketing Manager: *George Kane*

Cover Image: *Flight of the Butterfly,* 1955, Stanton Macdonald-Wright
Cover Design: *Karen Gourley Lehman*
Interior Design: *Dragonfly Design, Ron Kosciak*

ACKNOWLEDGMENTS:

KINCAID, JAMAICA "Annie John." Excerpt from "Gwen" from ANNIE JOHN by Jamaica Kincaid. Copyright © 1984, 1985 by Jamaica Kincaid. Reprinted by permission of Farrar, Straus & Giroux, Inc.

WALKER, ALICE "My Daughter Smokes," from LIVING BY THE WORD by Alice Walker. Copyright © 1987 by Alice Walker, reprinted by permission of Harcourt Brace & Company.

Acknowledgements are continued on pages 429–431, which constitute a continuation of the copyright page.

Copyright © 1994 by Houghton Mifflin Company. All rights reserved.

No part of this work may be reproduced or transmitted in any form or by any means, electronic or mechanical, including photocopying and recording, or by any information storage or retrieval system without the prior written permission of the copyright owner unless such copying is expressly permitted by federal copyright law. With the exception of non-profit transcription in Braille, Houghton Mifflin is not authorized to grant permission for further uses of copyrighted selections reprinted in this text without the permission of their owners. Permission must be obtained from the individual copyright owners as identified herein. Address requests for permission to make copies of Houghton Mifflin material to College Permissions, Houghton Mifflin Company, 222 Berkeley Street, Boston, MA 02116-3764.

Printed in the U.S.A.

Library of Congress Catalog Card Number: 93-78654

ISBN: 0-395-63682-5

23456789-AM-98 97 96 95 94

Contents

Guide to Focusing on the Writing Boxes — xiii

Preface — xv

Introduction — 3

The Writing Process — 4
    Inventing 4   Drafting 8   Revising 9   Editing 9

Your Writing Biography — 10

Revision Questions — 11

Editing Questions — 15

Theme 1
Connecting with the Family — 16

Making Discoveries — 19

Family Stories   ELIZABETH STONE — 20
    Family stories tell us about our backgrounds, provide role models, and give us self-esteem.

My Daughter Smokes ALICE WALKER 26
> Watching her daughter smoke makes the author think about how smoking has affected her family.

Only daughter SANDRA CISNEROS 34
> "I am the only daughter in a family of six sons. *That* explains everything."

My Father, "Dr. Pat" LINDSAY PATTERSON 41
> A brilliant, but unpredictable, father evokes fear and admiration in his two sons.

Amy Tan AMY LING 47
> Life experiences, good and bad, are the substance of this successful writer's work, and in writing about them she has learned to heal herself.

Mother Tongue AMY TAN 53
> The language one uses at home is not the same as the language one uses in school or in formal occasions, but it is the language of mother, family, and love.

Owls LEWIS NORDAN 64
> In telling about a childhood experience with his father, a man realizes the importance and danger of love.

Expanding Your Ideas: *Collaborative Writing Projects* 73

Theme 2
Fulfilling a Personal Dream 74

Making Discoveries 77

Contents

Running Toward Victory SUSANNA LEVIN 78
When she won the 800-meter run at the U.S. National Masters Track and Field Championships in July 1991, fifty-two-year-old Yvette La Vigne said she couldn't believe what she had done.

Iron Man DOUGLAS M. WEESE 84
Greg Barton from Washington State is an Olympic champion kayaker. Born with a physical limitation, he had the discipline and dedication to fulfill his dream of becoming an athlete.

Daughter of Invention JULIA ALVAREZ 90
Writing a speech creates family problems and turns out to be more complicated than Yolanda expected.

One Man's Kids DANIEL MEIER 100
Realizing his dream to be a first-grade schoolteacher is everything this young teacher expected, but his choice surprised some.

"They've Gotta Have Us" KAREN GRIGSBY BATES 107
John Singleton, the director of *Boyz N the Hood* discusses movie making, being black in Hollywood, and the power of writing to reach out to others.

This Lady Came Down from the Mountains ROBERT DRAPER 114
Lou Crabtree, a seventy-eight-year-old Appalachian woman, has fulfilled her dream to become a famous writer whose stories and poems tell about real-life experiences.

Three Thousand Dollars DAVID LIPSKY 123
A college student spends his tuition money and creates a family dilemma about paying for college.

Expanding Your Ideas: *Collaborative Writing Projects* 140

Theme 3
Affecting Someone Else's Life   142

Making Discoveries   145

Acts of Charity Spring from Rock of Honesty   WILLIAM ROBBINS   146
Returning a $400 check creates a friendship and a new meaning to life for two women and their families.

Thank You, M'am   LANGSTON HUGHES   152
A boy's attempt at robbery leads to a strange encounter and unexpected generosity.

Getting Involved   ANNA QUINDLEN   159
Decision to get involved in the near rape of a stranger leads to thoughts on involvement in our society.

I Wanted to Know Why   JONATHAN AMES   167
The suicide of an older, admired schoolboy alters the life of another boy.

Mothers with AIDS: A Love Story   PERRI KLASS   174
Pediatrician describes experiences of working with mothers and babies who have AIDS.

Another Kind of Sex Ed   SHARON A. SHEEHAN   182
Should sex education be about marriage, family, and commitment instead of only about condoms and birth control?

The Locker Room   SUSAN RICHARDS SHREVE   189
A group of strangers become friends as they reach out to one another.

Expanding Your Ideas: *Collaborative Writing Projects*   195

Contents

Theme 4
Changing Through Learning   198

Making Discoveries   201

The Sanctuary of School   LYNDA BARRY   202
A troubled child finds warmth, love, and her future vocation in school.

The Unwritten American Bargain   COLIN L. POWELL   209
The Chairman of the Joint Chiefs of Staff tells about the value of an education.

Annie John   JAMAICA KINCAID   216
A young girl describes how personal confidence and a writing assignment helped her succeed during her first day in a new school.

The Physician Who Healed Himself First   LINDA KRAMER   223
Becoming a famous pediatric surgeon was a struggle for Ben Carson, but his mother's courage and values helped him become the man he is today.

West Real   ALBERT ALVARO RÍOS   231
Born in Arizona into the two worlds of his Mexican father and British mother, Ríos arrived at school to be told that he may not speak Spanish.

Reading to Know   RICHARD RODRIGUEZ   239
What is the connection between reading and learning? Does one learn something only by reading it? Is an idea an idea only if it can be written down?

"It's Such A Pleasure to Learn"   WALLACE TERRY   248

    John Morton-Finney, the son of a former slave, at the age of 100 has eleven degrees, taught school until the age of eighty-one, and still practices law.

Expanding Your Ideas: *Collaborative Writing Projects*   257

Theme 5
Making a Social Commitment   258

Making Discoveries   261

The Poor Man's Superman, Scourge of Landlords   LARRY ROHTER   262

    Dressed in red tights, gold cape, and a mask, Super Barrio fights for the rights of the poor in Mexico City.

El Patrón   NASH CANDELARIA   269

    Sometimes standing up for one's rights means taking a stand against one's own father and against the system.

Aliza: Breaking Silence   ALIZA MOLDOFSKY   281

    A fourteen-year-old victim of incest tells her story to help others and to free herself.

The Right Thing to Do at the Time   GEORGE GARRETT   288

    A small-town southern lawyer believes in telling the truth and in taking on bigotry in his own way.

Pan Asian Repertory Theatre's Tisa Chang   FERN SIEGAL   297

    Tisa Chang established a theater that employs Asian-American actors and produces plays presenting Asian-American themes.

Contents

Meet Du Pont's 'In-House Conscience'   JOSEPH WEBER   303
    Faith A. Wohl has changed Du Pont into a company that cares for its employees and their families.

The Voice of the Land Is in Our Language   310
    Joseph Nicholas left his job as a barber to return to the Passamaquoddy Indian reservation to make sure that the language and culture of his people were preserved for future generations.

Expanding Your Ideas: *Collaborative Writing Projects*   317

Theme 6
Reaching Out to the Community   320

Making Discoveries   323

Coat for the Homeless Is Shelter, Too   MICHAEL DECOURCY HINDS   324
    A college professor requires his students to create projects that benefit the community. This time they have come up with a unique approach to helping the homeless.

Two Institutions Solve Common Problem   331
    Animal Therapy helps unwanted animals, and lonely seniors in a nursing home find love and affection.

Cinderellas in Toe Shoes   DAVID GROGAN AND JANE SUGDEN   338
    Diana Byer gives free ballet lessons to children from a homeless shelter.

Learning the Art of Bringing Up Baby   SALLY JOHNSON   344
    The Addison County Parent-Child Center program in Vermont helps parents learn to care for their children and get better jobs.

The Value of Volunteering   CHARLES A. LARSON   351
A nationwide commitment of two years on the part of every young American would help solve many of the country's problems and would benefit the volunteers as well.

Merit Gets Them Nowhere   ALBERT SHANKER   358
Women are better educated and more prepared for the job market than ever, but they still get paid less than men.

The Hiroshima Maiden   MARILYN KRYSL   365
Young victim of U.S. bombing of Hiroshima in August 1945 comes to the United States for medical help.

Expanding Your Ideas: *Collaborative Writing Project*   373

Moonlight Shadow   BANANA YOSHIMOTO   375
Through sharing her grief with others who have experienced pain, a young woman learns to cope with a great loss.

APPENDIX I
Focusing on Editing   407

APPENDIX II
Organizations and Activities to Make a Difference   419

Acknowledgments   429

Index   433

Guide to Focusing on the Writing Boxes

Theme 1
The Introduction	23
The Conclusion	31
General to Specific: Deduction	38
The First, Second, and Third Person	50
The Thesis Statement	60
Narration	69

Theme 2
Journalistic Writing	81
Cause and Effect	87
Point of View—Types of Narrators	97
Showing Versus Telling	104
Describing a Place	119

Theme 3
Writing a Step-by-Step Process Essay	149
Dialogue Writing	156

Writing a Definition Essay	163
Telling Facts from Opinions	179
Writing a Comparison-and-Contrast Essay	186

Theme 4

Chronological Order	206
Writing a Persuasion Essay	212
Describing a Person	228
Figures of Speech	236
Interviewing	254

Theme 5

Audience Awareness	278
Specific to General—Induction	284
Tone	293
Order of Importance	307
Analyzing	313

Theme 6

Describing an Object	328
Sentence Variety	335
Describing an Event	341
Making Connections Between Ideas	348
Writing a Summary	362
Word Choice	369

Preface

Making a Difference: A Reader for Writers is designed to empower students by improving their writing abilities and increasing their personal activism, thus providing a background for academic success. The readings have been carefully selected to enhance students' self-esteem and to help them realize that they can make a difference in their families, schools, communities, and in their own lives. By reading and writing about people who have discovered the strength of their personal resources—in writing, acting, listening, and caring—students can discover the power of determination. The apparatus in this book enables them to discuss, write, and explore the many ways in which they can use their talents and interests to make positive changes in the worlds in which they live.

SPECIAL FEATURES

Making a Difference includes several features intended to fulfill both the personal and academic needs of students.

- **Diverse, High Interest Reading Selections**   The readings have been chosen both as models of good writing and for their effectiveness in motivating students to solve problems, answer their own questions, and feel that they have something to contribute about real and relevant issues.

- **Coverage of the Writing Process**   The introduction describes the writing process and contains checklists of revision and editing questions that students can use as they revise their own writing. The apparatus leads students through prewriting, drafting, and revising.

- **Focus on Writing Instruction**   Boxed instructional tips within the exercises relate directly to the writing techniques modeled in the selection and required in the writing assignments. A guide to instructional boxes makes it easy for students to locate information on strategies that will be useful for college assignments across the disciplines.

- **Emphasis on Critical Thinking Skills**   Each selection is followed by questions designed to help students think critically about what they have read and to place the information in their personal context for understanding their world and evaluating the issues.

- **Collaborative Writing Projects**   Each theme ends with suggestions for collaborative projects in which small groups or the whole class can work together to do research, to interview, and to write.

- **A Longer Reading**   To encourage students to apply their reading and writing skills to longer, more involved selections, *Moonlight Shadow*, a novelette by the acclaimed young Japanese writer Banana Yoshimoto, has been included at the end of the text. Chosen for its high interest and readability, this story from *Kitchen* deals with love, loss, and the healing that comes from friendship and inner strength.

STRUCTURE OF THE TEXT

The Thematic Organization

The forty-two fiction and non-fiction selections are organized into six themes that highlight people who have overcome challenges and made a contribution to their world.

Connecting with the Family presents the experiences of living in, growing up in, and discovering one's individuality in a family.

Fulfilling a Personal Dream shows how different individuals found the discipline and perseverance to realize their ambitions and goals.

Preface

Affecting Someone Else's Life tells about various people who reached out to others in critical moments in their lives.

Changing Through Learning illustrates the influence of schooling on our values, our feelings, and our self-esteem.

Making a Social Commitment shows how standing up for what one believes can change the world in small and large ways.

Reaching Out to the Community focuses on people who have made the world a better place by looking for solutions to the complex issues of living together.

The Apparatus

The extensive apparatus focuses thinking, discussing, and writing on the issues and ideas presented in each theme.

Making Discoveries   Before beginning each theme, students explore how their personal experiences relate to the theme, discuss these with peers, and then share them with the entire class. Students learn to move from the specific to the general in their discovery of values and concepts.

Exploring Your Ideas   Before reading each selection, students write in their journals about their feelings, ideas, and prior knowledge about a subject.

Headnote about the Author   A brief background sketch of the author and the context in which the selection was written is provided.

Discussing the Selection   This section focuses students' attention on the content and meaning of what they have read.

Thinking Critically   Students are given an opportunity to explore personally and critically how what they have read fits into their prior experience and knowledge of the world.

Focusing on the Writing   These questions lead students to an awareness of writing conventions and how writers employ various techniques. This section includes the unique Focusing on the Writing boxes that highlight particular writing strategies.

Creating Your Own Text   These writing assignments provide opportunities for students to create their own writing based on the selection they have read, their journal writing, and the class discussions.

Revising Your Text   Students' attention is focused on ways of making their writing communicate their ideas and feelings more effectively.

Expanding Your Ideas   At the end of each theme, students work together on collaborative writing projects that place the theme in a more personal context.

The Appendixes

Focus on Editing   This appendix expands the "Focus on Editing" questions in the Introduction and explains the basic rules and conventions of correct writing.

Organizations and Activities to Make a Difference   This appendix lists resources, procedures, and organizations to give students strategies for becoming proactive. It includes names, addresses, phone numbers, and form letters to help students get started on making a difference in their communities.

ACKNOWLEDGMENTS

Writing a book is a process that involves the dedication and involvement of many people—from the early ideas to the realized product. *Making a Difference* would not exist without the support and creative vision of two superb editors, Susan Anker and Mary Jo Southern of Houghton Mifflin. The intelligence, patience, and editorial expertise of Managing Development Editor, Melody Davies, helped me turn an idea into a manuscript. As Project Editor, Danielle Carbonneau's artistic and aesthetic sensibility transformed this manuscript into a beautiful and usable book.

I would also like to thank the reviewers who participated in the process of making this book. Deborah Barberousse, Horry-Georgetown Technical College, SC; Pamela Morey Bourgeois, California State University-Northridge, CA; Marsha Childers, Delgado Community College, LA; Patricia Derby, Chabot College, CA; David Hanson, Minneapolis Community College, Minneapolis, MN; Patricia H. Johnson, J. Sargeant Reynolds Community College, VA; Julie Full-Lopez, Southern Illinois University at Edwardsville, IL; Katie Smith, Riverside Community College, CA; Judith L. Merrell, Community College of Allegheny-Boyce Campus, PA; Jane Maher, Nassau Community College, NY; Sandy Olsen, University of Dubuque, IA; Bonnie Orr, Wenatchee Valley College, WA; Dorothy G. Smith, Midlands Technical College, SC; Linda Weeks, Dyersburg State Community College, TN.

On a personal level, I would like to thank my colleagues in the Department of Academic Skills at Hunter College for their encouragement, support, and suggestions, but particularly, I would like to mention Teri Haas, Miriam Delgado, Gail Gordon, Ruth Rose, Vanita Vactor, Mary Small, and Bernice Baxter. Finally, I thank Alan Robbins, my husband and friend, for being there and making it all worthwhile.

Introduction

Making a Difference: A Reader for Writers contains reading selections and writing projects that will interest you, stimulate your thinking, and perhaps even inspire you to make changes in your own life and in the world that surrounds you.

People write for many reasons. We write to convey our thoughts and to express our feelings. We write to communicate with others. We write to learn, so we can understand ourselves and understand the world in which we live.

All the writing we do, whether in a classroom, at home, on the train, at work, or even at a party, takes place in a context. The *context* includes the place in which we write, the time in history in which we live, and the culture and society of which we are a part. Each of these influences the style and content of our writing.

All writing also has a *purpose*. The purpose can involve completing a paper in order to pass a course or writing personal notes to help us remember and learn new information. It may involve tasks such as writing letters to get into college, to apply for job interviews, to acquire information, or to keep in touch with important people. Or writing can involve such simple tasks as creating a shopping list or "things to do" list.

Thirdly, writing always involves an *audience*. Most of us write differently when we know our writing will be read by a teacher, a boss, a classmate, a friend, a lover, or just for ourselves. We choose our words and express our ideas in different ways depending on the audience for whom we are writing.

Finally, our personal *experiences* influence our writing by affecting our perceptions of the world. Each of us has a unique way of presenting ideas. No two people see any event in exactly the same way, nor do they write about the world in identical terms.

With these basic elements in mind, it is a good idea to ask yourself a few questions each time you get ready to write:

- Why am I writing this?
- Who will read this?
- What ideas do I want to communicate?

THE WRITING PROCESS

Writing is a process involving many activities. The writing process is frequently divided into four parts: **inventing, drafting, revising,** and **editing.** We can investigate each of these separately, but keep in mind that these different aspects of writing are interconnected and overlap throughout the process of writing because writing is a recursive process. This means that it involves starting, stopping, going back over ideas, and rewriting and revising while you are still working on your draft.

Inventing

The inventing part of the writing process involves choosing a subject and narrowing down that subject to a topic about which the writer has some knowledge and ideas.

Many writers have problems with this part of the process because they have trouble getting started. It is often difficult to invent or generate enough ideas about a topic to begin writing about it. Here are a few techniques you can use to come up with ideas and get started writing your papers.

Brainstorming To brainstorm, you do just what the words imply—you create a storm of ideas. To begin with, relax: this lets new ideas come into your mind. Do not judge your ideas at this point; just write them down. You can brainstorm by yourself, with a classmate, or in a small or large group. (One person can take notes, or you each may want to keep your own notes.) Experiment with brainstorming in different settings to see which way works best for you.

To brainstorm, start with a topic or subject that interests you. Then list any words and phrases that come into your mind as you think about the topic. Even if the ideas seem slightly off the subject or strange, write them down anyway. Let one idea lead to the next. Don't write down full sentences. Just write down the ideas as they occur.

After ten minutes or so of brainstorming, read through your list of ideas. Notice any words, phrases, or ideas that connect or are similar. Begin to organize your thoughts by copying them into groups of related words, phrases, or ideas.

As you read through these groups, write in the appropriate place any new ideas about your subject that occur to you. Set aside ideas that don't seem to fit in any category. Which groups have the most entries in them? Decide whether the groups with the smallest number of entries can be combined into another group or can be added to or dropped. Use these groups of words to develop a theme for your writing.

Once you have decided on a theme, organize the ideas from your brainstorming into an order that seems logical. Ask yourself the following questions:

- What do you want to communicate to your reader about your subject?
- Which specific idea is the main or most important point you want to make?
- What major ideas support, explain, or define your main point?
- In what order should you introduce your supporting ideas?
- Which ideas explain the supporting points?
- Which ideas still need more support?
- What idea belongs at the end of the draft to tie together your ideas and make your major point?

Copy your ideas into an organized brainstorming list that you can read and use. Use this list to help you write your first draft.

Clustering To cluster ideas, write a word or phrase from your topic on a blank piece of paper. By yourself or with a classmate, write down words, phrases, or ideas that come into your mind about the main idea. Write them on the page, and circle them. Draw a line connecting the circle to the main idea or to a related idea. (See the example.)

```
                    home  school  clustering      beginning  middle  end
        new
        ideas       freewriting                        main
                              rereading   organization  idea
        keeping        reading
        a journal                                           support
                    inventing         drafting
                                                            evidence
        brainstorming       writing
                    with
        alone      a peer                           revising
                         editing
                                                      reread
        punctuation              spelling      add                reorder
                                                new    delete     ideas
                                               ideas   ideas
        fragments  run-ons  grammar  verbs        rewrite
```

Once you have created this kind of cluster, look at it carefully, as you did with brainstorming, to organize the ideas you will use in your writing.

Freewriting   To do freewriting, put your pen or pencil on the page, and for five to ten minutes, without stopping, write anything that comes into your mind. Keep writing even if you are only writing nonsense words or ideas. You may even write "I can't think of anything to write" over and over again until you get a new idea. The purpose is to stimulate the flow of your words and ideas.

Some writers also do *focused freewriting*. To do this, write down a word, phrase, or topic. Look at it for about thirty seconds, put your pen to the paper, and begin to write. Write about whatever comes into your mind, but sometimes looking at the key word, phrase, or idea focuses your thinking and stimulates your writing.

After you finish freewriting, read over to yourself what you have written or share it with a classmate. Ask yourself

Introduction 7

- What ideas stand out in the freewriting? Why?
- Which ideas in this freewriting would you like to develop into a longer essay or story?
- How can you connect your ideas to the topic you are going to write about?
- What one idea from the ones you already selected can you use to get started writing?

If you do not find any ideas that relate to the topic you were trying to write about, write about something else—about an idea that has emerged from your freewriting. Discuss this idea with your teacher before going ahead with your essay or story.

Journalistic Thinking   To do journalistic thinking, most reporters for newspapers and magazines ask certain basic questions about their topic as they prepare to write about it: "Who?" "What?" "Where?" "When?" "Why?" and "How?"

Before you begin writing, copy down these words, skipping lines between them. Then, using each of these words, make a list of questions relating to your topic. For example, if you are writing about a person you can ask

- WHO is this essay about?
- WHAT happened to this person?
- WHERE did it happen?
- WHEN did it happen?
- WHY is it important? WHY should my reader be interested in my story?
- HOW did this event affect the person? HOW do I want it to affect the reader?

For practice, also write other questions that you could ask that would be helpful if you were writing about a place or an event.

When you use this technique to help you get started, just write down the ideas, words, or phrases that will help you think about and focus on your topic. Read through these answers before writing your first draft. The answers will help you develop new ideas about the topic.

Keeping a Journal   Experiment with keeping several types of journals for different purposes. Many writers keep journals or notebooks to help them remember their ideas. Some people keep daily journals to record their experiences or remember important events. Some people keep special journals for exploring ideas or feelings.

Each chapter in this book begins with a suggestion for writing in your own journal. You also should write in your journal after you have read each selection. When you do, think about the following questions:

- Have your ideas changed because of the reading?
- Did you learn anything in the reading?
- Do you have a quotation from the reading that you want to save? If so, copy it into your journal and write about why you want to remember it.

Reading To get the most out of reading, keep in mind the idea that writing and reading are interconnected. Reading helps stimulate your ideas and make connections to new ideas. Before you begin to write, it may be useful to re-read selections from this or other books. To inspire new thoughts and make connections, it can also be helpful to read a classmate's writing. As part of the writing process, most writers go back and reread what they have already written. You may want to reread earlier journal entries or other pieces of personal writing. Good writers are usually good readers.

Keep in mind that the invention techniques just described will help you to write about something that really interests you or about which you have something to write. If you can't answer the questions, or if you get bored as you are doing it, consider moving on to another topic. These techniques will stop you from wasting your time trying to write an essay or story about which you have little to write. They will also help you find ideas about subjects that interest you.

Drafting

Drafting is the part of the writing process in which the first draft or rough version is written. Your work in the invention stage will help you construct a good first draft. So before beginning the draft, look back over the notes you wrote during the invention stage.

These notes are useful for planning your first draft. Make a decision about your main idea or the most important point you want to make in your essay.

Introduction 9

Or, if you are writing a story, decide on the natural point at which to begin. Mark these places in your notes with a star (*) so you can find them easily.

Keep in mind that writing has a *Beginning*, a *Middle*, and an *End*. It is useful to develop a basic idea of these three parts of your writing before you begin. Look through your notes and order your ideas by writing letters (*B, M, E*, for instance) or numbers or by drawing arrows in your notes. Since these are for you to use, it is only important that you understand your own code.

Write notes to yourself about specific details or ideas that you want to develop or add as you write the draft.

These codes and notes are to help you organize. Be prepared to make changes as you write. You may discover new ideas or find that your original organizing structure does not work. Having thought out what you want to write helps you **focus** on your main idea, **find evidence and support** for what you want to say, and **come to a conclusion** when you have made your point. Keep in mind that this is a rough or first draft. After rereading it alone or with a friend, most writers revise their first draft.

Revising

The revising part of the writing process involves rereading and rethinking what has already been written. Almost all writers make some changes as they go along. The changes may involve vocabulary choice, word order, sentence order, and/or paragraph order. They may even involve eliminating whole ideas and replacing them with new ones. Revising occurs both during the drafting stage and after the first draft is completed. Some writers prefer to reread their completed first drafts with a classmate or peer; others prefer to do this alone. To help them revise their writing, many writers use revision questions such as the ones on pages 11 to 14.

Editing

Editing is the stage in the writing process that involves proofreading to locate and correct errors in grammar, word choice, spelling, punctuation, and style. The goal is to create a text that is as correct as possible so that readers will understand the ideas presented in your writing. Use the editing questions on page 15 to help you proofread and edit. If you have specific difficulties, use the "Focus on Editing" section on page 407 to help you improve your editing abilities.

YOUR WRITING BIOGRAPHY

You have been reading and writing for many years. Although some experiences were more successful than others, they all have influenced you in some way. To understand yourself as a writer, it is helpful to think about some of these earlier experiences. Use the following questions to help you focus on your writing process. To help you write your writing and reading biography, answer only the questions that are appropriate to you.

1. What kind of writing do you do the most? When do you do it? Is there any special place in which you like to write?
2. What is the most interesting writing assignment you ever had in school? What class was it in? How did you go about fulfilling the assignment? What did you like the most about it?
3. What is the first time you remember listening to someone reading a story to you? What do you remember about the story? Where were you? How did you feel?
4. What was your favorite story when you were younger? Why did you like this story?
5. What kind of material do you most enjoy reading? What favorite book or story have you read recently? What did you like about it?
6. How did you learn to read? How did the experience make you feel?
7. How did you learn to write? How did the experience make you feel?
8. Do you prefer to write at home or in school? Why?
9. What experience in writing stands out in your mind? Why is this important to you?
10. Is there anything you would like to change about your writing and reading habits? Why? What would help you make this change?

R E V I S I O N   Q U E S T I O N S
WRITING AN ESSAY: WORKING WITH A PEER

WRITER'S NAME: _____

READER'S NAME: _____

TITLE OR SUBJECT OF ESSAY: _____

DRAFT NUMBER: _____

DATE: _____

1. What did you like most in this essay?

2. What in the beginning of the essay makes you want to read more?

3. What is the main idea of the essay?

4. What specific evidence or ideas did the writer use to support that main idea?

5. What example or evidence was the strongest? Why?

6. What example or evidence was the weakest? Why?

7. How does the essay end? What in the ending ties the ideas from the beginning and middle together?

8. Were there parts of the essay you did not understand? Were there any words that confused you? Does the writer repeat any ideas too many times?

9. What would you like to know more about when the writer revises this essay?

10. What did you learn about the writer or the subject from reading this essay?

REVISION QUESTIONS
WRITING AN ESSAY: WORKING ALONE

WRITER'S NAME: _____

TITLE OR SUBJECT OF ESSAY: _____

DRAFT NUMBER: _____

DATE: _____

1. What do you like most in this essay?

2. What did you include in the beginning of the essay to make someone want to read more?

3. What is the main idea of the essay?

4. What specific evidence or ideas did you use to support that main idea?

5. What example or evidence was strongest? Why?

6. What example or evidence was weakest? How can you change it and make it stronger?

7. How does the essay end? What in the ending ties together or restates the ideas from the beginning and middle?

8. What did you learn about yourself or your subject from writing this essay?

REVISION QUESTIONS
WRITING A STORY: WORKING WITH A PEER

WRITER'S NAME: _____

READER'S NAME: _____

TITLE OR SUBJECT OF STORY: _____

DRAFT NUMBER: _____

DATE: _____

1. What specific details in this story do you remember? Why?

2. What characteristics of the person(s) described stand out in your mind? Why?

3. If there are several characters, which did you like the most? Which did you like the least? Explain your choices to the writer.

4. What do you recall about the place where the events occurred? What specific words or phrases helped you to see or feel the place from the description given by the writer?

5. What is the mood or feeling of the story? What words or ideas in the story make you feel this way?

6. List two descriptive words or phrases that were meaningful to you as a reader. Explain your choices.

7. Was there anything in the story that you did not understand or could not follow?

8. What could the writer add to make this story stronger?

9. What could the writer delete to make the story stronger?

10. What did you learn from reading this story?

REVISION QUESTIONS
WRITING A STORY: WORKING ALONE

WRITER'S NAME: _____

TITLE OR SUBJECT OF STORY: _____

DRAFT NUMBER: _____

DATE: _____

1. What specific details in this story are most important to you? How did you make them stand out in your writing?

2. What characteristics did you include to make each person stand out as an individual?

3. If there are several characters, which one did you like most? Which one did you like least? How do these preferences come across in your writing?

4. What specific words or phrases did you use to help your reader see or feel the place in which your story is set?

5. What is the mood or feeling of the story? What words or ideas in the story did you use to create this feeling?

6. List two descriptive words or phrases that were meaningful to you as a writer. Explain your choices.

7. Is there part of the story that does not seem clear? What can you do to explain this part better?

8. What could you add to make this story more powerful and affecting?

9. What could you delete to make this story stronger?

10. What did you learn from writing this story?

EDITING QUESTIONS

WRITER'S NAME: _____

TITLE OF DRAFT: _____

DRAFT NUMBER: _____

DATE: _____

1. Is each paragraph indented?

2. Does each sentence begin with a capital letter? Did you capitalize all of the words that need capitalizing? (See page 408 for a list.)

3. Does each sentence end with one of the following punctuation marks: period, question mark, or exclamation mark?

4. Is each sentence complete with a subject and a verb?

5. Does each verb agree with its subject? Does each verb have a final "-s" or "-ed" when necessary?

6. Are there any fragments? (Be careful when you use such words as *although, because, if, when, who,* or *that.* See page 411.)

7. Are there any run-on sentences or comma splices?

8. Do your pronouns (*I, he, she, it, they, we, you, her, his, them, theirs, its*) agree with the nouns to which they refer?

9. Is your voice consistent? (If you use *he, she,* or *they,* for example, you should not change to *you* or *we.*)

10. Are all the words spelled correctly? (Use a dictionary or the spell-check feature on your computer to help with this task.)

11. Did you choose the best words to convey your meaning? Did you eliminate biased or sexist language?

12. Did you overuse words? Could some of these words be replaced with a synonym or a pronoun?

Our relationships with our families are our first relationships with others in the world. From them, we learn about who we are and about who we can be.

Theme 1

Connecting with the Family

Readings

"Family Stories"
BY ELIZABETH STONE

"My Daughter Smokes"
BY ALICE WALKER

"Only daughter"
BY SANDRA CISNEROS

"My Father, 'Dr. Pat'"
BY LINDSAY PATTERSON

"Amy Tan"
BY AMY LING

"Mother Tongue"
BY AMY TAN

"Owls"
BY LEWIS NORDAN

"Family Stories," by Elizabeth Stone, explains the values of writing our family stories. She writes about her great-grandmother and how the stories she heard about her have made a difference in Stone's life today.

In "My Daughter Smokes," Alice Walker uses writing to examine the destructive force of smoking and tobacco in her family. Her essay helped convince her daughter to stop smoking.

"Only daughter," by Sandra Cisneros, examines the relationship of a father and daughter who finally communicate through her writing and his pride in her work.

"My Father, 'Dr. Pat,'" by Lindsay Patterson, is a memoir about a young man and his successful, but demanding, father. In sharing his father's eccentricities, Patterson comes to a better understanding of his father's motivations and desires.

In her minibiography "Amy Tan," Amy Ling shows how Tan's childhood experiences have contributed to the themes of her writing.

In "Mother Tongue," Amy Tan describes how her relationship with her mother is revealed in the language in which they communicate.

"Owls," by Lewis Nordan, is a story about a childhood memory that may or may not be true. Through the recollection of this memory, the narrator reflects on the ways that our early lives enable us to understand and love one another.

Making Discoveries

In Your Journal

Write in your journal about a family that you have seen on television or in the movies, or have read about in a book that matches your idea of what a family should be. Describe what you like about this family. Describe how people talk to each other in the family. Use one story from their lives to illustrate how they resolve problems.

With a Classmate

Talk to your classmate about the family you have chosen. Explain why you chose this family. What do the families you each have chosen have in common? In what ways are they different?

With Your Class

Discuss some of the families you selected. Using specific examples, what do the families have in common? How do they differ? Arrange the specific details into general categories that can be used to describe families. Make a list of these general categories. What does this list tell you about what the people in your class value in family life?

EXPLORING YOUR IDEAS

Think back into your childhood, to hearing someone tell a story about a person in your family. Write as much as you can remember of the story and the person(s) who told the story. Where were you when you heard it? Were you supposed to be listening? What part of the story did you enjoy most? What did the story make you feel about your family?

Family Stories

ELIZABETH STONE

The following is from Elizabeth Stone's book *Black Sheep and Kissing Cousins: How Our Family Stories Shape Us*, published in 1988. It describes the special power of writing and sharing family stories to understand our families and ourselves. Stone is an associate professor of English and media studies at Fordham University's College at Lincoln Center in New York City.

The storyteller takes what he tells from experience—his own or that reported by others. And he in turn makes it the experience of those who are listening to his tale.

—WALTER BENJAMIN,
"The Storyteller," in *Illuminations*

In the beginning, as far back in my family as anyone could go, was my great-grandmother, and her name was Annunziata. In the next generation, it would be my grandmother's first name. In the generation after that, in its anglicized form, Nancy, it would be my aunt's first name and my mother's middle name, and in the generation after that, my sister's middle name as well. I never met that first Annunziata, but my mother often told me a family story about her which, as a child, I knew as well as I knew the story of Cinderella and loved better.

Annunziata was the daughter of a rich landowner in Messina, Sicily [Italy], so the story went, and she fell in love with the town postman, a poor but talented man, able to play any musical instrument he laid eyes on. Her father heard about this romance and forbade them to see each other. So in the middle of one night—and then came the line I always waited for with a thrill of pleasure—she ran off with him in her shift.

I didn't know what a shift was and didn't want my settled version of the story disrupted by any new information. I loved the scene as I saw it: in the background was a house with a telltale ladder leaning against the second-story window. In the foreground was my great-grandmother, like some pre-Raphaelite maiden, dressed in a garment white and diaphanous and flowing, holding the hand of her beloved as she ran through a field at dawn, toward her future, toward me.

As a child, I was on very close terms with that story. I loved and admired my family—my grandmother especially—and as I saw it, her mother had been the start of us all. I never thought about any of my other great-grandparents or who they were. My grandfather, my mother's father, had died long before I was born; so I didn't think about him in any way that would bring him or his parents to life for me. As for my father, his parents had come from Austria, but he wasn't close to them, so I certainly wasn't. Nothing to build on there.

As a further refinement, I have to add that I paid absolutely no attention to the framed picture of my great-grandmother hanging over my grandmother's bed. That was just an old woman who, despite the fact that she happened to look like Sitting Bull, was of no interest to me. It was years before I realized that the person in the frame and the one in the story were the same. For me, it was always the stories that held the spirit and meaning of our family.

The first appeal of that story, then, was that it seemed to be the story of our genesis as a family. But there was a second appeal as well, and it was that my great-grandmother was everything I would have made her if I were inventing her. She was spunky, dazzlingly defiant, and I was sure, beautiful. Later, when I understood more about class and money, I admired her for having chosen my poor but talented great-grandfather in the first place. She was principled and egalitarian, someone I wanted to be like, hoped maybe I already was a little like, and most important, felt I *could* be like. She wasn't distant like a film star or imaginary like a fairy-tale heroine. She was real. And she was my relative.

Other family stories stayed with me, too. Some were old and ancestral but some were new, about my mother's generation or mine. None was elaborately plotted; some relied only on a well-developed scene—like the one in which my great-grandfather and his half-dozen sons were playing music after dinner in the courtyard as people came "from miles around" to listen. And still others were simply characterizations of people—"you had one ancestor who was a court musician" or "you had another ancestor who was an aide to Garibaldi." These qualified as stories in the way haiku qualify as poems. Almost any bit of lore about a family member, living or dead, qualifies as a family story—as long as it's significant, as long as it has worked its way into the family canon to be told and retold.

These stories last not because they're entertaining, though they may be; they last because in ways large and small they matter. They provide the family with esteem because they often show family members in an attractive light or define the family in a flattering way. They also give messages and instructions; they offer blueprints and ideals; they issue warnings and prohibitions. And when they no longer serve, they disappear. ■

DISCUSSING THE SELECTION

1. In paragraphs 1 and 2, Stone provides details that she thinks will make her readers interested in reading more. What details does Stone tell her readers about her great-grandmother?

2. Why does Stone perceive her great-grandmother as the "start of us all"? What evidence does she give to support this idea?

3. What particular qualities does Stone credit to her great-grandmother? How do you explain her reaction to her great-grandmother's photograph?

4. According to Stone, what are some of the reasons why family stories last?

Stone *Family Stories* 23

THINKING CRITICALLY

1. Stone tells her readers that "Annunziata" and its anglicized version, "Nancy," are popular names in her family. What is the origin of your name? Were you named after a family member? If so, what do you know about that person?

2. Stone admires her great-grandmother and views her as a role model. Who in your family serves as a role model or guide for you? Tell the story of this person to the class so they will understand this person's importance in your life.

3. In your experience, in what ways do family stories have different meanings for children and for adults?

4. Stone states that as a child, she didn't want her "settled version" of the story of her great-grandmother disrupted by new information. Many children feel this way. Have you ever had a similar experience when you tell stories to children you know?

FOCUSING ON THE WRITING

The Introduction p12

The introductory paragraph is important to the writer and to the reader. It should

- gain the reader's interest so the reader will want to read more.
- present the thesis or point of view of the essay.
- present the major ideas that will be developed in the rest of the essay.

Writers can use a variety of techniques to introduce their ideas, including

- telling a story.

- asking a question.
- making a general statement.
- quoting from a respected source.
- defining a word or concept.

1. Which techniques does Stone use to introduce this selection? What is the purpose of including the Walter Benjamin quotation? How did it make you feel as a reader?

2. Using another of the techniques described in the box, rewrite the introduction to this selection. Then compare the two introductions. Which do you prefer, and why?

3. One way writers make their points is by illustrating their ideas with stories or anecdotes. How does Annunziata's story illustrate Stone's point that family stories provide esteem?

4. Where does the first transition from Stone's personal family story to her general idea about family stories occur? In what other parts of the selection does Stone make the transition from the personal to the general? How do these transitions affect you as a reader?

CREATING YOUR TEXT

1. Write a family story that is important to you. Reread the journal entry you wrote before you read the Stone selection. The journal entry may suggest the story you want to develop further. Include as many details as you can recall from the story. Describe the people involved, the place in which the story occurred, and the step-by-step events of the story. In your conclusion, explain why this story is important to your understanding of your family. Share some of these family stories with your class.

2. Write a story about family events that you remember happening one way but that your family describes in a different way. Describe the two versions in detail (read the directions for the preceding exercise). In your conclusion, explain why you think the story has changed over time and what you think this story means to your family. Share some of these family stories with your class.

3. Write an essay describing some of the family stories you have listened to in class. What do these stories have in common? In your conclusion, explain why you remember or prefer particular stories.

love story
harmony!-

REVISING YOUR TEXT

Share your first draft with a classmate. Looking at the revision questions on page 11 or 13, decide what to keep and what changes to make when you write your second draft. Share your second draft with your class.

Focus on your introduction. Try writing several introductions using different techniques mentioned in the box on pages 23–24. Read them over with a classmate to help you decide which is most effective.

EXPLORING YOUR IDEAS

Have you ever done anything that upset or disappointed your family? Write in your journal about what you did, whom it upset, and how you dealt with the problem. What did you learn about yourself from the experience?

My Daughter Smokes

ALICE WALKER

Born in Georgia, Alice Walker now lives north of San Francisco, California. She writes essays, poems, and short stories, but is best known for her novel *The Color Purple*. She has won many awards for her writing. "My Daughter Smokes" was originally published in her book of essays, *Living by the Word* (1988).

My daughter smokes. While she is doing her homework, her feet on the bench in front of her and her calculator clicking out answers to her algebra problems, I am looking at the half-empty package of Camels tossed carelessly close at hand. Camels. I pick them up, take them into the kitchen, where the light is better, and study them—they're filtered, for which I am grateful. My heart feels terrible. I want to weep. In fact, I do weep a little, standing there by the stove holding one of the instruments, so white, so precisely rolled, that could cause my daughter's death. When she smoked Marlboros and Players I hardened myself against feeling so bad; nobody I knew ever smoked these brands.

She doesn't know this, but it was Camels that my father, her grandfather, smoked. But before he smoked "ready-mades"—when he was very young and very poor, with eyes like lanterns—he smoked Prince Albert tobacco in cigarettes he rolled himself. I remember the bright-red tobacco tin, with a picture of Queen Victoria's consort, Prince Albert, dressed in a black frock coat and carrying a cane.

The tobacco was dark brown, pungent, slightly bitter. I tasted it more than once as a child, and the discarded tins could be used for a number of things; to keep buttons and shoelaces in, to store seeds, and best of all, to hold worms for the rare times my father took us fishing.

By the late forties and fifties no one rolled his own anymore (and few women smoked) in my hometown, Eatonton, Georgia. The tobacco industry, coupled with Hollywood movies in which both hero and heroine smoked like chimneys, won over completely people like my father, who were hopelessly addicted to cigarettes. He never looked as dapper as Prince Albert, though; he continued to look like a poor, overweight, overworked colored man with too large a family; black, with a very white cigarette stuck in his mouth.

I do not remember when he started to cough. Perhaps it was unnoticeable at first. A little hacking in the morning as he lit his first cigarette upon getting out of bed. By the time I was my daughter's age, his breath was a wheeze, embarrassing to hear; he could not climb stairs without resting every third or fourth step. It was not unusual for him to cough for an hour.

It is hard to believe there was a time when people did not understand that cigarette smoking is an addiction. I wondered aloud once to my sister—who is perennially trying to quit—whether our father realized this. I wondered how she, a smoker since high school, viewed her own habit.

It was our father who gave her her first cigarette, one day when she had taken water to him in the fields.

"I always wondered why he did that," she said, puzzled, and with some bitterness.

"What did he say?" I asked.

"That he didn't want me to go to anyone else for them," she said, "which never really crossed my mind."

So he was aware it was addictive, I thought, though as annoyed as she that he assumed she would be interested.

I began smoking in eleventh grade, also the year I drank numerous bottles of terrible, sweet, very cheap wine. My friends and I, all boys for this venture, bought our supplies from a man who ran a segregated bar and liquor store on the outskirts of town. Over the entrance there was a large sign that said COLORED. We were not permitted to drink there, only to buy. I smoked Kools, because my sister did. By then I thought her toxic darkened lips and gums glamorous. However, my body simply would not tolerate smoke. After six months I had a chronic sore throat. I gave up smoking, gladly. Because it was a ritual with my buddies—Murl, Leon, and "Dog" Farley—I continued to drink wine.

My father died from "the poor man's friend," pneumonia, one hard winter when his bronchitis and emphysema had left him low. I doubt he had much lung left at all, after coughing for so many years. He had so little breath that, during his last years, he was always leaning on something. I remember once, at a family reunion, when my daughter was two, that my father picked her up for a minute—long enough for me to photograph them—but the effort was obvious. Near the very end of his life, and largely because he had no more lungs, he quit smoking. He gained a couple of pounds, but by then he was so emaciated no one noticed.

When I travel to Third World countries I see many people like my father and daughter. There are large billboards directed at them both: the tough, "take-charge," or dapper older man, the glamorous, "worldly" young woman, both puffing away. In these poor countries, as in American ghettos and on reservations, money that should be spent for food goes instead to the tobacco companies; over time, people starve themselves of both food and air, effectively weakening and addicting their children, eventually eradicating themselves. I read in the newspaper and in my gardening magazine that cigarette butts are so toxic that if a baby swallows one, it is likely to die, and that the boiled water from a bunch of them makes an effective insecticide.

My daughter would like to quit, she says. We both know the statistics are against her; most people who try to quit smoking do not succeed.[1]

There is a deep hurt that I feel as a mother. Some days it is a feeling of futility. I remember how carefully I ate when I was pregnant, how patiently I taught my daughter how to cross a street safely. For what, I sometimes wonder; so that she can wheeze through most of her life feeling half her strength, and then die of self-poisoning, as her grandfather did?

But, finally, one must feel empathy for the tobacco plant itself. For thousands of years, it has been venerated by Native Americans as a sacred medicine. They have used it extensively—its juice, its leaves, its roots, its (holy) smoke—to heal wounds and cure diseases, and in ceremonies of prayer and peace. And though the plant (as most of us know it) has been poisoned by chemicals and denatured by intensive mono-cropping and is therefore hardly the plant it was, still, to some modern Indians it remains a plant of positive power. I learned this when my Native American friends, Bill Wahpepah and his family, visited with me for a few days and the first thing he did was sow a few tobacco seeds in my garden.

Perhaps we can liberate tobacco from those who have captured and abused it, enslaving the plant on large plantations, keeping it from freedom and its kin, and forcing it to enslave the world. Its true nature suppressed, no wonder it has become deadly. Maybe by sowing a few seeds of tobacco in our gardens and treating the plant with the reverence it deserves, we can redeem tobacco's soul and restore its self-respect.

Besides, how grim, if one is a smoker, to realize one is smoking a slave.

There is a slogan from a battered women's shelter that I especially like: "Peace on earth begins at home." I believe everything does. I think of a slogan for people trying to stop smoking: "Every home a smoke-free zone." Smoking is a form of self-battering that also batters those who must sit by, occasionally cajole or complain, and helplessly watch. I realize now that as a child I sat by, through the years, and literally watched my father kill himself: surely one such victory in my family, for the rich white men who own the tobacco companies, is enough. ■

[1] Three months after reading this essay my daughter stopped smoking.

DISCUSSING THE SELECTION

1. Before you discuss the selection with your class, write for five minutes about the essay. What ideas did Walker present that stand out in your mind? What did you learn from reading this family story?

2. What words or ideas in the first paragraph tell you that the author is upset about her daughter's smoking? Why is the author so troubled about her daughter's smoking Camel cigarettes?

3. What family stories does Walker include that explain why she is so upset about her daughter's smoking?

4. Why does the author include the fact that she herself smoked at one time in her life?

5. Why does the author include the information about the Native Americans in this essay?

THINKING CRITICALLY

1. The footnote on page 29 tells us that Walker's daughter stopped smoking three months after reading this essay. What specific points in the essay do you think made her give up smoking? Why do you think it took her three months to give it up?

2. Have you or anyone you know well ever tried to give up a habit because it was upsetting to others? What steps did you or the other person take to break the habit? Was the habit broken?

3. Why do you think Walker did not just tell her daughter that she could not smoke at home? What do you think the effects of telling her that would have been?

4. What connections do you find between the Walker essay and the Stone selection, "Family Stories," on page 20?

FOCUSING ON THE WRITING

The Conclusion

The closing paragraph of your writing ties together the important points of your essay and draws a final conclusion for your readers. It may be short, humorous, or formal. You want to help your reader understand the meaning and significance of what you have written.

Reread your draft and decide if you have tied together loose ends and if you have made a clear point. Keep in mind that it is not always necessary to write a specific conclusion paragraph. Often your writing ends naturally after you have made your last point.

1. Reread Alice Walker's conclusion to this essay. How does it tie together the main points of the essay she has written? How does her conclusion make you feel?

2. When we write to persuade, we try to prove our point, we try to change a reader's opinion, and/or we try to clarify a controversial issue. To do this, we have to include strong support or evidence and enough of it to convince our readers of our ideas. What support does Walker offer to prove to her readers that smoking is not good for the health? What support does Walker give to prove that smoking is a problem beyond her own family concerns?

3. In addition to trying to persuade her daughter to stop smoking, Walker is trying to persuade her reader to consider smoking in a particular way.

Reread the essay and decide what evidence Walker provides that best expresses her main idea about smoking.

CREATING YOUR TEXT

1. Write an essay in which you use a family story or stories to describe a dangerous but common habit or behavior of a person you know. In your essay, tell the way this habit or behavior has affected this person's life. In your conclusion, include advice that can help other people deal with this problem.

2. In an essay, describe a situation in which you have tried to give up a bad habit or behavior. What steps did you take to break the habit? Which steps were most successful? Which steps were most difficult for you? In your conclusion, move from your specific situation to the general by providing advice to help someone who is trying to give up a similar habit or behavior.

3. Some political activists have said that advertisements for smoking and alcoholic beverages are aimed at young people more than at any other age group. Examine the advertisements for these products displayed on billboards, in public transportation, and in magazines. Write an essay in which you explain what specific details suggest the age of the audience at which they are targeted? In your essay, discuss how these advertisements affect you as a consumer. What advice would you offer friends who are trying to decide whether to begin smoking or drinking?

REVISING YOUR TEXT

After writing your first draft, reread it and think about ways to revise what you have written. To do this, review your writing by going over the revision questions on page 12. In addition, ask yourself the following questions:

Does my essay contain specific examples? What tense have I used to tell these personal stories?

Does my essay move from the specific to make a general point that would be of interest to many readers?

How does my conclusion connect to the body of my essay? Does it tie together my ideas?

EXPLORING YOUR IDEAS

Divide your journal page into two columns. At the top of one column, write "Fulfilling My Own Dreams," and for the other column write "Fulfilling My Family's Dreams for Me." Spend the next five minutes filling in the columns with any ideas that come into your mind. Reread what you have put in the lists, and write a brief description of yourself, explaining what you have learned about yourself from these lists.

Only daughter

SANDRA CISNEROS

Sandra Cisneros was born in Chicago, the daughter of a Mexican father and a Mexican-American mother. She has written many essays, short stories, and novels and is best known for her book *The House on Mango Street*. This essay appeared in *Glamour* magazine in November 1990. Cisneros now lives in San Antonio and is working on a new novel, *Caramelo*.

1 Once, several years ago, when I was just starting out my writing career, I was asked to write my own contributor's note for an anthology. I wrote: "I am the only daughter in a family of six sons. *That* explains everything."

2 Well, I've thought that ever since, and yes, it explains a lot to me, but for the reader's sake I should have written: "I am the only daughter in a *Mexican* family of six sons." Or even: "I am the only daughter of a Mexican father and a Mexican-American mother." Or: "I am the only daughter of a working-class family of nine." All of these had everything to do with who I am today.

3 I was/am the only daughter and *only a* daughter. Being an only daughter in a family of six sons forced me by circumstance to spend a lot of time by myself because my brothers felt it beneath them to play with a *girl* in public.

But that aloneness, that loneliness, was good for a would-be writer—it allowed me time to think and think, to imagine, to read and prepare myself.

Being only a daughter for my father meant my destiny would lead me to become someone's wife. That's what he believed. But when I was in the fifth grade and shared my plans for college with him, I was sure he understood. I remember my father saying, "*Que bueno, mi'ja,* that's good." That meant a lot to me, especially since my brothers thought the idea hilarious. What I didn't realize was that my father thought college was good for girls—good for finding a husband. After four years in college and two more in graduate school, and still no husband, my father shakes his head even now and says I wasted all that education.

In retrospect, I'm lucky my father believed daughters were meant for husbands. It meant it didn't matter if I majored in something silly like English. After all, I'd find a nice professional eventually, right? This allowed me the liberty to putter about embroidering my little poems and stories without my father interrupting with so much as a "What's that you're writing?"

But the truth is, I wanted him to interrupt. I wanted my father to understand what it was I was scribbling, to introduce me as "My only daughter, the writer." Not as "This is my only daughter. She teaches." *Es maestra*—teacher. Not even *profesora*.

In a sense, everything I have ever written has been for him, to win his approval even though I know my father can't read English words, even though my father's only reading includes the brown-ink *Esto* sports magazines from Mexico City and the bloody *¡Alarma!* magazines that feature yet another sighting of *La Virgen de Guadalupe* on a tortilla or a wife's revenge on her philandering husband by bashing his skull in with a *molcajete* (a kitchen mortar made of volcanic rock). Or the *fotonovelas*, the little picture paperbacks with tragedy and trauma erupting from the characters' mouths in bubbles.

A father represents, then, the public majority. A public who is disinterested in reading, and yet one whom I am writing about and for, and privately trying to woo.

When we were growing up in Chicago, we moved a lot because of my father. He suffered bouts of nostalgia. Then we'd have to let go of our flat, store the furniture with mother's relatives, load the station wagon with baggage and bologna sandwiches and head south. To Mexico City.

We came back, of course. To yet another Chicago flat, another Chicago neighborhood, another Catholic school. Each time, my father would seek out the parish priest in order to get a tuition break, and complain or boast: "I have seven sons."

He meant *siete hijos,* seven children, but he translated it as "sons." "I have seven sons." To anyone who would listen. The Sears Roebuck employee who sold us the washing machine. The short-order cook where my father ate his ham-and-eggs breakfasts. "I have seven sons." As if he deserved a medal from the state.

My papa. He didn't mean anything by that mistranslation, I'm sure. But somehow I could feel myself being erased. I'd tug my father's sleeve and whisper: "Not seven sons. Six! and *one daughter.*"

When my oldest brother graduated from medical school, he fulfilled my father's dream that we study hard and use this—our heads, instead of this—our hands. Even now my father's hands are thick and yellow, stubbed by a history of hammer and nails and twine and coils and springs. "Use this," my father said, tapping his head, "and not this," showing us those hands. He always looked tired when he said it.

Wasn't college an investment? And hadn't I spent all those years in college? And if I didn't marry, what was it all for? Why would anyone go to college and then choose to be poor? Especially someone who had always been poor.

Last year, after ten years of writing professionally, the financial rewards started to trickle in. My second National Endowment for the Arts Fellowship. A guest professorship at the University of California, Berkeley. My book, which sold to a major New York publishing house.

At Christmas, I flew home to Chicago. The house was throbbing, same as always; hot *tamales* and sweet *tamales* hissing in my mother's pressure cooker, and everybody—my mother, six brothers, wives, babies, aunts, cousins—talking too loud and at the same time, like in a Fellini film, because that's just how we are.

I went upstairs to my father's room. One of my stories had just been translated into Spanish and published in an anthology of Chicano writing, and I wanted to show it to him. Ever since he recovered from a stroke two years ago, my father likes to spend his leisure hours horizontally. And that's how I found him, watching a Pedro Infante movie on Galavision and eating rice pudding.

There was a glass filmed with milk on the bedside table. There were several vials of pills and balled Kleenex. And on the floor, one black sock and a plastic

Cisneros *Only daughter*

urinal that I didn't want to look at but looked at anyway. Pedro Infante was about to burst into song, and my father was laughing.

I'm not sure if it was because my story was translated into Spanish, or because it was published in Mexico, or perhaps because the story dealt with Tepeyac, the *colonia* my father was raised in and the house he grew up in, but at any rate, my father punched the mute button on his remote control and read my story.

I sat on the bed next to my father and waited. He read it very slowly. As if he were reading each line over and over. He laughed at all the right places and read lines he liked out loud. He pointed and asked questions: "Is this So-and-so?" "Yes," I said. He kept reading.

When he was finally finished, after what seemed like hours, my father looked up and asked: "Where can we get more copies of this for the relatives?"

Of all the wonderful things that happened to me last year, that was the most wonderful. ∎

DISCUSSING THE SELECTION

1. Make a list of as much as you can remember about Sandra Cisneros's background. Share and compare your list with a classmate. What did you both remember? Discuss why knowing this about her was important to understand her essay.

2. Why does Cisneros include the Spanish phrase *"siete hijos"* when she writes that her father says he has seven sons?

3. What expectations does the father have for his sons in this essay? What expectations does he have for his daughter? What does Cisneros tell her readers about her mother in this essay?

4. In the last paragraph Cisneros writes, "Of all the wonderful things that happened to me last year, that was the most wonderful." What wonderful

things has she already told her reader about? What is the most wonderful? Why?

THINKING CRITICALLY

1. Are boys treated differently from girls in your family? Use specific examples to explain your answer.

2. Do you think male and female children should be treated differently? Should there be different expectations for them?

3. Cisneros tells the reader that her father wants his children to use their heads, not their hands. Explain the difference as you see it. Do you think your family feels the same way? If so, why? If not, what is their attitude toward your life work?

4. Write your own contributor's note describing yourself in one sentence. Then, as Cisneros did, rewrite it. Read the variations. Choose the one you prefer. How did you decide which one to choose?

FOCUSING ON THE WRITING

General to Specific: Deduction

One way to order your ideas is to present a general statement or main idea and then to follow this with specific ideas or details that support this statement. This type of organization is called "deductive reasoning" or "illustration." Academic writing and scientific writing are often organized this way.

To do this, state your main idea or general statement early in your writing. Follow it with details that *expand, illustrate, clarify,* or *support* it. Your details can be in the form of a story, a comparison, facts, or description. Make sure you have enough details so your reader understands your point of view.

Words and phrases that are used include *for example, for instance, besides, in addition, another, furthermore, along with, together with,* and *another.*

1. Cisneros begins this essay with the general statement "I am the only daughter in a family of six sons. *That* explains everything." What specific details does she include to support her main idea?

2. In paragraph 2, she rewrites her general statement several times. What are the differences in meaning for the other three sentences she presents?

3. In the title of this selection, "Only daughter," Cisneros does not capitalize both words, as we usually do when we write a title. How does this lower-case *d* reflect the meaning of her story?

4. Reread the selection, identifying all the questions. For example, "After all, I'd find a nice professional eventually, right?" After you have found all the questions, decide to whom these questions are addressed. Does Cisneros answer them? Why does she include these questions in this essay?

5. Writers choose their words carefully; they can tell you whether something is important or not, valued or not, by the choice of words. Reread the selection, noting all the words that Cisneros uses to refer to writing. Make a list of them. Which of these words describe writing as a serious profession, and which make writing seem unimportant and silly? Look at the context in which each word is used, and decide why she uses a particular word in each case.

CREATING YOUR TEXT

1. Reread the lists you wrote in your journal entry, noticing the similarities and differences between the two lists. Write an essay in which you focus on what you must do to fulfill your own dreams and still satisfy some of your family's dreams for you. In your essay, describe the steps you would have to take. In your conclusion, explain what you have learned about yourself and your family from writing this essay.

2. "Of all the wonderful things that happened to me last year, that was the most wonderful." Write an essay describing an experience that you had, and use the preceding quotation as part of your conclusion.

3. Write an essay in which you compare the life and personality of Cisneros's father to that of a member of your family *or* another parent about whom you have read in this book. What experiences in their lives are similar? Do they have similar aspirations for themselves or for their families? What differences do you find in their personalities? In your conclusion, explain whether you think they would like each other and why.

REVISING YOUR TEXT

When you finish your first draft, on your own or with a classmate read the revision questions on page 11 or 12 and discuss the places where your draft succeeds and where it can be improved. Write your second draft to share with the class. When you reread your draft, notice the way you organized your ideas.

Did you begin with a general statement or main idea? If so, what is it? Where is it located in your draft?

What details did you include to support, illustrate, or explain your main idea?

My Father, "Dr. Pat"

LINDSAY PATTERSON

Born in Louisiana, Lindsay Patterson now lives in New York City. Early in his career, he was an editorial assistant to Langston Hughes (see Hughes story on page 152). He also was a co-host of radio and television programs. At present, he writes essays and short stories and teaches writing.

In American literature, very little has ever been written about the black middle class, particularly the Southern black middle class, which, when I was growing up, contained some of the most complex and colorful characters in American life.

Among them, I believed, was my father, a madly brilliant free spirit who entered college at 16 and medical school at 18, and did not quit until he had received three medical degrees. But when I knew him he was only a dentist (a black medical doctor had already established a successful practice in our town) and a pharmacist who concocted exotic but practical remedies, his best-known remedy being Dr. Pat's Log Cabin Cough Syrup, a dark brown liquid with a sweet taste and a powerful kick that was guaranteed to root out the most stubborn colds and that sold like wildfire.

In addition to being a man of medicine, he was a master showman. Every

Sunday afternoon he would fill the family car with cardboard cases of his Log Cabin Cough Syrup and visit four or five churches, where he was always called on "to render a few remarks," which he began by complimenting the "sisters" on their fine appearance and the "brothers" for having the foresight and wisdom to choose such bewitching creatures. When the congregation grew still, his face grew serious, and he proclaimed in ringing tones that "Negroes should always scratch each other's backs, so we can all live on Easy Street!"

The churches were mainly wood-gray structures on the edge of cotton fields beside small bleak cemeteries, and during my father's "remarks" white-uniformed ushers passed out pink and green circulars that contained his photograph, a list of his medical degrees, and an aphorism or two ("A bird in the hand is worth two in the bush"). Another circular was white and also contained his photograph and the poem "Lift Every Voice and Sing," but no mention of James Weldon Johnson as the author.

In his "remarks" he recited his own poetry, as well as that of Shakespeare and Milton, to make the point that blacks should love and support each other, especially their professional men. To illustrate this point he would always command me and my brother to stand. "Here are my two boys," he would boom. "One is going to be a doctor and the other a lawyer, but I need your help. They're as much mine as yours, and with the Lord's help we're going to raise them right. If you ever see them doing anything wrong, you have my permission to whip their butts and when they get home I'll whip them some more!"

The applause, the foot stomping and amens were always deafening, while my brother and I wept, for we knew that my father, who had a vile, sometimes uncontrollable temper, was as good as his word.

His purpose on earth, I was convinced, was to corrupt life. While other kids were plied with fairy tales and ghost stories, he burdened our minds with Tolstoy and Shakespeare and the Bible. He screened our playmates, burned our comic books, forbade Sunday movie-going and looked upon dancing as a mortal sin, yet when my brother turned seven he decided that it was time for his firstborn to learn the "scientific facts of life." But my brother was so overwhelmed by this knowledge about "the real birds" and "the real bees," he blabbed it to everyone, including his first grade teacher, who was so horrified that at the end of the school term she flunked him.

My father was a very restless man, and it was only after his death that I learned that he had established thriving dental or medical practices in three other places before settling in our small Louisiana hometown during the late 1930's, and that in each town he had married and divorced before moving on to the next. His third wife, though, had flatly refused to dissolve their union until he had threatened to have her "put away" and declared insane.

Marriage to my mother produced perhaps the happiest period in his life, but after she died he became strangely obsessed with finding a wife who held a master's degree. He eventually discovered this educational marvel in a six-foot-two haughty amazon from St. Louis, who after one month of marriage found his "two brats" a nuisance and small-town life a bore.

My father, however, expressed no remorse or disappointment at her sudden departure, for he too had begun to tire of life in our town, even though he had done extremely well financially, and had built what many claimed was "the best house in town." He was also the only black man who was never called "boy," and who was invited (as a professional courtesy) to sit in White Only waiting rooms. Yet, he never was an Uncle Tom, which was perhaps why the "brothers and sisters" tried vainly to persuade him to "stay put" for the good of them all.

But the promise of a new world to conquer proved, even at the age of 60, irresistible, and he set out once again to create his own extraordinary universe. Six months later, however, he was dead. Time was his only unbiased enemy. ■

DISCUSSING THE SELECTION

1. Patterson believes that his father was a complex person whose actions are not easily judged as right or wrong. What examples in the story support Patterson's belief and convince you that Patterson's father was a complex character?

2. Compare Cisneros's father (see page 34) to Patterson's father by asking such questions as: In what ways has each father fulfilled or not fulfilled

his dreams? What role has education played in each man's life? What indicates whether each father was or was not easy to communicate with? What in each selection indicates that the father was proud of his family? What indicates that the father worked hard? What other similarities and differences between these men did you notice as you read these two selections?

3. What does Dr. Pat expect of his sons? What does he do to make sure that his sons meet these expectations? How do you think Dr. Pat would feel about the fact that his son, Lindsay Patterson, is a writer and a teacher of writing? What in the selection supports your idea?

4. What characteristics does Dr. Pat have that make him respected by both blacks and whites? What does Dr. Pat mean when he says, "Negroes should always scratch each other's backs, so we can all live on Easy Street!"

5. What is an Uncle Tom? What does this term mean in the context of this story?

THINKING CRITICALLY

1. Why would you want or not want a father like Dr. Pat? Explain your answer, referring to particular events in the story.

2. What in the story tells you that the townspeople saw Dr. Pat differently from the way his own children saw him? If you have ever known anyone who had a "public" personality that was very different from his or her "private" personality, tell the class about that person and the effect he or she had on you.

3. What in the story reveals Dr. Pat's attitudes toward women? Have you ever met anyone who had attitudes toward women that were similar to Dr. Pat's? Do you think these attitudes should change? If so, how would you go about trying to change them?

FOCUSING ON THE WRITING

1. What specific details in this family story describe the writer's father?

2. What anecdotes or stories does Patterson include to explain his father's personality?

3. In paragraph 2, Patterson illustrates the general idea that his father was "a madly brilliant free spirit" with specific details. List the supporting details that prove this point.

4. In paragraph 3, the writer generalizes that his father "was a master showman." List the supporting details that prove this.

5. In paragraph 4, Patterson describes the events he experienced in detail. Reread that paragraph, and then list the words that describe the churches and the people in them.

6. In paragraph 1, Patterson places his story in a historical and literary context. How does he use this context to convince the readers that his story is important? Does this introduction make you want to read more, or do you prefer that a writer begin by just telling the story? Illustrate your answer by referring to other stories you have read.

CREATING YOUR TEXT

1. Write a story describing a person you have met or heard about in your family who is "bigger than life." Include as many details as necessary to draw a word picture that illustrates the complexity and colorfulness of the person.

2. Write a story telling about your personal hero, a person whom you admire,

look up to, and hope to be like someday. Explain why you chose this person, what the person has done, and what you are doing to make yourself more like this person.

3. Write a story about a person who has a "public" self that differs from his or her "private" self. Describe the person in detail, and explain why you think the person presents him- or herself in different ways.

REVISING YOUR TEXT

Review the first draft of your writing on your own or with a partner while looking at the revision questions for a story on page 13 or 14. In addition, think about the following questions:

Did you include descriptive details so your reader can almost see the person(s) you are describing?

Did you include a story or anecdote that helps the reader get a picture of the person(s) you are describing?

Did you make it clear why the person is interesting or important to you?

EXPLORING YOUR IDEAS

Make a list of five events in your life that stand out in your mind. These five events can have occurred at any time and may not have seemed important when they happened. After you have chosen and listed the five events, choose one of these. Write a paragraph in which you explain why you have selected it and its impact on who you are today.

Amy Tan

AMY LING

The following minibiography of Amy Tan was excerpted from Amy Ling's book *Between Worlds: Women Writers of Chinese Ancestry,* published in 1990. The writer described, Amy Tan, is well known for her 1988 novel of interconnecting stories *The Joy Luck Club* and her 1991 novel *The Kitchen God's Wife.*

Amy Tan was born in Oakland, California, in 1952; her parents had emigrated from China in 1949, leaving behind three young daughters. They had planned to find a place to live first and then send for the daughters, but the Communist Revolution prevented their carrying out this plan. Despite years of effort on her mother's part, contact was lost. Not until Amy was 12 did she learn of the existence of these sisters. The lost, absent daughters haunted the mother, in whose mind they became the perfect, good daughters, and their example was raised aloft to haunt Amy Tan, the bad, present daughter. "A few years ago, we found them," says Amy Tan in an interview with Susan Kepner [in 1989]. "It was an incredible experience. We met them in China, and now one of them is here. They write to me in Chinese, and my mother reads the letters to me."

Amy Tan's life has been marked by death and change. When Amy was 15, her 16-year-old brother died of a brain tumor; the following year, her engineer–Baptist minister father also died of a brain tumor. Her grief-stricken mother, believing that their house in Santa Clara was imbalanced in *feng shui* (wind and water), fled with her two remaining children to Switzerland, where Amy attended the College Monte Rosa Internationale in Montreux and from which she nearly eloped with an escaped mental patient who claimed to be a German army deserter. Back in the United States, she completed her bachelor's and master's degrees in English and linguistics at San Jose State University, where she met her husband, Lou DeMattei, now a tax attorney. She studied one year toward a Ph.D. in linguistics at the University of California at Berkeley, but the sudden murder of a close friend brought to the fore all the grief and anger over the deaths of her father and brother that she had suppressed for five years. She dropped her studies and took a position as a language development specialist working with handicapped children, where she was rewarded by what she considered a miracle: a two-year-old blind boy who had never spoken spoke to her. She then took up freelance writing and joined a writing group out of which *The Joy Luck Club* grew.

When visiting a Buddhist retreat in Marin County [in northern California] once with her husband, Amy Tan told Kepner she was amazed to see so many people "trying to learn how to act Chinese. . . . I couldn't help thinking, 'If you really want to learn how to act Chinese, go live with a Chinese mother for twenty years. Then you'll act Chinese.'" What she had heard from her Chinese mother for 20 years boiled down to three precepts: "First, if it's too easy, it's not worth pursuing. Second, you have to try harder, no matter what other people might have to do in the same situation—that's your lot in life. And if you're a woman, you're supposed to suffer in silence." Tan adds that she was never good at the last precept. She further explains that Chinese mothers map out your life and won't take no for an answer. If you tell them to "'shut up'" "you could be held as an accessory to your own murder. Or worse . . . to their suicide." "So the ground rule is, *there is no way the daughter wins.*". . .

Though all the stories of *The Joy Luck Club* mothers are poignant, the most affecting one is Suyuan Woo's. She had been forced to leave behind twin baby girls when she was running away on foot, in panic and exhaustion, from Japanese soldiers during World War II. In the clothes of these babies, she hid jewels to pay for their care, her photograph, name, and the address of her family in Shanghai so that the babies could later be returned. But her house was bombed, her family totally annihilated, and all her efforts to recover her children were in vain. For 40 years, from America, she tried to find these lost daughters in China; at last, they were found and wrote to her, but not before her sudden death. Her daughter Jing-mei is asked to go to China to tell these sisters whom she has never met all about their mother. These sisters live in the motherland that Jing-mei has never known, and Jing-mei has lived with the mother that the sisters have never known. But when Jing-mei is first asked by her mother's friends from the Joy Luck Club to go to China on this mission, her immediate response is bewilderment: "What will I say? What can I tell them about my mother? I don't know anything. She was my mother" (Tan, page 40). ∎

DISCUSSING THE SELECTION

1. The title of Amy Ling's book from which this minibiography was excerpted is *Between Worlds: Women Writers of Chinese Ancestry*. Why do you think Ling decided to write about Amy Tan? What worlds is Amy Tan caught between? What evidence does Ling present that supports your answer?

2. Many writers use events from their family stories in their writing, whether their writing is fiction or not. According to Ling, what events from her family experiences does Tan use in the story of Suyuan Woo? How does she change the events to fictionalize them?

3. Tan explains the three precepts that her mother taught her. If you didn't know what a precept was, how did you figure it out from the selection?

4. List the three precepts that Tan's mother taught her to live by.

5. Make a list of the five most important events that are included in Ling's minibiography of Amy Tan. What would you like to know about Amy Tan that is not included in this selection?

THINKING CRITICALLY

1. Make a list of three precepts that are important in your life.

2. Are any of the precepts that Tan's mother taught her similar to ones that have influenced your life? How or from whom did you learn the precepts that govern your life? In what ways, if any, have they changed as you have gotten older?

3. "And if you're a woman, you're supposed to suffer in silence" is the third precept by which Tan is supposed to live. What is your response to this precept? Are there societies in the world in which this precept is true? Can you think of any situations in which it is thought that if you are a man, you are supposed to suffer in silence?

4. What did you learn from reading this minibiography that explains why Tan's mother was so important to her? What personal characteristics does Tan's mother have that make her a memorable character to you?

FOCUSING ON THE WRITING

The First, Second, and Third Person

When writing in the first person, writers use *I* or *we* as the subject. This is usually the most personal style of writing and is used for autobiographies and for some stories and essays.

In the second person, writers use *you* as the subject. This creates a style of writing that is very informal and almost conversational.

In the third person, writers use a person's name, or *one, she, he, it,* or *they* to refer to the subject. This is the most formal style and is often

> used in academic essays and in research papers. It is also used in biographies and in much fiction writing.
>
> Once you have begun your essay, try as much as possible to be consistent in maintaining the same person throughout.

1. In what person is "Amy Tan" written? Why? In what person would an autobiography be written? What other differences would you expect to find in a biography and an autobiography?

2. Compare the writing in "Amy Tan" with "Only daughter" using this chart:

	Ling	Cisneros
Written in the first person		
Written in the third person		
Written primarily in the past tense		
Based on research		
Based on memory		

   As a reader, which selection did you prefer? Why?

3. What connection between themes do you find in the first paragraph and in the last paragraph of this selection?

CREATING YOUR TEXT

1. Reread your journal entry written before you read the Ling selection, and choose one of the events from your own life. Write an accurate story of the event, including description to make the event come alive.

2. Reread your journal entry, and choose one of the events from your own life. Write a fictional account of it, changing some elements in the story to make the story more interesting, exciting, or less personal.

3. Write an essay explaining the origin of three precepts you live by and explaining some decisions you have based on these precepts.

REVISING YOUR TEXT

When you finish your first draft, share it with a classmate or in a small group. Together, read the revision questions on pages 11–14 and decide where your writing is successful and where it needs revision to make it clearer and more effective.

In which person did you write your draft? Why?

Try rewriting a paragraph in a different person. How does this change the meaning of your essay?

ADDITIONAL PROJECT

Write a minibiography of one of the writers whose work you admired as you read it in this book. To begin, go to your college library and read book reviews, articles about the person, and/or a reference guide to writers. You can discuss other research possibilities with a librarian.

EXPLORING YOUR IDEAS

Think about the way you talk at home or with your friends or in school. Write in your journal about any differences you notice in your informal patterns of speech (at home or with friends) and your formal patterns of speech (at school or on a job interview). What do you like most about your informal language? What do you like most about your formal language?

Mother Tongue

AMY TAN

Born in Oakland, California, Amy Tan now lives in San Francisco, California, with her husband. She has written essays, short stories, and novels. She is best known for *The Joy Luck Club* (1988). This essay appeared in *The Threepenny Review*.

1. I am not a scholar of English or literature. I cannot give you much more than personal opinions on the English language and its variations in this country or others.

2. I am a writer. And by that definition, I am someone who has always loved language. I am fascinated by language in daily life. I spend a great deal of my time thinking about the power of language—the way it can evoke an emotion, a visual image, a complex idea, or a simple truth. Language is the tool of my trade. And I use them all—all the Englishes I grew up with.

3. Recently, I was made keenly aware of the different Englishes I do use. I was giving a talk to a large group of people, the same talk I had already given to half a dozen other groups. The nature of the talk was about my writing, my life, and my book, *The Joy Luck Club*. The talk was going along well enough, until I remembered one major difference that made the whole talk sound

wrong. My mother was in the room. And it was perhaps the first time she had heard me give a lengthy speech, using the kind of English I have never used with her. I was saying things like, "The intersection of memory upon imagination" and "There is an aspect of my fiction that relates to thus-and-thus"—a speech filled with carefully wrought grammatical phrases, burdened, it suddenly seemed to me, with nominalized forms, past perfect tenses, conditional phrases, all the forms of standard English that I had learned in school and through books, the forms of English I did not use at home with my mother.

Just last week, I was walking down the street with my mother, and I again found myself conscious of the English I was using, the English I do use with her. We were talking about the price of new and used furniture and I heard myself saying this: "Not waste money that way." My husband was with us as well, and he didn't notice any switch in my English. And then I realized why. It's because over the twenty years we've been together I've often used that same kind of English with him, and sometimes he even uses it with me. It has become our language of intimacy, a different sort of English that relates to family talk, the language I grew up with.

So you'll have some idea of what this family talk I heard sounds like, I'll quote what my mother said during a recent conversation which I videotaped and then transcribed. During this conversation, my mother was talking about a political gangster in Shanghai who had the same last name as her family's, Du, and how the gangster in his early years wanted to be adopted by her family, which was rich by comparison. Later, the gangster became more powerful, far richer than my mother's family, and one day showed up at my mother's wedding to pay his respects. Here's what she said in part:

"Du Yusong having business like fruit stand. Like off the street kind. He is Du like Du Zong—but not Tsung-ming Island people. The local people call putong, the river east side, he belong to that side local people. That man want to ask Du Zong father take him in like become own family. Du Zong father wasn't look down on him, but didn't take seriously, until that man big like become a mafia. Now important person, very hard to inviting him. Chinese way, came only to show respect, don't stay for dinner. Respect for making big celebration, he shows up. Mean gives lots of respect. Chinese custom. Chinese social life that way. If too important won't have to stay too long. He come to my wedding. I didn't see. I heard it. I gone to boy's side, they have YMCA dinner. Chinese age I was nineteen."

You should know that my mother's expressive command of English belies how much she actually understands. She reads the *Forbes* report, listens to *Wall Street Week,* converses daily with her stockbroker, reads all of Shirley MacLaine's books with ease—all kinds of things I can't begin to understand. Yet some of my friends tell me they understand 50 percent of what my mother says. Some say they understand 80 to 90 percent. Some say they understand none of it, as if she were speaking pure Chinese. But to me, my mother's English is perfectly clear, perfectly natural. It's my mother tongue. Her language, as I hear it, is vivid, direct, full of observation and imagery. That was the language that helped shape the way I saw things, expressed things, made sense of the world.

Lately, I've been giving more thought to the kind of English my mother speaks. Like others, I have described it to people as "broken" or "fractured" English. But I wince when I say that. It has always bothered me that I can think of no way to describe it other than "broken," as if it were damaged and needed to be fixed, as if it lacked a certain wholeness and soundness. I've heard other terms used, "limited English," for example. But they seem just as bad, as if everything is limited, including people's perceptions of the limited English speaker.

I know this for a fact, because when I was growing up, my mother's "limited" English limited *my* perception of her. I was ashamed of her English. I believed that her English reflected the quality of what she had to say. That is, because she expressed them imperfectly her thoughts were imperfect. And I had plenty of empirical evidence to support me: the fact that people in department stores, at banks, and at restaurants did not take her seriously, did not give her good service, pretended not to understand her, or even acted as if they did not hear her.

My mother has long realized the limitations of her English as well. When I was fifteen, she used to have me call people on the phone to pretend I was she. In this guise, I was forced to ask for information or even to complain and yell at people who had been rude to her. One time it was a call to her stockbroker in New York. She had cashed out her small portfolio and it just so happened we were going to go to New York the next week, our very first trip outside California. I had to get on the phone and say in an adolescent voice that was not very convincing, "This is Mrs. Tan."

And my mother was standing in the back whispering loudly, "Why he don't send me check, already two weeks late. So mad he lie to me, losing me money."

And then I said in perfect English, "Yes, I'm getting rather concerned. You had agreed to send the check two weeks ago, but it hasn't arrived."

Then she began to talk more loudly. "What he want, I come to New York tell him front of his boss, you cheating me?" And I was trying to calm her down, make her be quiet, while telling the stockbroker, "I can't tolerate any more excuses. If I don't receive the check immediately, I am going to have to speak to your manager when I'm in New York next week." And sure enough, the following week there we were in front of this astonished stockbroker, and I was sitting there red-faced and quiet, and my mother, the real Mrs. Tan, was shouting at his boss in her impeccable broken English.

We used a similar routine just five days ago, for a situation that was far less humorous. My mother had gone to the hospital for an appointment, to find out about a benign brain tumor a CAT scan had revealed a month ago. She said she had spoken very good English, her best English, no mistakes. Still, she said, the hospital did not apologize when they said they had lost the CAT scan and she had come for nothing. She said they did not seem to have any sympathy when she told them she was anxious to know the exact diagnosis, since her husband and son had both died of brain tumors. She said they would not give her any more information until the next time and she would have to make another appointment for that. So she said she would not leave until the doctor called her daughter. She wouldn't budge. And when the doctor finally called her daughter, me, who spoke in perfect English—lo and behold—we had assurances the CAT scan would be found, promises that a conference call on Monday would be held, and apologies for any suffering my mother had gone through for a most regrettable mistake.

I think my mother's English almost had an effect on limiting my possibilities in life as well. Sociologists and linguists probably will tell you that a person's developing language skills are more influenced by peers. But I do think that the language spoken in the family, especially in immigrant families which are more insular, plays a large role in shaping the language of the child. And I believe that it affected my results on achievement tests, IQ tests, and the SAT. While my English skills were never judged as poor, compared to math, English could not be considered my strong suit. In grade school I did moderately well, getting perhaps B's, sometimes B-pluses, in English and scoring perhaps in the sixtieth or seventieth percentile on achievement tests. But those scores were not good enough to override the opinion that my true abilities lay in math and science, because in those areas I achieved A's and scored in the ninetieth percentile or higher.

This was understandable. Math is precise; there is only one correct answer. Whereas, for me at least, the answers on English tests were always a judgment call, a matter of opinion and personal experience. Those tests were constructed around items like fill-in-the-blank sentence completion, such as, "Even though Tom was _____, Mary thought he was _____." And the correct answer always seemed to be the most bland combinations of thoughts, for example, "Even though Tom was shy, Mary thought he was charming," with the grammatical structure "even though" limiting the correct answer to some sort of semantic opposites, so you wouldn't get answers like, "Even though Tom was foolish, Mary thought he was ridiculous." Well, according to my mother, there were very few limitations as to what Tom could have been and what Mary might have thought of him. So I never did well on tests like that.

The same was true with word analogies, pairs of words in which you were supposed to find some sort of logical, semantic relationship—for example, "*Sunset* is to *nightfall* as _____ is to _____." And here you would be presented with a list of four possible pairs, one of which showed the same kind of relationship: *red* is to *stoplight*, *bus* is to *arrival*, *chills* is to *fever*, *yawn* is to *boring*. Well, I could never think that way. I knew what the tests were asking, but I could not block out of my mind the images already created by the first pair, "*sunset* is to *nightfall*"—and I would see a burst of colors against a darkening sky, the moon rising, the lowering of a curtain of stars. And all the other pairs of words—red, bus, stoplight, boring—just threw up a mass of confusing images, making it impossible for me to sort out something as logical as saying: "A sunset precedes nightfall" is the same as "a chill precedes a fever." The only way I would have gotten that answer right would have been to imagine an associative situation, for example, my being disobedient and staying out past sunset, catching a chill at night, which turns into feverish pneumonia as punishment, which indeed did happen to me.

I have been thinking about all this lately, about my mother's English, about achievement tests. Because lately I've been asked, as a writer, why there are not more Asian Americans represented in American literature. Why are there few Asian Americans enrolled in creative writing programs? Why do so many Chinese students go into engineering? Well, these are broad sociological questions I can't begin to answer. But I have noticed in surveys—in fact, just last week—that Asian students, as a whole, always do significantly better on math achievement tests than in English. And this makes me think that there are other Asian-American students whose English spoken in the home might also be described as "broken" or "limited." And perhaps they also have teachers who are steering them away from writing and into math and science, which is what happened to me.

Fortunately, I happen to be rebellious in nature and enjoy the challenge of disproving assumptions made about me. I became an English major my first year in college, after being enrolled as pre-med. I started writing nonfiction as a freelancer the week after I was told by my former boss that writing was my worst skill and I should hone my talents toward account management.

But it wasn't until 1985 that I finally began to write fiction. And at first I wrote using what I thought to be wittily crafted sentences, sentences that would finally prove I had mastery over the English language. Here's an example from the first draft of a story that later made its way into *The Joy Luck Club*, but without this line: "That was my mental quandary in its nascent state." A terrible line, which I can barely pronounce.

Fortunately, for reasons I won't get into today, I later decided I should envision a reader for the stories I would write. And the reader I decided upon was my mother, because these were stories about mothers. So with this reader in mind—and in fact she did read my early drafts—I began to write stories using all the Englishes I grew up with: the English I spoke to my mother, which for lack of a better term might be described as "simple"; the English she used with me, which for lack of a better term might be described as "broken"; my translation of her Chinese, which could certainly be described as "watered down"; and what I imagined to be her translation of her Chinese if she could speak in perfect English, her internal language, and for that I sought to preserve the essence, but neither an English nor a Chinese structure. I wanted to capture what language ability tests can never reveal: her intent, her passion, her imagery, the rhythms of her speech and the nature of her thoughts.

Apart from what any critic had to say about my writing, I knew I had succeeded where it counted when my mother finished reading my book and gave me her verdict: "So easy to read." ∎

DISCUSSING THE SELECTION

1. Write the words "home language" or "mother tongue" in the middle of a blank piece of paper (see the discussion of clustering on page 5), and circle the words. For the next five minutes, write down any word or phrase that comes into your mind. Circle the new words and phrases, and connect the circles to "mother tongue" in the middle. Looking at your clusters, which words best describe what "home language" or "mother tongue" means to you? Compare your response with other students in your class.

2. As a class, look at your clustering and list four reasons why Amy Tan uses her "mother tongue" when she talks with her mother. Which is the most important reason? How did you decide? What do your answers tell you about the relationship that Tan and her mother share?

3. In paragraph 2, Tan writes, "And I use them all—all the Englishes I grew up with." What supporting details in the next paragraphs illustrate the different Englishes Tan learned?

4. According to Tan, why is she troubled by the terms "broken," "fractured," and "limited" as applied to the way some people speak English? How does she think these terms affect people's perceptions of her mother and herself? What examples does she include in her essay to illustrate her point?

5. Why, according to Tan, did she do better on math achievement tests than on English achievement tests? What difficulties did Tan have when she took the English tests? How does she relate these difficulties to her "mother tongue"?

6. Tan writes that when she was younger she was ashamed of her mother's English. What details does she include to show that she has changed? What changed her perception of her mother?

THINKING CRITICALLY

1. How many different Englishes do you know and speak? Where do you speak each one? How did you learn each one? In which do you feel the most relaxed? Why?

2. In paragraph 2, Tan describes the characteristics of a writer. What are those characteristics? What other characteristics do you think are important?

3. Have you ever felt embarrassed by a friend's or a family member's language or actions? What was your experience? How did you handle the situation? How did you feel about it in the end?

4. After reading the minibiography of Amy Tan and then reading her essay, have you changed your mind about her in any way? Which did you prefer reading? Why?

FOCUSING ON THE WRITING

The Thesis Statement

The thesis statement or main idea is a statement of the purpose or controlling idea of the essay. It presents the writer's attitude or position about a topic that will be supported and developed in the essay.

Although the thesis statement may be stated anywhere in the writing or may even be implied—that is, not directly stated, but understood by the readers—many writers find that writing the thesis statement as the first or last sentence in the introductory paragraph helps them organize and focus their writing from the beginning.

Tan *Mother Tongue*

1. What is the thesis statement or main idea of this essay? Where does Tan state this? How did you know this was the thesis or main idea?

2. Where in the essay does Tan compare or present similarities? What details or examples does she use to make comparisons? Where does she contrast or present differences? What details or examples does she use to make contrasts?

3. In paragraphs 11 and 12, Tan includes an example of her mother's speech and her translation into formal English:

    Mother: Why he don't send me check, already two weeks late. So mad he lie to me, losing me money.
    Tan's translation: Yes, I'm getting rather concerned. You had agreed to send the check two weeks ago, but it hasn't arrived.

    Copy down any other examples of such comparison in Tan's essay. Why do you think Tan includes examples of the way her mother actually speaks in this essay? What other writers do you know who use dialect or accented English to show how people really speak? Do you enjoy reading books in which writers do this? Why or why not?

4. How do you explain the fact that Amy Tan realized that she should become a writer when her boss told her that her worst skill was writing?

5. Paragraph 9 begins, "I know this for a fact, . . ." What does the word *this* refer to? How did you know? Look at the beginnings of the other paragraphs in this essay. Notice how ideas are connected from one paragraph to the next.

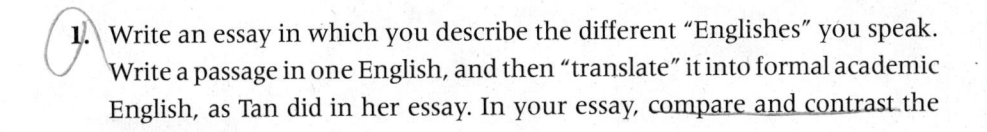

✵ CREATING YOUR TEXT

1. Write an essay in which you describe the different "Englishes" you speak. Write a passage in one English, and then "translate" it into formal academic English, as Tan did in her essay. In your essay, compare and contrast the

different Englishes. Think about the people with whom you speak the various varieties of English and why. Explain what you have gained from knowing more than one English.

2. Rap music uses words and rhythm to make music. Write out a rap lyric that you know or have written yourself. Write out the meaning of the lyric in formal academic English. Read over both varieties, and compare the feeling you get from each. Explain why one expresses a particular feeling better than the other.

3. Do you think all students need to learn to speak, read, and write in formal academic English? Write an essay in which you describe how you found your experiences of learning to speak, read, and write in formal academic English different from learning the less formal spoken English. Do you think students *should* be taught formal academic English? Why or why not?

4. Amy Tan has the responsibility for speaking for her mother in many formal situations, such as in school, at the hospital, and in government offices. Write an essay in which you describe an experience when you had to speak for another person because the person did not know the language or was uncomfortable speaking in public. Explain how the experience made you feel and what it taught you about yourself and the other person.

REVISING YOUR TEXT

Show your first draft to the classmate with whom you created the subject or question. Discuss the areas in which your draft is interesting and exciting. Discuss the areas in which it seems repetitive or needs help. Go over the revision questions on page 11 to give you some ideas for ways to improve your second draft. Share your second draft with the class.

In addition, ask yourself the following questions:

What is your thesis statement? Where is it placed in the essay?

Does this draft compare (present similarities) or contrast (present differences)? If so, where in the writing does each occur? Why did you compare or contrast at that point in your essay?

Are the examples you have chosen to illustrate your comparison and/or contrast strong and clear?

Do you have enough examples to make your point?

EXPLORING YOUR IDEAS

Write about a strange and yet memorable experience that occurred with someone in your family or someone you know well. As part of your writing, explain what made the experience special to you. Include a description of the setting or place, the time of day, and any other details that bring the feeling of the experience back to you.

Owls

LEWIS NORDAN

Born in Mississippi, Lewis Nordan now lives in Pittsburgh, Pennsylvania. He has written a novel, *The All-Girl Football Team,* and many short stories, including "Owls." This story concerns a father-and-son relationship and the odd nature of love.

Once when I was a small boy of ten or eleven I was traveling late at night with my father on a narrow country road. I had been counting the number of beers he drank that night, nine or ten of them, and I was anxious about his driving.

Neither of us had spoken for a long time. What was there to say: the beers, the narrow road, the stubble fields, a bare bulb shining out in the darkness from a porch far back from the road, the yellow headlights? What was there to talk about? The car held the road on the curves; the heater was making its familiar sound.

Then I saw a road sign, bright yellow and diamond-shaped, and on it I read the word SLOW. My father kept on driving at the same speed and did not slow down, though I knew he had seen the sign.

So I was bold. I said, "Did you see that sign?"

Immediately my father let up on the gas and the car began to slow down. He said, "You're right. We should go back."

He pulled his car onto the berm and stopped and looked back over his left shoulder for safety and then pulled out onto the road again and made a U-turn.

I was frightened. I said, "Why are we going back?"

My father shifted the gears, and we began driving back in the direction we had come. "The sign," he said. "I'm going back to see the sign."

I said, "Why? Why are we doing that?"

He said, "Isn't that what you meant? Didn't you want to go back?"

I said, "I wanted you to slow down. I was afraid."

We drove on in the darkness for a minute. My father said, "The sign didn't say SLOW."

I said, "It didn't? I thought it said SLOW."

My father said, "It said OWLS."

So we kept driving and I didn't argue. I listened to the quiet sound of the heater fan. I saw the red eyes of a rabbit on the roadside. I saw the stubble fields. For one second I believed I had lived a very long hard life and that I was all alone in the world.

Then the sign came into view again: the back of the sign, of course. My father slowed the car and pulled over far to the right, and when he had come to a complete stop he checked over his shoulder for safety and made another U-turn so that we might face the sign again and read its message. The headlights made the sign huge and bright.

My father had been right. The sign said OWLS.

We kept sitting there for a long time. The engine was running; there was a small vibration.

Then my father turned off the engine. The early spring night air was cold, but he rolled down the windows.

I knew my father wanted me to be quiet. I'm not sure how I knew this. I knew he wanted us to listen. I scarcely breathed, I was listening so hard. I did not move at all.

Then I heard the owls overhead. I heard the soft centrifugal buffeting of their feathers on the night air. I heard a sound from their owl throats so soft I believed it was their breathing. In my mind I counted them and thought that they were many. The owls were circling and circling and circling in the air above us.

I don't know what I believed would happen. I think I believed I would feel the fingers of my father's hand touch my arm, the sleeve of my shirt. I believed I would turn to him and for the first time in my life I would know what to say. I would tell him all my secrets. I believed my father would say "I love you." This was what it meant to sit in a car with your father in the middle of the night and listen to a flock of owls while looking at a diamond-shaped sign that said OWLS.

Then he rolled up his window, and so I rolled up mine. In the darkness he said, "You know, your mother is a terrible housekeeper."

We only sat there looking at the OWLS sign. I knew things would not go well after this.

And so then he started up the car and we drove away, back along the dark road, and we did not say anything else to each other that night, and he drank a few more beers.

All I mean to say is this: Many years later I fell in love with a woman, and she was beautiful and strange. One afternoon, after we had made our love, we lay in a band of sunlight that fell across our bed and I told her the story of my father and the dark road and the sign that said OWLS.

I said, "You don't believe me, do you."

The woman said, "Have you ever told this story to anyone before?"

I said, "I told my mother. That same night, after my father and I got home and my mother came upstairs to tuck me in."

The woman said, "Tell me again about your room, then, with the fake stars on the ceiling."

I told her what she already knew. I said, "It was an attic room, with a slanted ceiling. A desk and even my clothes drawers were built into the wall to save space. There was a crawl space in the back of my closet, where I sat sometimes, in the rafters. On the ceiling above my bed were pasted luminous decals of stars and the planets and the moon. Saturn had rings. A comet had a funny tail."

She said, "Tell me again about the real moon."

I said, "The moon outside my window."

She said, "How large was it?"

I said what I had said to her many times. I said, "It was a peach-basket-sized moon."

She said, "And you were lying in your bed, with the fake stars shining down on you and the peach-basket moon outside your window, and then—"

I said, "I heard my mother coming up the stairs to tuck me in."

She said, "Your mother had been worried about you, out in the car with your father when he had been drinking."

I said, "Yes, she had been worried. She would never say this."

She said, "What did she say?"

I said, "She said, 'Did you have a nice time with Daddy tonight?'"

She said, "What did you say?"

I said, "I told her the story about seeing the sign. About stopping and listening to the owls in the air."

She said, "What did your mother say then?"

I said, "She said, 'That's about like your daddy.'"

She said, "Your mother didn't believe you?"

I said, "She was right. There was no OWLS sign. It's ridiculous. There is no way to hear OWLS in the air. And anyway, think about the coincidence of a drunk man and his oversensitive kid stopping at just the moment the owls happen to be flying above a sign."

She said, "Hm."

I said, "And you know that thing my father said. That thing about 'Your mother is a terrible housekeeper'?"

She said, "Mm-hm."

I said, "That's part of an old joke we used to hear in the South when I was a boy. The punch line is, 'My wife is a terrible housekeeper; every time I go to piss in the sink it's full of dirty dishes.'" I said, "I think I made the whole thing up."

She said, "Where did the owls come from?"

I said, "I'm not sure. Do you remember in *Winnie-the-Pooh*, the character named Owl?"

She said, "Yes."

I said, "Remember, somewhere, in one of those books, we learn that Owl's name is misspelled on a sign as WOL. Maybe that's where I got the idea. I just happened to think of the book. Jesus. It's possible I made this whole thing up."

She said, "Are rabbits' eyes really red?"

I said, "I don't know. I saw a blind dog in my headlights one time, and its eyes looked red. Christ."

The way the sunlight fell across this bed was . . . well, I was so much in love.
She said, "Was your father magic?"
I said, "I wanted him to be."
She said, "He might have been."

Now she looked at me, and it was the night of the owls all over again. The car's heater, the vibration of the engine, the red eyes of the rabbit, the stubble fields, the music of the odd birds in flight, the OWLS sign before me. And also the feeling that there was someone beside me to whom I could tell my most terrible secret and the secret would be heard and received as a gift. I believed my clumsy drunken inexpert father, or my invention of him, had prepared me for this magic. The woman beside me said, "I love you."

In that moment every good thing I had expected, longed to feel with my father, I felt with her. And I also felt it with my father, and I heard his voice speak those words of love, though he was already a long time dead. He was with me in a way he could not be in life.

For one second the woman and I seemed to become twins, or closer than twins, the same person together. Maybe we said nothing. Maybe we only lay in the band of sunlight that fell across our bed. Or maybe together we said, "There is great pain in all love, but we don't care, it's worth it." ■

DISCUSSING THE SELECTION

1. After reading this story, what do you know about "father"? From the information you can put together from the story, describe the man. What is his relationship to his son? What is his relationship to his wife?

2. What do you know about the boy? Describe him. How does he feel about his father? about his mother? How does he feel about falling in love now that he is an adult?

3. What in the story suggests that the mother and father do not trust each other?

4. What in the story suggests that the boy wants to trust his father? What does the boy want to tell his father? What does he hope his father will say to him? What prevents this from happening?

5. What is the man's "most terrible secret"?

6. Why does the woman want to know about the man's childhood? Why does she ask him if he has told the story to anyone else before? What details does she like to hear over and over again? Why does he tell her the story about the owls was not true?

THINKING CRITICALLY

1. Do you think the sign said "SLOW" or "OWLS"? Explain your answer, using the story or your own experience with life.

2. Did the man make up the story about the owls, his father, and himself as a boy? Have you ever made up a story or even exaggerated something that happened to you in your life? Why do people do this?

3. To you as a reader, what is the meaning of the last sentence in the story: "There is great pain in all love, but we don't care, it's worth it"?

FOCUSING ON THE WRITING

Narration

People have probably been telling stories since the origin of language. When writers tell stories, they try to keep a few ideas in mind.

> Stories are about people or characters.
>
> - Describe them carefully.
> - Make them seem real.
>
> Stories have plots.
>
> - Tell what happened in time order unless there is an important reason to tell it in another order.
>
> Stories happen somewhere.
>
> - Describe the location so the reader can see it through your eyes.
>
> Stories have a beginning, a middle, and an end.
>
> - The beginning usually sets out the situation.
> - The middle gives more details and sometimes adds new situations.
> - The end resolves the situation in some way.

1. In paragraph 1, in two sentences, Nordan gives his reader a lot of information about the story he is about to tell. What information does he give about the following?
   The characters in the story
   The time of day
   The setting or place
   The feelings of the narrator
   The reason for the feelings

2. Where in the story does the time shift? What words does Nordan use to indicate to his reader that the time in the story has changed and that the boy is now a man?

3. In paragraph 31, which begins, "I told her what she already knew," Nordan describes his childhood room in detail. Copy the descriptive words that draw a word picture to help a reader "see" the room. Write a short description of a room that is familiar to you and include as many details as you think you need to draw a word picture of that room. Share it with

a classmate, and discuss with each other whether the room becomes real in your description.

CREATING YOUR TEXT

1. Spend five minutes freewriting about this story and what experiences in your own life it made you think about. To do this (see pages 6–7), open to a blank page and start to write down any ideas that come into your mind. This activity may help you remember a story or a person you can use in your writing. It may also help you relax as you write. The only requirement is that you write for the entire five minutes without stopping to reread, judge, or edit what you have written.

2. Read through your freewriting and through the journal entry you wrote before you read "Owls." Write a story telling about a childhood experience that confused you and that even today you do not entirely understand. In your conclusion, explain why the experience remains confusing to you and how, if in any way, your adult perceptions help you to clarify the experience.

3. Some people recall that when they were children, they could not communicate with their parents. Others feel that it is more difficult for adult children to communicate with their parents. Decide how you feel about this, and write an essay in which you use supporting details from your own life or from stories you have read that explain why you feel as you do.

4. Part of growing up involves forgiving adults for some of the mistakes that they made. Explain what the narrator of the story learned about himself and his family through telling this family story, *or* tell your own family story and explain what you have learned about yourself or your family by writing and thinking about this experience.

REVISING YOUR TEXT

Review the first draft of your writing by reading the draft alone or with a classmate and then going over the revision questions on page 11 or 12 if you have written an essay or on page 13 or 14 if you have written a story.

In addition, think about the following questions as you read the narrative section of what you have written:

What details do you provide to make each person unique or special?

What events do you describe? In what order did you present them? What details did you include to make these events interesting to read about?

Where does the story take place? What details have you included to describe the place?

Does your story have a beginning, a middle, and an end? How does the end relate to the beginning? If you have written an essay, how does the story relate to your main idea in the essay?

EXPANDING YOUR IDEAS

Collaborative Writing Projects

1. With a classmate, discuss the various family stories you have read in this theme. Together, decide on two people, each from a different selection, whom you would like to introduce to each other. Discuss the characteristics of each individual and what they might say to each other. Together, write a draft imagining their first meeting. What do you think they would say to each other? What would they learn from each other? Are there any specific areas about which they would have disagreement, or any specific areas about which you feel sure they would agree? What details from the selection made you feel this way? Rewrite the draft describing their first meeting until you both feel ready to share it with other classmates.

2. Next, meet in a small group of three or four students. After reading all the drafts from project 1 carefully, choose one you especially like. As a group, read the revision questions on page 14 and revise the writing into a second draft to share with the whole class.

3. Each group will read its draft to the whole class. Then, as a class, choose one draft that everyone particularly enjoys. Together, on the computer if you have a networking system or on the chalkboard, all students can work together revising the group draft to make it clearer and more interesting. You may decide to submit the final draft of the story to a college magazine or newspaper as a class project.

As we move toward adulthood, we develop a vision of ourselves and of the goals we have for our lives. The ways in which we fulfill these goals mark us as unique human beings.

Theme 2

Fulfilling a Personal Dream

Readings

"Running Toward Victory"
BY SUSANNA LEVIN

"Iron Man"
BY DOUGLAS M. WEESE

"Daughter of Invention"
BY JULIA ALVAREZ

"One Man's Kids"
BY DANIEL MEIER

"'They've Gotta Have Us'"
BY KAREN GRIGSBY BATES

"This Lady Came Down from the Mountains"
BY ROBERT DRAPER

"Three Thousand Dollars"
BY DAVID LIPSKY

"Running Toward Victory," by Susanna Levin, tells about Yvette La Vigne, who in her fifties became stronger and more confident because of her newfound ability to run and compete.

In some ways La Vigne's achievement is similar to that of "Iron Man," in which Douglas M. Weese tells about a kayaker, Greg Barton, who learned that physical discipline could help him fulfill his dreams. Barton learned discipline early in life, to overcome a physical limitation.

"Daughter of Invention," by Julia Alvarez, describes the beginning of a writer's life: Yolanda must regain her voice after losing it to satisfy her father's demands.

"One Man's Kids," by Daniel Meier, describes a young man's confrontation of stereotypes in fulfilling his dream of becoming a first-grade teacher.

Karen Grigsby Bates, in her article "'They've Gotta Have Us,'" tells us about John Singleton, a young filmmaker who writes and directs films that present his view of the problems of urban society today.

In "This Lady Came Down from the Mountains," Robert Draper describes the life and times of a newly discovered 78-year-old writer, and shows that the dream of personal fulfillment is ageless.

Our values and views about honesty are questioned in "Three Thousand Dollars" as David Lipsky challenges us to think about how fulfilling one's personal needs can impinge on and create problems for those close to us.

Making Discoveries

In Your Journal

Write in your journal about a person that you know, have seen on television or in the movies, or have read about in a book, who has fulfilled a personal dream that matters to you. Describe what you admire about this person. Describe the steps the person took to fulfill his or her dream. Describe any setbacks this person had. Describe how the setbacks were overcome. Explain why you have selected this person and what the person's story means to you.

With a Classmate

Talk to your classmate about the person you have selected. Explain why you chose this person. What do the individuals you each chose have in common? What is unique about each individual you selected?

With Your Class

Discuss some of the individuals you each selected. What do these people have in common? Decide what elements your classmates focused on when they made their decisions, and make a list of these. What does this list tell you about the values held by the members of your class?

EXPLORING YOUR IDEAS

Is there an athletic activity you have always wanted to try but still have not tried yet? Write about the athletic activity and why you would like to try it someday. Why haven't you tried it yet? What would get you to try it? Write about this activity and your feelings about it.

Running Toward Victory

SUSANNA LEVIN

Susanna Levin published this article in the March–April 1992 issue of *Ms.* magazine. It tells about an athlete and marathon runner who began running at the age of forty-seven.

When Yvette La Vigne crossed the finish line first in the 800-meter run at the U.S. National Masters Track & Field Championships last July [1991], she says, "I couldn't believe what I had just done."

What La Vigne did was run a perfect race and win a national title in her first year of competing in track. The 52-year-old from Los Angeles came from behind in the final turn to beat Jane Arnold, of Connecticut, by a stride. The day before, Arnold had beaten La Vigne soundly in the 5,000 meters, and La Vigne went to the track expecting to lose again. "She was really tough," says La Vigne, who has only been running for four years.

On the advice of some other runners, La Vigne stayed with Arnold for the first lap and a half of the two-lap race. "I knew she was worried because just as we went into the turn she looked around, and I was gaining," she says. La Vigne felt her confidence rise, and as the two runners came out of the turn, she pulled ahead of Arnold. "When I took that second step in front of her, then I knew. I thought, I'm not going to let her catch me. I dug down deep, and I could hear my coach from L.A. talking to me, and everything everyone else had ever said to me," says La Vigne. "I just tried to remember to pump those arms and lift those legs."

She crossed the line just seconds ahead of Arnold. Some other runners from Los Angeles were there, waiting for her with outstretched arms. "I believe they were as happy as I was," she says. "It was total elation."

It is not a scene that La Vigne would have imagined just a few years ago. "Not in my wildest imagination," she laughs. "It surprises me, the things I'm accomplishing at this age, at 52. I never knew I was competitive, and I have never made a commitment to anything like this."

Her commitment includes getting up at 4 A.M. to run with a few other members of Renaissance Runners, L.A.'s largest African American running club. She puts in a five- to eight-mile run four mornings a week before going to work as a substitute elementary school teacher. "It gives me the extra energy I need to keep up with the stress of the job. The needs are so great in the inner city. As a substitute, you're dealing with a different group of children each day, and there's only so much influence you're going to have on them."

Although she says she was always health conscious, La Vigne was 47 and completely untrained when some friends encouraged her to try to run the L.A. Marathon. She ran the marathon with some other club members; their camaraderie and guidance got her through that first race and beyond.

"My group took me along slowly, so I finished without any problems," she says. A month later, she came in second in her age division at the Long Beach Marathon, and she was hooked. She's run 12 marathons, and won several of them in her age group.

Last year, a friend suggested she try running on the track. "He told me what a positive experience Nationals was. He encouraged me because he thought I had the ability," La Vigne recalls. Soon she was commuting 45 minutes during L.A.'s hellish rush hour to do grueling speed workouts on the track with a coach from the California Institute of Technology. "It's something I love to hate," she laughs. "It's intense, and not as enjoyable as taking the long runs, but there are two or three people doing the same workout, and we just pull one another through it," she says.

All that effort was rewarded when she won her Nationals victory, although La Vigne is quick to point out that when she and Arnold met up again a few months later, the Connecticut runner came out on top. "We've struck up a runners' friendship," says La Vigne of her competitor. "I look forward to seeing her at the next meet."

La Vigne is still running marathons, still seeking decreasing times. Running gives her great joy, she says, and fills her with energy. It has also given her a new, deeper confidence in herself, and reaffirmed her belief that hard work pays off. "I try to instill this in the children I work with. They come from such poverty, and I try to tell them that you can succeed in spite of all this, as long as you're determined to work at it," she says. "I tell them it does not come easy." ■

DISCUSSING THE SELECTION

1. What in this selection tells the reader that La Vigne was athletically fit, although untrained, when she ran her first marathon?

2. What experiences does she have with the competition runner Jane Arnold? At the end of the article, what does La Vigne say she feels about Arnold?

3. In the article, what specific steps are described that La Vigne takes to prepare herself for competition running?

4. What in the article tells the reader that La Vigne benefits from the relationships she has developed in running?

5. How does La Vigne use in her everyday job the principles she has learned from running?

THINKING CRITICALLY

1. What does being "athletically fit" or "in condition" mean to you? What athletic activity do you do every day, three times a week, or once a week?

If you do not do any athletic activity, what would you like to do if you had the time or ability?

2. Have you ever been in an athletic competition? What was the competition? How did you feel when you won or lost? Did you feel differently when you were younger than when you were older? If so, why?

3. What does this article suggest about age as a factor in becoming physically active? If you know any older person who is still or has recently become involved in an athletic activity, tell the class about the person(s) and about his or her athletic experiences.

FOCUSING ON THE WRITING

Journalistic Writing

Journalistic writing is found in newspapers, magazines, and in many nonfiction books. The purpose of journalistic writing is to inform readers about a subject.

To do this, the writer answers *who, what, where, when, why,* and *how* questions about the subject covered in the article. Readers expect this information to be provided directly and clearly.

1. Find answers to the following journalistic questions by rereading the article. As you do so, notice where the answers are located in the article.

    a. *Who* is the article about?

    b. *What* is happening to that person?

    c. *What* specific information do you know about the subject of this article? *What* facts does the writer present? *Why* are these important to the article?

    d. *Where* do the events in the article take place?
    e. *When* do they take place?
    f. *Why* are these events important or worth finding out about?
    g. *How* do these events affect the lives of the main character and of the reader(s)?

2. What is the thesis statement or main idea of this selection? Where is it located? What supporting details or information does Levin provide to support her main idea?

3. What is the purpose of the introduction to this selection? Which style of introduction did Levin use? (See pages 23–24 for more information on writing an introduction.)

CREATING YOUR TEXT

1. Reread the journal entry you wrote before reading the article about Yvette La Vigne. Write an essay in which you tell the reader about the athletic activity you would like to try and the particular steps you would take to become competent in the activity. In your conclusion, explain why you have not tried the activity yet and why you think it would be a good experience for you to do so.

2. Most athletes do not compete in competitions or get accepted onto professional teams. They feel pleasure in simply performing better with practice. Each small victory is called a "personal best." On the top of your page, write "Personal Bests." Make a list of your own personal bests. These do not have to be only athletic. You may think of personal bests in school, at home, at work, or with your friends. Choose one of these personal bests, and write an essay in which you describe what you did and the events that led up to your success. Explain why this personal best was important to you.

3. Some people believe that sports, especially school sports, have become too competitive. They think that there should be more emphasis on "personal

bests" instead (see question 2) or on getting better for self-improvement rather than on competing and winning. Write an essay in which you discuss what you think about competition and competitive sports. Is there too much emphasis on competition in school sports? Is there a difference between what people gain from self-discipline and what they gain from competing with others?

REVISING YOUR TEXT

When you have finished writing your first draft, share it with a classmate. Discuss what you have written, focusing on the strong points and on parts of the essay that need improvement. Then together review the essay by going over the revision questions on page 11.

In addition, create *who, what, where, when, why,* and *how* questions that relate to your topic. Reread your essay, noticing whether you have answered these questions in your writing. Make the changes you think will improve your draft. Share this draft with your class.

EXPLORING YOUR IDEAS

Think about an activity you tried that was hard for you at first, but at which you got better and better as you practiced. Write about your experience with this activity. How did you feel when you first tried it? How did you improve your performance? Why did you keep trying to get better? What advice would you give someone who was thinking about trying that activity for the first time?

Iron Man

DOUGLAS M. WEESE

In this article, which appeared in *Horizon Air* in March 1992, Douglas Weese tells about an athlete who has succeeded despite physical limitations.

Before moving to the Northwest [in 1988], Olympic kayaker Greg Barton did most of his training in Newport Harbor in Southern California. Today, most of his workouts are on Washington's beautiful Lake Samish near Bellingham. As far as training grounds go, not bad, not bad at all.

Barton's real training, however, came on his Daddy's hog farm in Homer, Michigan, getting up before dawn to feed the animals, fill their troughs, all whether he wanted to or not. Every day. The Midwest work ethic is deeply rooted, and he's proud of it.

"A lot of fair weather athletes can train in good conditions, but the ones who succeed are those who can get past the thousands of excuses not to train," says Barton, a flawless technician renowned for pulling away from the pack down the stretch. "Some are willing to do half the work, but it's that final bit that only a few are willing to do."

Barton is not just one of the few; he is the only American to win an Olympic gold medal in kayaking. He did it on Seoul's Han River in 1988, edging Australia's Grant Davies in the 1,000-meter flatwater by .005 seconds. Just 90 minutes later, he got back in the water and stunned onlookers by picking up another gold, this time in the 10,000-meter doubles. In the 1984 Los Angeles Games, his bronze finish was America's first medal since 1964.

Barton realizes that most people see only the fleeting moments of Olympic glory, athletes stepping up to receive medals or taking victory laps. Others don't feel the fatigue and the pain or see the sacrifices made while chasing Olympic rainbows. They don't know what it's like to work out twice a day for 335 days last year, either on the water or in the weight room. "The main thing that makes him really good is his life discipline," says his coach, Paul Podgorski.

Barton was born with clubfeet, his bones fused in three separate surgeries between the ages of 10 and 13. The operations actually made things worse. He lost mobility completely in one ankle, and one leg ultimately wound up shorter than the other. Although he managed to participate in cross country in high school, he's since broken bones in his feet attempting to run too much.

The fact that kayaking is almost exclusively an upper-body sport was purely coincidental.

"Looking back, I was lucky I chose kayaking, but it really happened by chance," says Barton, who began canoeing on family vacations in Upper Michigan and Canada. His parents raced in canoe marathons as a mixed team, while his older brother, Bruce, went on to compete on the 1976 U.S. Olympic kayak team.

"It [clubfeet] may have made me more dedicated because I realized I had to overcome obstacles and struggle day to day to do what others took for granted. When training and hard times hit, I know I've gone through hard times before."

While his chances of winning a medal are good, repeating his double-gold performance in Barcelona is no sure thing. Norway's Knut Holmann has won the 1,000-meter world championships the past two years, while Barton finished third in 1991 behind Ferenc Csipes of Hungary. Barton finished fourth in 1990.

Barcelona . . . will be Barton's last Olympic competition. A summa cum laude graduate at the University of Michigan, Barton works as a mechanical engineer for Ocean Kayak in Ferndale, Washington. He's 32 years old and eager to get on with life. Only two other American paddlers have made the Olympic team four times.

"Sometimes you wonder why you're doing it. I've sacrificed a lot, put my career on hold and spent a lot of time away from family and friends," he says. "But I still have the desire to be the best and know hard work is what it takes to get there. I know in five or 10 years I'll be glad I did." ■

12

DISCUSSING THE SELECTION

1. What details in this article convince you that the title "Iron Man" is a good description of Greg Barton?

2. What are clubfeet? How does Greg Barton look on the fact that he was born with clubfeet? What evidence in the selection influenced your interpretation?

3. What steps are revealed in this article that could help one to become a successful athlete? Which steps are similar to those you read about in any other selections in this class or in other readings outside of class?

4. What is Greg Barton's daily routine? How does Barton make himself go through this routine every day?

THINKING CRITICALLY

1. Coach Paul Podgorski says that the main thing that makes Barton "really good is his life discipline." How do you define a "disciplined" athlete? How do you define a "talented" athlete? Explain the differences between the two.

2. Name an athlete that you think of as "disciplined," one that you see as "talented," and one that you see as a combination of these. Explain your choices.

3. Almost everyone knows of at least one person such as Greg Barton who has had to overcome a physical problem to reach a goal. Discuss the person you know, the goal, and the steps the person took to fulfill the goal.

FOCUSING ON THE WRITING

Cause and Effect

One way that writers organize their ideas is called *cause and effect*. In this method, the author tries to make connections between a result and the event(s) that led to this result.

To explain something through cause and effect, some writers develop their ideas with chronological or time order to show how one event led to another. Some use description or narration. However, keep in mind that it is difficult to state with certainty that a particular event "caused" a specific response. Life is complicated, and there are almost always multiple reasons—immediate, obvious reasons and distant, underlying reasons—to explain why something occurred. Make your connections as logical and believable as possible.

Some words used to establish cause and effect are *as a result, consequently, for this reason, due to, therefore, because, since,* and *the reason why.*

1. In this article, Weese presents as *cause* the events that lead to the *effect,* which is that Barton is a dedicated and disciplined athlete. Reread paragraphs 1 to 4 and locate the events that Weese mentioned that lead a reader

to see Barton as dedicated and disciplined. With a classmate, list the specific events mentioned in these paragraphs. Are the connections between the causes and effects convincing to you as a reader?

2. Where in this essay does Weese establish a cause-and-effect relationship using a specific word or phrase? For ideas, look at the box on cause and effect.

3. Notice the time shifts in this article. What tenses are in the first paragraph? Why is there a change in tense in this paragraph? In what tense is paragraph 2 written? paragraph 3?

4. The author never explains what a "kayak" is or what the difference is between a kayak and a canoe. If you were not sure about this, what did you do to find the answer? Explain the difference to someone in your class who still is unsure.

5. Many words in this article refer to the hard work of becoming a successful athlete. Make a list of these words. Try to use some of these words when you write an essay about this subject.

CREATING YOUR TEXT

1. Write an essay in which you use your journal entry as a springboard for writing. In the essay, describe an activity you tried that was hard for you at first, but at which you got better and better as you practiced. What caused you to attempt this activity? What effect has this activity had on your life? How did you feel when you first tried it? How did you improve your performance? Why did you keep trying to get better? What advice would you give someone who was thinking about trying that activity for the first time?

2. Write an essay in which you explain what caused you to enroll in college. Then describe the effect this action has had on your life up to now.

3. Write an essay in which you compare and contrast the steps taken by Greg Barton to those taken by Yvette La Vigne (see page 78) to prepare for athletic competition. What do both athletes do to prepare themselves? What differences do you notice in reading the two articles? In your conclusion, include what you as a reader have learned about what it takes to be a competitive athlete.

4. Write an essay in which you describe a sports figure who is important to you. Tell about the person's background, ability, special game, and whatever else makes this person your sports hero.

5. Shannon Cate, one of the best female basketball players in the United States, once said that sports teach a person discipline, and how to deal with people, jealousy, being in the limelight, and accepting authority figures. Write an essay in which you agree or disagree with Cate's statement, giving examples supporting your point of view.

REVISING YOUR TEXT

Share your first draft with a partner, looking at the revision questions on page 11. Together, decide what is strong in your writing and what changes you want to make when you write your second draft.

If you used the cause-and-effect method of organizing your ideas, discuss with a classmate whether the cause-and-effect relationship you described is believable and logical. If not, how can you improve the connection? Remember to think about other underlying or more distant causes that related to the event. What words and phrases did you use to establish the cause-and-effect relationship?

Theme 2 Fulfilling a Personal Dream

EXPLORING YOUR IDEAS

Write about an experience you had in which you made a compromise to get something that was important to you. In your writing, explain why your goal was so important. Explain why you feel you were willing to compromise, and think about whether you would do the same thing again.

Daughter of Invention

JULIA ALVAREZ

Julia Alvarez was born in the Dominican Republic and came to the United States when she was ten years old. She now lives in Middlebury, Vermont, where she teaches writing at Middlebury College. She has written many stories and essays, but is best known for her novel *How the García Girls Lost Their Accents* (1991), from which the following story is excerpted.

In ninth grade, Yoyo was chosen by her English teacher, Sister Mary Joseph, to deliver the Teacher's Day address at the school assembly. Back in the Dominican Republic growing up, Yoyo had been a terrible student. No one could ever get her to sit down to a book. But in New York, she needed to settle somewhere, and since the natives were unfriendly, and the country inhospitable, she took root in the language. By high school, the nuns were reading her stories and compositions out loud in English class.

But the spectre of delivering a speech brown-nosing the teachers jammed her imagination. At first she didn't want to and then she couldn't seem to write that speech. She should have thought of it as "a great honor," as her father called it. But she was mortified. She still had a slight accent, and she did not like to speak in public, subjecting herself to her classmates' ridicule. It also took no great figuring to see that to deliver a eulogy for a convent full of crazy, old, overweight nuns was no way to endear herself to her peers.

But she didn't know how to get out of it. Night after night, she sat at her desk, hoping to polish off some quick, noncommittal little speech. But she couldn't get anything down.

The weekend before the assembly Monday morning Yoyo went into a panic. Her mother would just have to call in tomorrow and say Yoyo was in the hospital, in a coma.

Laura tried to calm her down. "Just remember how Mister Lincoln couldn't think of anything to say at the Gettysburg, but then, bang! *Four score and once upon a time ago,*" she began reciting. "Something is going to come if you just relax. You'll see, like the Americans say, *Necessity is the daughter of invention.* I'll help you."

That weekend, her mother turned all her energy towards helping Yoyo write her speech. "Please, Mami, just leave me alone, please," Yoyo pleaded with her. But Yoyo would get rid of the goose only to have to contend with the gander. Her father kept poking his head in the door just to see if Yoyo had "fulfilled your obligations," a phrase he had used when the girls were younger and he'd check to see whether they had gone to the bathroom before a car trip. Several times that weekend around the supper table, he recited his own high school valedictorian speech. He gave Yoyo pointers on delivery, notes on the great orators and their tricks. (Humbleness and praise and falling silent with great emotion were his favorites.)

Laura sat across the table, the only one who seemed to be listening to him. Yoyo and her sisters were forgetting a lot of their Spanish, and their father's formal, florid diction was hard to understand. But Laura smiled softly to herself, and turned the lazy Susan at the center of the table around and around as if it were the prime mover, the first gear of her attention.

That Sunday evening, Yoyo was reading some poetry to get herself inspired: Whitman's poems in an old book with an engraved cover her father had picked up in a thrift shop next to his office. *I celebrate myself and sing myself.... He most honors my style who learns under it to destroy the teacher.* The poet's words shocked and thrilled her. She had gotten used to the nuns, a literature of appropriate sentiments, poems with a message, expurgated texts. But here was a flesh and blood man, belching and laughing and sweating in poems. *Who touches this book touches a man.*

That night, at last, she started to write, recklessly, three, five pages, looking up once only to see her father passing by the hall on tiptoe. When Yoyo was done, she read over her words, and her eyes filled. She finally sounded like herself in English!

As soon as she had finished that first draft, she called her mother to her room. Laura listened attentively while Yoyo read the speech out loud, and in the end, her eyes were glistening too. Her face was soft and warm and proud. "*Ay*, Yoyo, you are going to be the one to bring our name to the headlights in this country! That is a beautiful, beautiful speech. I want for your father to hear it before he goes to sleep. Then I will type it for you, all right?"

Down the hall they went, mother and daughter, faces flushed with accomplishment. Into the master bedroom where Carlos was propped up on his pillows, still awake, reading the Dominican papers, already days old. Now that the dictatorship had been toppled, he had become interested in his country's fate again. The interim government was going to hold the first free elections in thirty years. History was in the making, freedom and hope were in the air again! There was still some question in his mind whether or not he might move his family back. But Laura had gotten used to the life here. She did not want to go back to the old country where, de la Torre or not, she was only a wife and a mother (and a failed one at that, since she had never provided the required son). Better an independent nobody than a high-class houseslave. She did not come straight out and disagree with her husband's plans. Instead, she fussed with him about reading the papers in bed, soiling their sheets with those poorly printed, foreign tabloids. "*The Times* is not that bad!" she'd claim if her husband tried to humor her by saying they shared the same dirty habit.

The minute Carlos saw his wife and daughter filing in, he put his paper down, and his face brightened as if at long last his wife had delivered the son, and that was the news she was bringing him. His teeth were already grinning from the glass of water next to his bedside lamp, so he lisped when he said, "Eh-speech, eh-speech!"

"It is so beautiful, Cuco," Laura coached him, turning the sound on his TV off. She sat down at the foot of the bed. Yoyo stood before both of them, blocking their view of the soldiers in helicopters landing amid silenced gun reports and explosions. A few weeks ago it had been the shores of the

Dominican Republic. Now it was the jungles of Southeast Asia they were saving. Her mother gave her the nod to begin reading.

Yoyo didn't need much encouragement. She put her nose to the fire, as her mother would have said, and read from start to finish without looking up. When she concluded, she was a little embarrassed at the pride she took in her own words. She pretended to quibble with a phrase or two, then looked questioningly to her mother. Laura's face was radiant. Yoyo turned to share her pride with her father.

The expression on his face shocked both mother and daughter. Carlos's toothless mouth had collapsed into a dark zero. His eyes bored into Yoyo, then shifted to Laura. In barely audible Spanish, as if secret microphones or informers were all about, he whispered to his wife, "You will permit her to read *that?*"

Laura's eyebrows shot up, her mouth fell open. In the old country, any whisper of a challenge to authority could bring the secret police in their black V.W.'s. But this was America. People could say what they thought. "What is wrong with her speech?" Laura questioned him.

"What ees wrrrong with her eh-speech?" Carlos wagged his head at her. His anger was always more frightening in his broken English. As if he had mutilated the language in his fury—and now there was nothing to stand between them and his raw, dumb anger. "What is wrong? I will tell you what is wrong. It show no gratitude. It is boastful. *I celebrate myself? The best student learns to destroy the teacher?*" He mocked Yoyo's plagiarized words. "That is insubordinate. It is improper. It is disrespecting of her teachers—" In his anger he had forgotten his fear of lurking spies: each wrong he voiced was a decibel higher than the last outrage. Finally, he shouted at Yoyo, "As your father, I forbid you to make that eh-speech!"

Laura leapt to her feet, a sign that *she* was about to deliver her own speech. She was a small woman, and she spoke all her pronouncements standing up, either for more protection or as a carry-over from her girlhood in convent schools where one asked for and, literally, took the floor in order to speak. She stood by Yoyo's side, shoulder to shoulder. They looked down at Carlos. "That is no tone of voice—" she began.

But now, Carlos was truly furious. It was bad enough that his daughter was rebelling, but here was his own wife joining forces with her. Soon he would be surrounded by a houseful of independent American women. He too leapt from the bed, throwing off his covers. The Spanish newspapers flew across the room. He snatched the speech out of Yoyo's hands, held it before the girl's wide eyes, a vengeful, mad look in his own, and then once, twice, three, four, countless times, he tore the speech into shreds.

"Are you crazy?" Laura lunged at him. "Have you gone mad? That is her speech for tomorrow you have torn up!"

"Have *you* gone mad?" He shook her away. "You were going to let her read that . . . that insult to her teachers?"

"Insult to her teachers!" Laura's face had crumpled up like a piece of paper. On it was written a love note to her husband, an unhappy, haunted man. "This is America, Papi, America! You are not in a savage country anymore!"

Meanwhile, Yoyo was on her knees, weeping wildly, collecting all the little pieces of her speech, hoping that she could put it back together before the assembly tomorrow morning. But not even a sibyl could have made sense of those tiny scraps of paper. All hope was lost. "He broke it, he broke it," Yoyo moaned as she picked up a handful of pieces.

Probably, if she had thought a moment about it, she would not have done what she did next. She would have realized her father had lost brothers and friends to the dictator Trujillo. For the rest of his life, he would be haunted by blood in the streets and late night disappearances. Even after all these years, he cringed if a black Volkswagen passed him on the street. He feared anyone in uniform: the meter maid giving out parking tickets, a museum guard approaching to tell him not to get too close to his favorite Goya.

On her knees, Yoyo thought of the worst thing she could say to her father. She gathered a handful of scraps, stood up, and hurled them in his face. In a low, ugly whisper, she pronounced Trujillo's hated nickname: "Chapita! You're just another Chapita!"

It took Yoyo's father only a moment to register the loathsome nickname before he came after her. Down the halls they raced, but Yoyo was quicker than he and made it into her room just in time to lock the door as her father threw his weight against it. He called down curses on her head, ordered her on his authority as her father to open that door! He throttled that doorknob, but all to no avail. Her mother's love of gadgets saved Yoyo's hide that night. Laura had hired a locksmith to install good locks on all the bedroom doors after the house had been broken into once while they were away. Now if burglars broke in again, and the family were at home, there would be a second round of locks for the thieves to contend with.

"Lolo," she said, trying to calm him down. "Don't you ruin my new locks."

Finally he did calm down, his anger spent. Yoyo heard their footsteps retreating down the hall. Their door clicked shut. Then, muffled voices, her mother's rising in anger, in persuasion, her father's deeper murmurs of explanation and self-defense. The house fell silent a moment, before Yoyo heard, far off, the gun blasts and explosions, the serious, self-important voices of newscasters reporting their TV war.

A little while later, there was a quiet knock at Yoyo's door, followed by a tentative attempt at the door knob. "Cuquita?" her mother whispered. "Open up, Cuquita."

"Go away," Yoyo wailed, but they both knew she was glad her mother was there, and needed only a moment's protest to save face.

Together they concocted a speech: two brief pages of stale compliments and the polite commonplaces on teachers, a speech wrought by necessity and without much invention by mother and daughter late into the night on one of the pads of paper Laura had once used for her own inventions. After it was drafted, Laura typed it up while Yoyo stood by, correcting her mother's misnomers and mis-sayings.

Yoyo came home the next day with the success story of the assembly. The nuns had been flattered, the audience had stood up and given "our devoted teachers a standing ovation," what Laura had suggested they do at the end of the speech.

She clapped her hands together as Yoyo recreated the moment. "I stole that from your father's speech, remember? Remember how he put that in at the end?" She quoted him in Spanish, then translated for Yoyo into English.

That night, Yoyo watched him from the upstairs hall window, where she'd retreated the minute she heard his car pull up in front of the house. Slowly, her father came up the driveway, a grim expression on his face as he grappled with a large, heavy cardboard box. At the front door, he set the package down carefully and patted all his pockets for his house keys. (If only he'd had Laura's ticking key chain!) Yoyo heard the snapping open of locks downstairs. She listened as he struggled to maneuver the box through the narrow doorway. He called her name several times, but she did not answer him.

"My daughter, your father, he love you very much," he explained from the bottom of the stairs. "He just want to protect you." Finally, her mother came up and pleaded with Yoyo to go down and reconcile with him. "Your father did not mean to harm. You must pardon him. Always it is better to let bygones be forgotten, no?"

Downstairs, Yoyo found her father setting up a brand new electric typewriter on the kitchen table. It was even better than her mother's. He had outdone himself with all the extra features: a plastic carrying case with Yoyo's initials decaled below the handle, a brace to lift the paper upright while she typed, an erase cartridge, an automatic margin tab, a plastic hood like a toaster cover to keep the dust away. Not even her mother could have invented such a machine!

But Laura's inventing days were over just as Yoyo's were starting up with her school-wide success. Rather than the rolling suitcase everyone else in the family remembers, Yoyo thinks of the speech her mother wrote as her last invention. It was as if, after that, her mother had passed on to Yoyo her pencil and pad and said, "Okay, Cuquita, here's the buck. You give it a shot." ∎

DISCUSSING THE SELECTION

1. In the story, what differences are presented between the father and his daughter in relation to attitudes toward teachers and toward authority in general? What causes these differences?

2. Reread this story, focusing on Yoyo's parents. Describe "Mami" or "Laura." Why does she help Yoyo rewrite the speech? What is her relationship to "Papi" or "Carlos" like? Describe Papi. Why does he get upset about Yoyo's first speech? What evidence in the story supports your ideas?

3. What do you find out about Yoyo from this story? What is her role in this story? Could Yoyo have accomplished what she did without Mami's help? What other stories do you know in which someone helps the main character fulfill a goal or a dream? Which of these stories would you recommend to other readers in your class? Explain why you think your classmates might enjoy these stories.

4. What is the significance of the typewriter at the end of the story?

THINKING CRITICALLY

1. In this story, Yoyo is a nickname for "Yolanda." What else does the word *yo-yo* mean? In what ways does this nickname describe the girl's character? If you have a nickname, tell the class what it is and how you got it. If you do not like your nickname, what have you done to stop people from calling you by that name?

2. Have you ever had an experience during which someone did something upsetting, as Papi does in this story? Explain your situation to the class, and tell how the situation was finally resolved.

3. Although Papi considers his daughter's delivering the speech to be a great honor, she is not as happy about the assignment as he is. Why? Have you ever had an experience in which family members felt happy about an event in your life that you felt less happy or satisfied about? Explain to the class.

FOCUSING ON THE WRITING

Point of View—Types of Narrators

The term "point of view" refers to the angle of the narrator or storyteller as a story is told. Some types of narrators include the following:

- The *omniscient narrator* (the storyteller tells the thoughts and feelings of *all* the characters and has a godlike intuition)
- The *limited omniscient narrator* (the storyteller tells the thoughts and feelings of only *one* character)

- The *objective (camera) view narrator* (the storyteller sees and records the action from the outside, from an unemotional angle; in this case, the narrator just tells the story without revealing the inner thoughts and feelings of any of the characters)

1. Do we know the inner thoughts and feelings of any of the characters in this story? What type of narrator is used in "Daughter of Invention"? What evidence in the story supports your answer?

2. Look at other stories in this book or any others you have written or read. Decide what type of narrator tells each story. Which types of stories do you usually prefer? Why?

3. Writers use words and tell about specific incidents in ways that make the readers feel for their characters. Sometimes writers prefer particular characters in their writing. Which character do you think Alvarez prefers in this story? Support your answer with evidence from the story.

4. "Daughter of Invention" is an example of *narrating* or telling a story. Stories are usually told in the past tense. Stories often tell the who, what, where, when, how, and why of an event. Where in "Daughter of Invention" does Alvarez answer the questions who, what, where, when, how, and why about the event she is narrating?

CREATING YOUR TEXT

1. Rewrite this story from the viewpoint of one character in the story, revealing that person's thoughts and feelings in detail.

2. Is there always a "generation gap" or difference in thinking and attitude between parents and children? Write an essay in which you take a point

of view and support it with your own experiences, the experiences of other people you know, or your readings.

3. The behavior of the father in "Daughter of Invention" is influenced by experiences in his native country. Write an essay describing a person whose behavior is affected by something that happened to that person in his or her past. Describe a particular event and how that person responds to it because of the earlier experience. What have you learned from knowing and observing that person?

4. In the end of the story, Papi gives Yoyo a typewriter and her writing career begins. In an essay, explain how writing with a typewriter or a computer has changed your writing. Tell your readers in what ways it has improved or worsened your writing, and explain why you think it did so.

REVISING YOUR TEXT

Review the first draft of your writing by going over the revision questions on page 12 if you have written an essay and on page 14 if you have written a story.

Notice "how" you tell your story. What point of view do you use? You may want to rewrite the story part of your essay from a different point of view. How does the point of view affect the telling of your story?

EXPLORING YOUR IDEAS

Write about any experience you have had working with, teaching, or caring for young childen. Focus on one experience in which you think you learned something about yourself and/or something about children. Describe your experience in as much detail as possible.

One Man's Kids

DANIEL MEIER

Daniel Meier teaches at a public elementary school in Boston, Massachusetts. He got his bachelor's degree from Wesleyan University in 1982 when he was twenty-three years old. Two years later, he received a master's degree from Harvard Graduate School of Education. Meier has written many essays about education and about his experiences, including "One Man's Kids," which originally appeared in the "About Men" series in *The New York Times*.

I teach first graders. I live in a world of skinned knees, double-knotted shoelaces, riddles that I've heard a dozen times, stale birthday cakes, hurt feelings, wandering stories and one lost shoe ("and if you don't find it my mother'll kill me"). My work is dominated by 6-year-olds. 1

It's 10:45, the middle of snack, and I'm helping Emily open her milk carton. She has already tried the other end without success, and now there's so much paint and ink on the carton from her fingers that I'm not sure she should drink it at all. But I open it. Then I turn to help Scott clean up some milk he has just spilled onto Rebecca's whale crossword puzzle. 2

While I wipe my milk- and paint-covered hands, Jenny wants to know if I've seen that funny book about penguins that I read in class. As I hunt for it 3 in a messy pile of books, Jason wants to know if there is a new seating arrangement for lunch tables. I find the book, turn to answer Jason, then face Maya, who is fast approaching with a new knock-knock joke. After what seems like the 10th "Who's there?" I laugh and Maya is pleased.

Then Andrew wants to know how to spell "flukes" for his crossword. As I get to "u," I give a hand signal for Sarah to take away the snack. But just as Sarah is almost out the door, two children complain that "we haven't even had ours yet." I stop the snack mid-flight, complying with their request for graham crackers. I then return to Andrew, noticing that he has put "flu" for 9 Down, rather than 9 Across. It's now 10:50.

My work is not traditional male work. It's not a singular pursuit. There is not a large pile of paper to get through or one deal to transact. I don't have one area of expertise or knowledge. I don't have the singular power over language of a lawyer, the physical force of a construction worker, the command over fellow workers of a surgeon, the wheeling and dealing transactions of a businessman. My energy is not spent in pursuing, climbing, achieving, conquering or cornering some goal or object.

My energy is spent in encouraging, supporting, consoling and praising my children. In teaching, the inner rewards come from without. On any given day, quite apart from teaching reading and spelling, I bandage a cut, dry a tear, erase a frown, tape a torn doll and locate a long-lost boot. The day is really won through matters of the heart. As my students groan, laugh, shudder, cry, exult and wonder, I do too. I have to be soft around the edges.

A few years ago, when I was interviewing for an elementary-school teaching position, every principal told me with confidence that, as a male, I had an advantage over female applicants because of the lack of male teachers. But in the next breath, they asked with a hint of suspicion why I chose to work with young children. I told them that I wanted to observe and contribute to the intellectual growth of a maturing mind. What I really felt like saying, but didn't, was that I loved helping a child learn to write his name for the first time, finding someone a new friend, or sharing in the hilarity of reading about Winnie the Pooh getting so stuck in a hole that only his head and rear show.

I gave that answer to those principals, who were mostly male, because I thought they wanted a "male" response. This meant talking about intellectual matters. If I had taken a different course and talked about my interest in helping children in their emotional development, it would have been seen as closer to a "female" answer. I even altered my language, not once mentioning the word "love" to describe what I do indeed love about teaching. My answer worked; every principal nodded approvingly.

Some of the principals also asked what I saw myself doing later in my career. They wanted to know if I eventually wanted to go into educational administration. Becoming a dean of students or a principal has never been one of my goals, but they seemed to expect me, as a male, to want to climb higher on the career stepladder. So I mentioned that, at some point, I would be interested in working with teachers as a curriculum coordinator. Again, they nodded approvingly.

If those principals had been female instead of male, I wonder whether their questions, and my answers, would have been different. My guess is that they would have been.

At other times, when I'm at a party or a dinner and tell someone that I teach young children, I've found that men and women respond differently. Most men ask about the subjects I teach and the courses I took in my training. Then, unless they bring up an issue such as merit pay, the conversation stops. Most women, on the other hand, begin the conversation on a more immediate and personal level. They say things like "those kids must love having a male teacher" or "that age is just wonderful, you must love it." Then, more often than not, they'll talk about their own kids or ask me specific questions about what I do. We're then off and talking shop.

Possibly, men would have more to say to me, and I to them, if my job had more of the trappings and benefits of more traditional male jobs. But my job has no bonuses or promotions. No complimentary box seats at the ball park. No cab fare home. No drinking buddies after work. No briefcase. No suit. (Ties get stuck in paint jars.) No power lunches. (I eat peanut butter and jelly, chips, milk and cookies with the kids.) No taking clients out for cocktails. The only place I take my kids is to the playground.

Although I could have pursued a career in law or business, as several of my friends did, I chose teaching instead. My job has benefits all its own. I'm able to bake cookies without getting them stuck together as they cool, buy cheap sewing materials, take out splinters, and search just the right trash cans for useful odds and ends. I'm sometimes called "Daddy" and even "Mommy" by my students, and if there's ever a lull in the conversation at a dinner party, I can always ask those assembled if they've heard the latest riddle about why the turkey crossed the road. (He thought he was a chicken.) ■

DISCUSSING THE SELECTION

1. Daniel Meier made an important decision about what he wanted in life. What is his decision? What reasons does he give his readers to explain his decision?

2. What made Meier feel he should work with children? What particular steps did Meier take to fulfill his dream of working with children?

3. To get his job and keep it, how does Meier alter his real reasons for wanting to teach? What else does he do to get the acceptance of those around him?

4. What examples does Meier provide to support the idea that men and women respond differently to his choice of profession?

THINKING CRITICALLY

1. We all reach particular turning points in our lives when we make decisions about our lives. Think about a time when you made an important decision about your life. Was there anybody who did not understand the decision you made for yourself? How did you convince such people to have confidence in your decision?

2. What personal abilities or strengths did Meier use to help him fulfill his dream? What personal abilities or strengths do you have that have helped you complete important and/or difficult projects? Explain to the class by

telling a story that illustrates a time when you were able to take an action because of these abilities or strengths.

3. Do you think particular jobs should be exclusively men's jobs or women's jobs? Why or why not?

wasp.

FOCUSING ON THE WRITING

Showing Versus Telling

Writers have choices. They can *tell* their readers how they think, or they can *show* their readers how they think, using examples of events that relate to or support their ideas.

Many readers remember the "showing" rather than the "telling" because showing brings the writing alive and helps the reader to identify with the writer. "Showing" also adds some drama and excitement to writing.

However, writers must be careful to balance their writing. They should not include too many "showing" stories, but should include just enough to make their writing lively and interesting. The stories should clearly relate or connect to the ideas the writers are trying to present.

1. Meier "shows" rather than "tells" throughout this essay. What examples does he include to let his readers know what it is like to teach first-graders? What examples does he include to let his readers know what men think about his work?

2. How does Meier combine "showing" and "telling" in his conclusion?

3. Meier uses comparisons in this essay. What specific examples does he use to compare the way he uses his energy as a teacher with the way lawyers,

construction workers, and businesspeople use energy? What is the difference between the meaning of these two sets of examples? What do these examples tell you about how Meier feels about his work?

4. Meier compares the responses of males and females talking with him in social settings. What specific examples does he give of each type of response? What is Meier "telling" his readers by "showing" them these responses?

5. When Meier goes for interviews, he presents what he classifies as a "male" response. What are the characteristics of such a response? What is Meier "telling" his readers that men expect of other men? Do you think he would act differently if he were being interviewed by a woman? Support your answer with evidence from his essay.

CREATING YOUR TEXT

1. Reread your journal entry to give you ideas as you write an essay describing your experience working with, teaching, or caring for children. Where were you? What was your role with the children? How did you care for them? Were there any problems? What did you learn from your experience? What advice would you give to someone who is planning to work with or teach young children?

2. For the next five minutes, create a cluster (see page 5) around the words "my career." At the end of the time, look at the words you have written. Read your cluster looking for ideas to use in an essay describing your future career. In the essay, explain how and why you chose this career direction and what you expect to accomplish in your future. What kind of courses do people need to take to enter the career you have chosen? What personality characteristics do they need? How will your background help you succeed in this field?

3. Do you think certain jobs should be restricted to members of one sex? Are there jobs that only men can do or only women can do? Write an essay in which you agree or disagree with the idea that some jobs should be restricted to members of one sex, given your own experiences, readings, or observations of others.

4. Explain why you think men should or should not have a place in elementary school teaching. Use your personal experiences, observations, or readings to support your ideas.

REVISING YOUR TEXT

When you finish your first draft, read the revision questions on page 11 or 14 on your own or with a partner. Review your draft, and decide what changes to make when you write your second draft.

Reread your draft alone or with a classmate, looking for examples of "showing" and of "telling." Make sure you have a balance of both.

EXPLORING YOUR IDEAS

Write about a movie you have seen that touched you in an important way. What about this movie makes it stand out in your mind? Would you recommend this movie to your teacher, your friends, and your family? Why or why not?

"They've Gotta Have Us"

KAREN GRIGSBY BATES

Karen Grigsby Bates wrote the article "'They've Gotta Have Us': Hollywood's Black Directors"—from which this reading is excerpted—for *The New York Times Magazine*, and it was published on July 14, 1991. Her article is about the writer and filmmaker John Singleton.

John Singleton, a 23-year-old black man, has the notoriously insular and mostly white Hollywood establishment purring.

It was just over a year ago that Singleton, then a student in the Filmic Writing Program at the University of Southern California [USC], sent his script for "Boyz," a coming-of-age story set in the tough Los Angeles neighborhood where he grew up, to Columbia Pictures. What followed has already become a Hollywood legend. When the Columbia chairman, Frank Price, offered to have the studio develop his script, Singleton agreed—with the understanding that he would direct it himself. "It's my story, I lived it," says Singleton. "What sense would it have made to have some white boy impose his interpretation on my experience?"

Not only did Singleton get a $6 million budget to direct "Boyz N the Hood," he signed a three-year contract with Columbia that enables him to make as many movies as he can during that period. . . .

Black film making goes back to the all-black Lincoln Motion Picture Company, established in Los Angeles around 1916. Then, during the Harlem Renaissance in the 1920's and into the 1940's, the independent producer and director Oscar Micheaux created many films for black audiences. These films—romances, comedies, dramas, and adventures—depicted black people in their rich variety, from the pious* bourgeoisie** to less savory characters. For the next 30 years there were sporadic Hollywood films about blacks—almost always directed by whites—and of course the ascension of Sidney Poitier. In the 1970's, the "blaxploitation" films—like "Super Fly"—became the first black movies to receive significant attention from the general public, though these films, too, were frequently made by whites. Star vehicles for Bill Cosby, Richard Pryor, and Eddie Murphy followed.

The current crop of films is breaking new ground in their subject matter and their politics. For the studios, these are tales from a new world, presented with an often harrowing, if occasionally hyperbolic,† realism. Such films as Spike Lee's "Jungle Fever," Mario Van Peebles' "New Jack City," "Hangin' With the Homeboys," a tale of the Bronx from the 28-year-old Joseph B. Vasquez, and "Straight Out of Brooklyn," the angry first feature from the startlingly precocious 19-year-old director, Matty Rich, are stridently‡ confrontational in their depiction of a problem-ridden urban culture in conflict with a white mainstream.

"Boyz N the Hood," the story of a group of teenagers growing to manhood on a block in south central Los Angeles beleaguered by drugs, crime and gang violence, stands squarely at the center of the trend. The film focuses on Tre Styles (played by Cuba Gooding Jr.), who has the advantage of a father's guidance, and two half brothers who don't. The brothers—Ricky, a football star (played by Morris Chestnut) favored by his mother, and Doughboy (a complex creation, stirringly portrayed by the rapper Ice Cube), whose intelligence and street eloquence do battle with a penchant§ for self-destruction—

---

*pious: religious.
**bourgeoisie: middle class.
†hyperbolic: exaggerated.
‡stridently: sharply, in a shrill manner.
§penchant: a taste or liking for something.

are ill fated, which may be a commentary on the plight of fatherless black families but one that is no less powerful for its didacticism.*

"Boyz N the Hood" is an ambitious film that fulfills much of its ambition, one that most critics have concurred deserves its good fortune for having arrived simultaneously with the Hollywood hunger for it.

Singleton himself seems to understand that. Slender and laconic to the point of being Cooper-esque, he masks a passion to bring the stories of the black communities to the screen. He concedes that five years ago, before Spike Lee's seminal low-budget first film, "She's Gotta Have It," proved that black-made films on black subjects could be financially successful, he'd have encountered resistance to his directing demand. And yet he bristles at any suggestions that his big break is the result of anything but creative talent. "Look," he says. "In this business you get hired for your vision, and your vision begins with your script. I'm a writer first, and I direct in order to protect my vision. 'Boyz' is a good story, a *real* story, and they wanted it. Simple as that."

Like Tre Styles, the protagonist in his film, Singleton grew up in south central Los Angeles. His mother, Sheila Ward, a sales executive for a pharmaceutical company, and father, Danny Singleton, a mortgage broker, never married. Nevertheless, they lived near each other and for several years he split his time between them.

Singleton began going to the movies early on—"I'm a child of 'Star Wars,' 'Raiders of the Lost Ark' and 'E.T.,'" he says—and decided to make them himself by the time he was 9.

He gorged on films by Orson Welles, François Truffaut, Steven Spielberg, Akira Kurosawa, John Cassavetes, Martin Scorsese, and Francis Ford Coppola. "The christening scene at the end of 'The Godfather' is my favorite," he says with uncharacteristic animation. Singleton imitates the priest's solemn recitation of the Roman Catholic christening vows: "'Michael Corleone, do you renounce Satan?' 'I do.' And at the same time everybody's getting shot! I *love* scenes like that. I strive toward saying things visually—that verbal stuff is for TV. In a way that scene in 'The Godfather' influenced how I ended 'Boyz.'"

In high school, he started to learn the inner workings of Hollywood. "Somebody told me that the film business was controlled by literary proper-

---

*didacticism: teaching manner.

ties," he says. "After that, I worked to strengthen my writing skills." And that's when things took off.

He won a spot in the prestigious Filmic Writing Program at U.S.C. By the time he graduated in 1990, he had made a few 8-millimeter short films, but, more important, he had won several writing awards. The powerful Creative Artists Agency [C.A.A.] signed him while he was still an undergraduate. It was his agent, Bradford W. Smith at C.A.A., who sent the script of "Boyz" to Columbia in May 1990. 13

Given the material, it seems remarkable that "Boyz N the Hood" and the other so-called homeboy movies have found their way through the cultural cocoon of Hollywood's executive offices to the screen. Sean Daniel, a white independent producer and former production executive at Universal Pictures, says studios continue not to know what the next big "It" is, which is to the advantage of as-yet-untested people who want to make movies. ■ 14

DISCUSSING THE SELECTION

1. To what does the title of this article refer? What specific evidence in the article tells you what the title means?

2. In paragraph 4, Bates includes a brief history of black filmmaking. What differences are there between earlier black films and those made today? Which films mentioned in this article have you seen?

3. Many names in this article relate to the film business—the names of actors and actresses, directors, or films. Read the article again, underlining the names. Which people do you know something about? How can you find out about the others? Share any information you have with the rest of the class.

4. How did Singleton become a better writer? How did he learn to become a screenwriter?

THINKING CRITICALLY

1. What are three of your favorite movies? Do you prefer movies with serious themes? Why or why not?

2. Singleton states that his favorite movie scene is in *The Godfather*. What is your favorite scene in a movie? Explain the scene to your class, and tell why you chose it.

3. At an early age, Singleton knew he wanted a career in Hollywood. What were his early influences? What steps did he take to fulfill his dream? If you have a life goal, when did you know what you wanted to do with your life? What influenced you to choose your particular goal? What steps have you taken so far to make sure you will attain your goal?

4. If you were given the money and assistance to make a movie about any of the selections you have read in this book so far, which one would you choose? Why?

FOCUSING ON THE WRITING

1. Writers choose their words carefully to make an impact on their readers. In the first sentence, Bates uses the word *purring* to describe the white Hollywood reaction to Singleton. To what does the word *purring* usually refer? What other words could she have used to express a similar feeling? Why do you think she chose to use *purring* in this sentence?

2. In paragraph 4, Bates includes a brief history of black filmmaking, presented in chronological or time order. What effect does presenting this information in chronological order have on you as a reader?

3. The last sentence in paragraph 6 is very complicated but is important for understanding the meaning of "Boyz N the Hood." After rereading this sentence, answer the following questions:

   a. Does the mother prefer Ricky or Doughboy?
   b. Which of the boys is the athlete?
   c. Which of the boys is bright and speaks well?
   d. Which of the boys is doomed?
   e. Are the boys in trouble because they are motherless or fatherless?
   f. Bates thinks *Boyz N the Hood* is didactic or teaches a moral. What does she think is the moral of the movie?

CREATING YOUR TEXT

1. Imagine that you have received a letter from Hollywood producers offering you the opportunity to write a story for a movie to be produced in the near future. Describe your story in order to convince these producers that your movie should be made. What is the story? Who are the characters? What is the setting?

2. "Coming-of-age" stories and films tell about important moments when young people feel they have become adults. Write a "coming-of-age" story about yourself or about someone you know well. Include specific details so your readers can "see" the people you describe and the settings in which these stories take place.

3. Write an essay in which you tell the story of a movie you enjoyed watching. Explain to your readers why you chose this movie. What did you like about it? What did you find interesting about the characters? the story? the look of the movie? the music? Why should your readers go to see this movie?

4. Tell the story of someone else you know of or have read about who knew what he or she wanted to be at an early age. What was this person's

background? Did the person fulfill his or her dream? What is this person doing today? How do you know about this person's life? What have you learned from this person?

REVISING YOUR TEXT

Read your first draft with a classmate. Discuss its strengths and weaknesses. Then together go over the revision questions on page 11. In addition, think about the following questions:

Does your introduction make your reader want to read more? Would another introduction style be more effective?

Have you balanced specific or personal and general information in your draft?

Do you show by example and illustration as much as possible rather than tell your reader how to think about your subject?

What type of conclusion did you write? Would another style be more effective?

ADDITIONAL PROJECT

See *Boyz N the Hood* and another film mentioned in this article. Look for a similarity that shows you how Singleton was influenced by the other movie. Write an essay in which you explain how it influenced Singleton's movie.

> **EXPLORING YOUR IDEAS**
>
> Have you ever found out that someone you thought you knew well had an unexpected talent or ability? That's the focus of the story you are about to read. Write in your journal about the person who surprised you with a hidden talent or ability.

This Lady Came Down from the Mountains

ROBERT DRAPER

Robert Draper published this article in the *American Way* magazine of June 1, 1991. It deals with a recently discovered seventy-eight-year-old writer, Lou Crabtree, and the world she inhabits.

"I have written all my life," says Lou Crabtree, elongating the word "all" to suggest centuries of travail.* The stout, snow-haired, seventy-eight-year-old Appalachian woman leads me through her creaky Victorian cottage and into a room crammed with boxes and boxes of her life's work. She hands me a tray of fruits and cookies, and then falls into a chair at least as old as herself. "And you know who I showed it to? Nobody, that's who. I don't think even now the things I'm writing will see the light of day. They're in these boxes. I'm not very good at sending things out. I know that's part of being a writer, but I'm sorry. Now, some universities, they've wanted my stuff for their archives."

*travail: physical or mental hard work.

Crabtree's round face wrinkles at this. "I thought you had to be dead to be in the archives," she murmurs. "Oh, how I pray to God that I can live to the year 2000! There'll be so many changes! I've read somewhere that by the year 2020 a man will be allowed to have three wives."

Lou Crabtree slaps her knee and has a good laugh at this. The resident of tiny Abingdon, Virginia, makes it very easy for people not to take her seriously. It's hard to square her credentials—critically applauded short-story writer and poet, laureate* in literature of the state of Virginia—with her almost primitive innocence . . . until one reads her writing. Upon witnessing her incredibly raw, rare talent, two questions are begged. First, how did a hillbilly one-room schoolteacher learn how to write so well? And second, if Lou Crabtree could do it, are there others up there in the hills just like her as yet undiscovered?

As it is, the author of *Sweet Hollow* (LSU [Louisiana State University] Press, 1984) is hardly a household word herself. Yet considering her background and her refusal to peddle her work, it's a small miracle that anyone outside of southwestern Virginia knows who Lou Crabtree is. It happened, however, that in 1982 the acclaimed North Carolina novelist Lee Smith—who was busily at work on *Oral History*, a fictional dissection of a haunted Appalachian family—visited Abingdon to teach a writing workshop. The workshop attracted a handful of curious teenagers, bored housewives, literary would-bes, and an old woman who'd spent much of her life deep in the hollers outside of town.

"This lady came down from the mountains," recalls Smith, "and she told me: 'My name is Lou Crabtree, and I just *looovve* to write!' And she handed me this immense stack of paper, and of course I thought, oh boy. But then I read one of the stories, and I just couldn't believe the opening sentence:

"'Old Rellar had thirteen miscarriages and she named all of them.'"

The old woman's stories were all like that: unwashed and a little frightening, but hypnotically descriptive and as imaginative as any prose Smith had ever seen. Crabtree wrote about mountain superstitions, social rites, hardships, and yearnings as if she'd experienced them herself. And she had. As Smith got to know her student better, the whole of Lou Crabtree's bizarre life slowly revealed itself. Born in the river hills of Washington County, Virginia, in 1913.

---

*laureate: honored one.

The daughter of a deeply religious mother and a judge "who dispensed mountain justice, especially dog trials—when your dog bites somebody or runs off with the neighbor's sheep," according to Crabtree. A child who preferred to be alone, her friends consisted of the animals and flowers of the country, and she spent summer afternoons standing on the banks of the Holston River, gaping at the Cherokees who built stick-houses across the water. Educated in a one-room schoolhouse, and later—after attending Radford Normal School in town—employed as a teacher in yet another one-room schoolhouse, in Possum Hollow. Married to a farmer (who died in 1960), a mother of five, immersed in and all but broken by the primitive mountain lifestyle.

Throughout all this, somehow, she'd been writing, catching random snatches of thoughts and dreams on scraps of paper. Her work was all handwritten, and after reading it, Lee Smith took the pages back home to Chapel Hill and had them typed. Smith then sent the pages to a friend, then LSU Press managing editor Martha Lucy Hall. "The writing was just wonderful. She was a true primitive, with absolutely no pretense." Hall selected seven stories and published them under the title *Sweet Hollow* in 1984, just before Lou Crabtree's seventy-first birthday.

"That book has changed my life," Crabtree declares of the critically acclaimed collection, which has become one of the best-selling books of fiction in LSU Press' catalog. "Given me a new outlook. Given me money! Lord, I've gotten thousands of write-ups that I could never pay for. NBC put me on that show of theirs, *The Today Show*. And old Willard [Scott] said, 'I hope she gets to be a hundred.'

"Now I get to go to the universities and talk and read. They wanted me to come up to West Virginia University and my Lord, that's as far as De-troit! I don't fly, and the bus drive was too long, so I kept puttin' 'em off, and finally they said, 'We'll send a state car for you.' At that time I'd cut all my hair off. And my boy said, 'You cain't go, mama! With that short haircut in that state car, people are gonna think they're takin' you to the women's prison!' So I didn't go."

That Crabtree is hardly a high-toned product of the publishing industry is what makes her special. But her innocence makes her vulnerable as well. "For the same reason that writers like Lou are dumbfounded by the praise they acquire," says Martha Hall, "they're also very hurt by the criticism they receive." Indeed, Crabtree bristles at the *New York Times* review of *Sweet Hollow*—a generally glowing write-up that nonetheless chides the prose for being a little too heavy on the fauna and the flora. And when Crabtree sent a second book to LSU Press—a "town novel," reflecting her fascination with modern lifestyles, but completely abandoning the Appalachian mysticism that so fascinated her fans—Hall rejected it outright. Crabtree admits she didn't take the news well. "When I found out," she says, her voice low and lamenting, "I took off all my clothes and went outside and just rolled in the snow."

Crabtree never resubmitted the novel. But gradually she's overcome the sting of rejection, and a second collection of short stories—*The Village*, a revisitation of the fading mountain culture—is almost finished.

Still, it's the writer in Crabtree that maintains a curiosity in the evolving human condition. "I've changed with the times," she says, "and I've begun to write stories and poems about the woman who says: 'I'va done it, I'va done it, I didn't wanna do it but I'va done it, I went and had my boy's ears pierced.' And about the black man who wants the blonde woman. And homosexuals.

"And oh, I'm lost in space," she says, laughing at herself but continuing seriously: "I think there's great ignorance about space, and before people can understand it, the writers and poets are gonna have to write about it. Just like before I can understand computers, the poets are gonna have to explain 'em to me. So I've been writing about space in the common language."

Whether LSU Press is ready for a Lou Crabtree book of poems about space mutations remains to be seen. Crabtree doesn't seem preoccupied with the matter. She's thinking about space creatures even as her memory drifts to the dog trials, and to her old dog, Bobbi, who could sing opera; to the holy garden she once grew, with all the Biblical flowers, the rose of Sharon and the Gabriel's trumpet; to the snakehandlings and the woman who prayed for three years that blood might spurt out of her hands until her prayers were finally answered; to life before the malls, before the coal barons, back in her family's old log cabin, a few pieces of which still stand precariously in the depths of the holler. Lou Crabtree's thinking about distant past and distant future, and putting it down on paper, and squeezing it into boxes. ■

DISCUSSING THE SELECTION

1. What steps did Crabtree take to become a published writer?

2. What evidence does Draper provide that other writers helped Crabtree to succeed?

3. In paragraph 11, Draper writes about Crabtree, "But her innocence makes her vulnerable as well." What does this mean to you? What examples or supporting details does the writer include in the article to prove this statement to his readers?

4. According to Draper, how has Crabtree's background and culture influenced her writing?

5. What examples does the writer provide to convince his readers that Crabtree is a recognized and important writer?

THINKING CRITICALLY

1. Lou Crabtree is described as innocent and vulnerable. Describe a person you have met who has those characteristics. Has this person ever been hurt by people who may not be aware of his or her vulnerability?

2. If you or anyone you know has ever been rejected for anything or lost a contest or competition, how did the person react to the loss? What is the best way to cope with such loss?

3. How do you think Crabtree's friends and family feel when they find out that she has written about them? If you have ever written a story or essay about someone you know, did you show it to that person? Why or why not? If you did, what was the person's reaction?

4. How do you feel when you read someone else's writing? What do you feel best qualified to help them with? What do you feel most nervous about offering advice about?

5. Imagine that you are going to attend a writing workshop to help you write a story that is important to you. What story would you like to write? What writer from this book would you like to have as your teacher? Why did you choose this person?

FOCUSING ON THE WRITING

Describing a Place

When you prepare to write about a place, look at the place in person, with a photograph, or in your mind. Make notes about what makes this place interesting, unique, or worth describing. In your notes, write down the size, the colors, the textures, and the feeling of the place. Compare the place you are describing to other places you have seen.

Use your notes as you write about the place. In your writing, be sure to include enough details so your readers will be able to imagine the place. Finally, make sure your readers know why you want them to know about this place.

1. What descriptive words does Draper use to describe the place in which Crabtree lives? What feeling about this area do you get from these words? How does knowing about this place help you form a picture of Crabtree?

2. Which journalistic questions (see page 81) does Draper answer about Crabtree? In what part of the article does he answer them?

3. In this article, Draper presents the general idea about Crabtree that she

expresses as "I have written all my life." Then he includes specific facts and details that support the general idea (see pages 38–39 for more information about this). Reread the article, locating the general idea and the specific facts and details that give it support. With a classmate, list the specific facts and supporting details.

4. When Crabtree writes that "Old Rellar had thirteen miscarriages and she named all of them," she is showing her character in action rather than telling her reader what kind of person she is. (See the discussion of showing versus telling on page 104). Where in this article does Draper show Crabtree in action rather than tell his reader about her as a person?

5. In his *description* of Crabtree, Draper includes many details that come through the senses of sound, touch, sight, smell, and taste. What sensory details does Draper include about Crabtree? On a blank piece of paper, list characteristics of Lou Crabtree based on what you have read about her. Share your list with the class. What similarities and differences are there among the lists shared?

6. The introductory paragraph of "This Lady Came Down from the Mountains" contains quotations. Rewrite this paragraph substituting a third-person paraphrase of the quotations. For example:

    Original: "'I have written *all* my life,' says Lou Crabtree, elongating the word 'all' to suggest centuries of travail."
    Third-Person Version: Stressing the word *all*, Lou Crabtree says that she has written "all" her life.

    When you have finished doing this, reread the two versions and decide which you prefer and why.

CREATING YOUR TEXT

1. On the top of your page, for three minutes, list any unusual things you can do. Look through your list, and choose one ability you have that you

would like to share with your class. Write an essay in which you describe your ability. Explain how you learned to do it, and tell the story of a time in your life when your unusual ability helped you solve a problem or handle a difficulty. What did this incident teach you about yourself?

2. Write an essay in which you describe a place you have been that you think no one else in your class has ever seen in the way you have. Describe it in detail, to make the place come alive for your readers. Explain to your readers why you decided to write about this place.

3. Write an essay in which you describe a person who has an "unrewarded or unrecognized ability." It could be the ability to raise and love children, to cook, to fix a car, to paint a picture, to handle an emergency, or whatever ability you have observed and admire in someone you know. Bring the person alive as you write by using sensory details so the reader can almost see the person and what the person knows how to do.

REVISING YOUR TEXT

When you finish your first draft, on your own or with a classmate, read the revision questions on pages 11–12 and discuss where your draft succeeds and where it can be improved.

In addition, ask yourself the following questions:

Do you show rather than tell about the subjects about which you are writing?
Do you include both general and specific ideas in your writing?
Have you answered any questions you asked, furnished enough details so that the reader has new ideas about your subject, and provided enough details to make your subject interesting?
When you have answered these questions, write your second draft to share with your class.

ADDITIONAL PROJECT

Find *Sweet Hollow* in your school library or bookstore. Read one or more of Lou Crabtree's short stories. Write about the story, and share this writing with your class.

EXPLORING YOUR IDEAS

Write about an experience in which, to get something important, you or someone you know did something unethical or irresponsible. Explain the consequences of the action and what you learned from this incident.

Three Thousand Dollars

DAVID LIPSKY

David Lipsky, who lives in New York, has written many stories, including a novel, *Triangle*, and a collection of short stories entitled *Three Thousand Dollars*. He won the Henfield Prize for the title story, which also appeared in *The New Yorker*. Lipsky's story is about a college student who has learned to play his divorced parents against each other to get what he wants.

My mother doesn't know that I owe my father three thousand dollars. What happened was this: My father sent me three thousand dollars to pay my college tuition. That was the deal he and my mom had made. We'd apply for financial aid without him to get a lower tuition, and then he'd send me a check, and then I'd put the check in my bank account and write one of my own checks out to the school. This made sense not because my father is rich but because he makes a lot more money than my mother does—she's a teacher—and if we could get a better deal using her income instead of his, there was no reason not to. Only, when the money came, instead of giving it to the school, I spent it. I don't even know what I spent it on—books and things, movies. The school never called me in about it. They just kept sending these bills to my mother, saying we were delinquent in our payments. That's how my father found out. My mother kept sending him the bills, he kept looking on them for the money he'd sent me, and I kept telling him that the school's computer was making an error and that I'd drop by the office one day after class and clear it up.

So when I came home to New York for the summer my mother was frantic, because the school had called her and she couldn't understand how we could owe them so much money. I explained to her, somehow, that what we owed them was a different three thousand dollars—that during the winter the school had cut our financial aid in half. My mother called my father to ask him to send us the extra money, and he said that he wanted to talk to me.

I waited till the next day so I could call him at his office. My stepmother's in finance, and she gets crazy whenever money comes up—her nightmare, I think, is of a river of money flowing from my father to me without veering through her—so I thought it would be better to talk to him when she wasn't around. My father has his own advertising agency in Chicago—Paul Weller Associates. I've seen him at his job when I've visited him out there, and he's pretty good. His company does all the ads for a big midwestern supermarket chain, and mostly what he does is supervise on these huge sets while camera crews stand around filming fruit. It's a really big deal. The fruit has to look just right. My father stands there in a coat and tie, and he and a bunch of other guys keep bending over and making sure that the fruit is O.K.—shiny-looking. There are all these other people standing around with water vapor and gloss. One word from my father and a thousand spray cans go off.

When he gets on the phone, I am almost too nervous to talk to him, though his voice is slow and far off, surrounded by static. I ask him to please send more money. He says he won't. I ask why, and he says because it would be the wrong thing to do. He doesn't say anything for a moment and then I tell him that I agree with him, that I think he is right not to send the money. He doesn't say anything to acknowledge this, and there is a long pause during which I feel the distance between us growing.

Just before he gets off the phone, he says, "What I'm really curious about, Richard, is what your mother thinks of all this," and this wakes me up, because he doesn't seem to realize that I haven't told her yet. I was afraid to. Before I came home, I thought of about twenty different ways of telling her, but once she was right there in front of me it just seemed unbearable. What I'm afraid of now is that my father will find that out, and then he will tell her himself. "I mean," he says, "if I were her, I probably couldn't bear having you in the house. What is she planning to do? Isn't the school calling you up? I can't imagine she has the money to pay them. Isn't she angry at you, Rich?"

I say, "She's pretty angry."

"I hope so," my father says. "I hope she's making you feel terrible. When I talked to her on the phone yesterday—and we only talked for a couple of seconds—she seemed mostly concerned with getting me to give you this money, but I hope that deep down she's really upset about this. Tell her it's no great tragedy if you don't go back to school in the fall. You can get a job in the city and I'll be happy to pay your tuition again next year. I'm sorry, but it just doesn't feel right for me to keep supporting you while you keep acting the way you've been acting, which to me seems morally deficient."

My mother is tall, with light hair and gray, watery eyes. She is a jogger. She has been jogging for six years, and as she's gotten older her body has gotten younger looking. Her face has gotten older, though. There are lines around her lips and in the corners of her eyes, as if she has taken one of those statues without arms or a head and put her own head on top of it. She teaches art at a grammar school a few blocks up from our house, and the walls of our apartment are covered with her drawings. That's the way she teaches. She stands over these kids while she has them drawing a still life or a portrait or something, and if they're having trouble she sits down next to them to show them what to do, and usually she ends up liking her own work so much that she brings it home with her. We have all these candlesticks and clay flowerpots that she made during class. She used to teach up in Greenwich, Connecticut, which is where we lived before she and my dad got divorced, right before I started high school. Every summer, she and a bunch of other teachers rent a house together in Wellfleet; she will be leaving New York to go up there in six days, so I only have to keep her from finding out until then.

When I get off the phone, she is in the living room reading the newspaper. She gives me this ready-for-the-worst look and asks, "What did he say?"

I explain to her that I will not be going back to college in September. Instead, I will be staying in the apartment and working until I have paid the school the rest of the money.

My mother gets angry. She stands up and folds the paper together and stuffs it into the trash. "Not in this apartment," she says.

"Why not?" I ask. "It's big enough."

"A boy your age should be in college. Your friends are in college. Your father went to college. I'd better call him back." She walks to the phone, which sits on the windowsill.

"Why?" I ask quickly. "He said he wasn't going to do it."

"Well, of course, that's what he'd say to you. He knows you're afraid of him." She sees I'm going to protest this. "Who could blame you? Who wouldn't be afraid of a man who won't even support his own son's education?"

"He said he doesn't have the money."

"And you believe him?" she asks. "With two Volvos and a town house and cable TV? Let him sell one of his cars if he has to. Let him stop watching HBO. Where are his priorities?"

"I'm not his responsibility."

"Oh, no. You're just his son, that's all; I forgot. Why are you protecting him?"

I look up, and my mother's eyes widen a little—part of her question—and it feels as if she is seeing something in my face, so I realize I'd better get out of the room. "I'm not protecting him," I say. "It's just that you always want everything to be somebody's fault. It's the school's fault. It's nobody's fault. It's no great tragedy if I don't go back to school in the fall; you're the only person who thinks so. Why can't you just accept things, like everyone else?" I walk into my bedroom, shutting the door behind me. I lie on my bed and look up at the ceiling, where the summer bugs have already formed a sooty layer inside the bottom of my light fixture. My ears are hot.

Our apartment is small. There are only the two bedrooms, the living room, the bathroom, and the kitchen, and so if you want to be alone it's pretty impossible. My mother comes in after a few minutes. She has calmed down. She walks over to the air conditioner and turns it on, then waves her hand in front of the vents to make sure that cold air is coming out. I sit up and frown at her.

She sits down next to me and puts her arm around my shoulders. "I'm sorry you're so upset," she says. As she talks she rubs the back of my neck. "But I just think that there are a lot of things we can do before you have to go and look for a full-time job. There are relatives we can call. There are loans we can take out. There are a lot of avenues open to us."

"O.K., Mom."

"I know it must be pretty hard on you, having a father like this." She gives me time to speak, then says, "I mean, a man who won't even pay for his son's school."

"It's not that," I say. "It's not even that I'm that upset. It's just that I don't want us to be beholden to him anymore. I don't even like him very much."

My mom laughs. "What's to like?" she says.

I laugh with her. "It's just that he's so creepy."

"You don't have to tell me. I was married to him."

"Why did you marry him?" I ask.

"He was different when I met him."

"How different could he be?"

Mom laughs, shaking her head. Her eyes blank a little, remembering. She was twenty when she met my father—a year older than I am now. I imagine her in a green flannel skirt and blue knee socks. "I don't know," she says, looking past me. "Not very." We laugh together again. "I don't know. I wanted to get away from my parents, I guess."

"Who could blame you?" I say, but I can tell from a shift in her face that I have pushed too far. Her father died two years back.

"What do you mean?" she asks, turning back to me.

"I don't know," I say. "I mean, you were young."

She nods, as if this fact, remembering it, comes as something of a surprise to her. She blinks. "I was young," she says.

I get a job working at a B. Dalton bookstore. The manager has to fill out some forms, and when he asks me how long I will be working—for the whole year or just for the summer—I say, "Just for the summer," without thinking, and by the time I realize, he has already written it down and it doesn't seem worth the trouble of making him go back and change it. Still, I go through the rest of the day with the feeling that I've done something wrong. It's the store on Fifth Avenue, and it's not a bad place to work. I am sent to the main floor, to the middle register, where old women come in pairs and shuffle through the Romance section. I eat lunch in a little park a block from the store, where a man-made waterfall keeps tumbling down and secretaries drink diet soda. There is a cool breeze, because of the water. It is the second week of the summer, and on returning from lunch I am told I will have Wednesday off, because it is the Fourth of July.

Riding the bus home, I begin thinking that maybe my mother called my father anyway. It's terrible. The bus keeps stopping and people keep piling in, and meanwhile I am imagining their conversation going on. If I could make the bus go faster, maybe I could get home in time to stop them. I try to make mental contact with the bus driver by concentrating. I think, Skip the next stop; but he, out of loyalty to the other passengers or simple psychic deafness, doesn't, and instead the bus keeps stopping and people keep getting off and on. Walking into our building, I get the feeling everyone knows. Even the people on the elevator scowl. Maybe if I had told my mother myself, I would have softened it somehow. What would upset her now is not only the money—although the money would be a big part of it—but also that I tried to put something over on her. I am almost afraid to open our door. "Hello," I call, stepping inside.

As it turns out, my mother isn't home. There is a note on the table. She has gone shopping. I look at the note for a while, to see if I can figure anything out from it. For example, it is a short note. Would she usually write a longer one? It isn't signed "Love" or anything—just "Mom," in the scratchy way she draws her pictures.

I hang my jacket in the closet and then turn on my mom's answering machine. There is one hang-up, and then a message from my father. It makes my whole body go cold. His voice sounds farther away than when we talked the last time. "Richard?" he says. His voice is slow. "This is your father. I just wanted to call to see how things were going. I had an interesting discussion with your mother this afternoon, and we can talk about it later, if you'd like to. Call back if you get a chance." Then there is the clatter of his phone being hung up, and then a little electronic squawk as the connection is broken, which the machine has recorded. I play it again, but there is no way of telling just what he and Mom talked about. I walk into the bathroom and splash cold water on my face and look in the mirror. Then I try reading my mom's note again, but all I can really make it say is that she has gone to the supermarket.

My mother comes home, carrying two big bags of groceries. She pushes the door open with her shoulder. "Can you give me a hand?" she says.

I stand up and take the bags from her and carry them into the kitchen. They are heavy even for me. I hold them close to my chest, where the edges brush against my nose, giving me their heavy, dusty smell. My mom stands in the dining area. She rests one hand on the table. She is wearing running shorts and a T-shirt that on the front says "Perrier" and on the back has the name and date of a race she ran. "Any messages?" she asks me.

I look at her, but I can't tell anything from her face, either. She looks angry, but that could be just because it was hot outside, or because there was too long a line at the supermarket. "I didn't look," I answer. "Don't you even say hello anymore?"

"Hello," she says. She picks up her note and holds it so I can see. "You can throw this away, you know," she says. "Or are you saving it for any particular reason?"

"No, you can throw it away."

"That's nice. How about you throw it away?"

"I'm unloading the groceries right now."

She puts the note back down on the table and then walks into the living room. I unload the rest of the groceries. There is a box of spaghetti, Tropicana orange juice, brown rice, pita bread, a few plain Dannon yogurts. I put everything away and then I fold up the bags and stuff them into the broom closet, where we save them for garbage.

In the living room I hear my mom turn on the machine. There is the hang-up and then my father's message begins again. "Richard?" he says. "This is your father." I walk into the living room. Mom is standing over the machine, one hand on the buttons. "Oh, God," she says, in a bored way when she hears his voice, and she shuts it off. Then she turns around and looks at me. I am standing near the wall. "Why do you have that funny look on your face, Richard?" she asks.

I shrug. "How was your day?" I say.

"Bad." She steps over her chair and sits down on the sofa. From the way she arranged herself, I can tell she is upset. She keeps her arms folded across her stomach, and there is something compressed and angry about her face. The way her lips are pressed together—and also something around her eyes. "You want to make me some tea?"

"What happened?" I ask.

"Nothing happened. I ran. I went shopping. I spoke to your father."

I pull a chair over from the table and sit down across from her. I count to five and then ask, "What did he say?"

She shakes her head and laughs through her nose. "Oh, God. He was awful, Richard. Just awful. Right when he got on the phone, he started asking if you'd found a job, and then when I asked him if he was planning to pay the rest of your tuition he laughed and said of course not. He said it was time for you to learn to take care of yourself. He said it was going to be good for you. I couldn't talk to him. Really, Richard, he was awful. I mean it. Just awful."

"I told you not to call him."

"Well, then, I was stupid, Richard."

"Are you going to call him again?"

"How do I know if I'm going to call him again? Not if he keeps acting that way on the phone to me. But I can't pay the school myself." Her lips go back to being tight, and she pulls her arms closer together, so that each hand curls under the opposite elbow.

It occurs to me that what's pressing down on her face is the money we owe the school. "Did the school call again?" I guess.

She nods. "Yesterday."

"Don't call him," I say.

"Thanks, Richard. You want to get me some tea?"

"How about 'please'?"

"How about throwing that note away? Or are you planning to leave it there till Christmas?"

The next day, I get the same feeling that she has called my father again. I go outside during lunch to phone her. It is very hot, and the undersides of my arms are soggy. I have to walk about two blocks down Fifth Avenue before I can find a free phone, and then when I dial our number there is no answer. I think I may have dialed the number wrong, because even if no one is home there should still be the machine, but when I try again there is still no answer. As I hang up, I catch my reflection in the shiny front of the phone for a second and I look awful, sweaty. The rest of the day is terrible. I can hardly work. I keep ringing up the paperbacks as calendars and the children's books as software. On the way home, I think that even if my father didn't tell her I will have to tell her myself. I'm afraid that if I don't something awful will happen, like we'll never speak to each other again or something. But when I get home she is sitting on the sofa, reading the newspaper with her feet up on a chair, and when I walk into the living room she smiles at me, and it just doesn't seem like the right time. I take off my tie and blazer and then pour myself a glass of milk and sit down next to her. She smells like Ben-Gay—a strong, wintergreenish smell—which is what she rubs on her legs after running.

"How was your day?" she asks me. She has a mug of tea on the cushion next to her, and when I sit down she folds the newspaper and picks up the mug.

"Fine," I say. Then I ask, "Did you go somewhere? I tried calling around noon, but there was no answer."

"I drove up to Greenwich," she says.

"Why didn't you turn on the machine?"

"What are you, the police inspector? I didn't feel like it, that's why."

"But why'd you drive up to Greenwich?"

She laughs. "I feel like I should have one of those big lights on me." She brings her arms very close in to her sides and speaks very quickly, like a suspect: "I don't know. I don't know why I went up to Greenwich." She drinks from her cup, which she holds with both hands. Then she shakes her head and laughs.

We eat dinner. When we lived in Greenwich. she used to teach art in the summers, too. They had a summer day program, with a bunch of little kids running around—I was in it, too, when I was younger—and she used to take them out into the fields and have them draw trees and flowers. She hated it. While we are eating, I get the idea that maybe this is what she went up there for, to talk to someone about this job. Dinner is cool things: tuna fish and pita bread and iced coffee. My mother has a salad. We don't talk for a while. All we do is crunch.

"Why'd you go up to Greenwich?" I ask her again.

She looks up at me, a little angry. The rule, I know, is that we don't talk about anything once she has clearly finished talking about it. "I felt like it," she says. Then she forks some more salad into her mouth, and maybe thinks that her response is off key, because she says, "I had a great idea while I was up there, though."

"What?"

"I thought we could go up tomorrow. You know, for the Fourth of July. See the fireworks. I thought it'd be a lot of fun."

"It sounds great."

"Yes," she says, "I thought you'd like that."

I sleep late the next day, and when I wake up she has gone jogging. She has left me a note saying so, which I throw away. She comes back sweaty and happy, drinking a bottle of club soda, and I ask her why she isn't drinking tea, and we joke, and it all feels very nice, until I remember about Dad and the money and her job and then I feel awful again, because it seems as if all our talking and joking is going on in midair, without anything underneath it to hold it up. We eat lunch, and then my mom makes some sandwiches and we get into our car and drive up the thruway to Connecticut. It's fun seeing the place where you used to live. We drive by our old house, and it looks the same, though there are some toys in the backyard and some lawn furniture—chairs and a big wooden table—which we didn't own. I get this funny feeling while we are in the car that we could still be living inside, as a family; that my father could walk out on the lawn and wave to us, or that if we stayed long enough we might see ourselves going past a window or walking over to sit at that big table. When we get to the high school, cars are everywhere, loading and unloading, families carrying big plastic coolers filled with food. I ask my mother if it was always this popular. "Yes," she says. "You just don't remember." We have to drive up the street about two blocks to find a space. By the time we have taken our own cooler out of the trunk, two more cars have already parked in front of us.

The fireworks are always held at the same place. The people sit on the athletic field and the fireworks are set off from behind the baseball diamond about a hundred yards away. Thousands of people are sitting on blankets or walking around and talking to each other. It's like a scene from one of those movies where the dam bursts and everyone is evacuated to a municipal building, only instead of all their belongings the people here are carrying pillows and Cokes and Twinkies. We find a spot right in the middle of the field. Some kids are playing a game of tag. They keep running through the crowd, laughing, screaming, just barely missing the people on the ground, which of course is part of the fun. When one of the kids brushes against my mother's shoulder I can see that she wants to stop him, give him a talking to, but I ask her not to. I remember when I would have been playing, too.

There is a black platform in the center of the baseball field, and after about three-quarters of an hour a presentation begins. A fireman and a policeman and a man from the Chamber of Commerce walk back and forth to the microphone and give each other awards, for safety and diligence and community service. Then they step down and a group of boys and girls collect onstage, most of them blond, all of them in robes. The man from the Chamber of Commerce, wearing his silver community-service medal, introduces them as the Royal Danish Boys and Girls Choir, "all the way from Holland." Then he leaves the stage, and though I imagine that the children will sing Danish folk songs, or maybe European anthems, what they sing is a medley of Broadway show tunes, in English, designed around the theme of a foreigner's impressions of America: "Oklahoma!" and "Getting to Know You" and "Gary, Indiana," though it is hard to make out the exact words through their accents.

By the time they have finished, the sky has turned dark blue, with the moon hanging just to one side. The policeman and the fireman return with the man from the Chamber of Commerce. "Good evening," he says. His voice echoes all over the field. "We'd like to welcome all of you to this year's celebration of the Greenwich, Connecticut, Fourth of July. In keeping with the spirit of this very special day, we'd like all of you to rise for the singing of our national anthem." My mother and I stand to sing, and there is something nice about being part of this wave of people, of voices. During the last line, there is a popping sound like a champagne bottle opening, and a yellow streak rises over the platform, nosing its way into the sky. The words "and the home, of the brave" are lost in a chorus of "Oh's." We sit down again, en masse. I hand my mother her sweater. I can barely see her, but her voice comes from where I know she should be: "Thank you." The fireworks go off over the outfield, sometimes one, sometimes two or three at a time. Each one leaves a little shadow of smoke that the next one, bursting, illuminates. Some bloom like flowers; others are simply midair explosions, flashes. A few burst and then shoot forward, like the effect in *Star Wars* when the ship goes into hyperspace. Some are designed to fool us: One pops open very high in the air, sending out a circle of streamers like the frame of an umbrella; the crowd begins to "Ooh." Then one of these streamers, falling, pops open itself, sending out another series, and the rest of the crowd goes "Ah." Finally, one of those pops right over our heads, giving off a final shower of color, and the crowd whistles and applauds. The display gets more and more elaborate, until, for the last few minutes, there are ten or twenty rockets in the air at once, bursting and unfolding simultaneously. Everyone starts cheering, and the noises keep booming over us, making us duck our heads. The air smells like sulfur.

In the car, I am close to sleep. My mother is driving, outside it is dark, and I feel safe. The roads are crowded at first, but farther away from the school the traffic gets thinner, until we are driving alone down mostly empty roads. We seem to drive for a long time before joining up with the highway, where we become again simply one car among many.

"I'm working this summer," my mother announces after a little while.

I know, but I ask, "Where?" anyway.

"Here," she says. "At the school. I got my old job back."

"Mom."

She stops me. "I thought about it, and I decided that it really was important for me to have you in school right now. It was my decision to make, and I made it."

I turn to look at her. Her face is lit up by the meters in the dashboard. It's a surprise to remember that she has a body to go with her voice. I look at her profile, at her cheek, and at the skin underneath her chin beginning to sag. I remember how frightened she had been when we first moved to the city, how odd it had felt being in a house without my father's voice filling it, and how when we drove up to college for the first time last fall and she saw my name on top of my registration folder she walked out of the reception hall. I found her outside, on the main green, crying. "I can't believe we did it, we pulled it off," she said, meaning college.

"I just don't want to be a burden," I say now.

"You are," she says. "But it's O.K. I mean, I'm your mother, and you're supposed to be my burden." She turns to look at me in the dark. "I am your mother, aren't I?"

"As far as I know."

She laughs, and then we don't talk for a while. She turns on the air conditioner. I close my eyes and lean my head against the window. Every so often we hit a bump, which makes the window jiggle, which makes my teeth click together. "I'm sorry you have to work," I say.

"Look, you should be. Don't ask me to get rid of your guilt for you. If you feel guilty, that's fine. This was just important to me, that's all."

Her using the word *guilt* frightens me. I sit up and open my eyes. "What did Dad say to you on the phone?" I ask.

"Nothing. He said he wasn't going to pay for you. He said that he was doing the right thing. He said you understood. Do you?"

"No."

She nods, driving. "That's what I told your father. He said you should call him, if you want to. Do you?"

I laugh. "No."

She nods again. "I told him that, too."

She seems ready to stop talking, but I keep going. I want her to tell me that it's O.K., that she missed working outdoors, that she missed the little kids, missed Connecticut. "I just feel bad because now you can't go to Wellfleet for the summer."

My mother says, "Let's not talk."

We drive. Through the windshield everything looks purple and slick—the road and the taillights of the cars passing us and the slender, long-necked lights hanging over the highway. We seem sealed in, as if we are traveling underwater.

My mother reaches over and turns off the air conditioner. "There is something I want to talk to you about, Richard," she says.

"What?" I ask.

She keeps her face turned toward the highway. "If anything like this ever happens again, I want you to tell me immediately. Don't make it so I have to find out myself. This whole thing wouldn't have happened if you had told me about it in the spring. We could have gotten loans and things. As it is, we're stuck."

I don't say anything.

"If you ever have anything to tell me," she says, "tell me when it happens, O.K.? We're very close. You can tell me anything you want to. O.K.?"

She looks over at me. I try to keep my face from showing anything, and when I can't do that I look away, at my feet under the dashboard. It is an offer. I can tell her or not. The funny thing is, I can feel that she doesn't really want me to. If she has guessed, she doesn't want me to confirm it. And though I am relieved, it seems to me that if I don't tell her now I never will, and this thing will always be between us, this failure, my father's voice embedded in static.

I look up. We are passing under the George Washington Bridge.

"O.K.," I say. ■

DISCUSSING THE SELECTION

1. What do we learn about the parents in the beginning of the story that tells the readers they are willing to cheat the system, specifically the college, to save money? How is their behavior reflected in their son's behavior?

2. What do we know about the father in this story?
   Where does he live?
   What kind of work does he do?
   What is his relationship to his son?
   What is his relationship to his ex-wife?
   What is his relationship to his present wife?
   What is most important to him: money, responsibility, or honesty? Explain your answer with reference to the story.

3. What do we know about the mother in the story?
   Where does she live?
   What kind of work does she do?
   What is her relationship to her son?
   What is her relationship to her ex-husband?
   What is most important to her: money, responsibility, or honesty? Explain your answer with reference to the story.

4. What do we know about the son in the story?
   Where does he live?

What kind of work does he do?
What does he feel about college?
What is his relationship to his father?
What is his relationship to his mother?
What is most important to him: money, responsibility, or honesty? Explain your answer with reference to the story.

5. What specific events in the story tell the readers that the son is playing his parents' feelings against each other?

THINKING CRITICALLY

1. At the end of the story, Lipsky leaves his readers with uncertainty. Do you think the father has told the mother the real story? Do you think the son tells his mother what really happened? Do you think he should tell his mother? Explain your answers.

2. What one characteristic do you admire about each of the three characters in this story? Explain your answer.

3. How do you think divorce has affected this family? How would the story have changed if the family had all lived together?

4. What is the ultimate message of this story? What in this story might be considered offensive to some readers?

5. Why do some people try to find ways to abuse the system even though they know they may hurt others?

6. If you were asked to give advice to each of the three characters in this story, what advice would you give them? Why?

FOCUSING ON THE WRITING

1. What specific details does Lipsky provide to contrast the lifestyles of the two parents?

2. "Three Thousand Dollars" begins with the narrator, Richard, talking to the reader. What type of narrator does Lipsky use (see pages 97–98 for more information about narrator types) throughout the story? How would this story change if it were told from the mother's point of view? from the father's point of view?

3. Look at other stories in this book or any others that you have written or read before. Decide what type of narrator tells each story. Which types of stories do you usually prefer? Why?

4. Reread the last page. What is the effect of leaving the reader with final unanswered questions? Explain why this type of ending could be thought-provoking or upsetting to readers. If you prefer that Lipsky answer these questions in the story, explain why.

CREATING YOUR TEXT

1. Divorce can have a lasting effect on a family. Write an essay in which you tell the story of a family that has been through a divorce and how the split has affected the children and the adults in the family. What did you learn from writing about this?

2. If you discovered that the family in this story was cheating on their college financial aid application, would you have an obligation to notify the college about their unethical behavior? Could anyone else be hurt by their cheating about their financial information? In an essay, explain your decision and how you made it.

3. Are there two systems of justice in the United States, one for the poor and one for the rich? Write an essay in which you answer this question by referring to experiences of people around you, to cases you have read about in the newspaper, and to the behavior of the family in this story. What would you do to ensure that the justice system is equal for all?

4. Are there times when it is acceptable to lie? In an essay, explain your answer to this question by referring to your own feelings, experiences, readings, or observations of others.

REVISING YOUR TEXT

Review your first draft by going over the revision questions on page 11 or 12.

Make sure you have clearly stated your thesis statement or main idea. What evidence did you provide to support your main idea? How did you use the Lipsky story to support your main idea?

In your conclusion, do you provide a solution or do you leave your readers wondering? You may want to try writing several conclusions until you find the most effective one.

EXPANDING YOUR IDEAS

Collaborative Writing Projects

1. As a small-group project, find someone in your college who has recently completed a creative project—writing a book, making a film, completing a painting or sculpture, or any others you can discover. Ask the person if he or she is willing to meet with one or two students to discuss the project. If the person is willing, make an appointment to get together. Then develop interview questions (see page 276) that will help you understand the steps the person went through to fulfill the goal. Find out if the person will let you audiotape the interview. If not, someone should take notes. In any case, someone in the group needs to transcribe or write out the interview to share with the others. Then as a group, write about the person, focusing on the goal of completing the project and the steps involved in doing so. After showing it to the person you interviewed, you may submit your finished piece to the school newspaper for publication.

2. In a small group, find out more information about one of the people that you have read about in this Theme. For example, you can read one of Lou Crabtree's stories, read news reports of the 1992 summer Olympics to see how Greg Barton did, watch one of Singleton's films, or read more of *How the García Girls Lost Their Accents.* You can go to the library and read other articles about any of these people. Take notes as you gather information. In your group, discuss together what you have found out by doing this additional research. As a group, write a short paper revealing your source(s) and what you have discovered. In your paper, explain what this teaches you about relying on only one piece of information to understand a person, project, or event. Share what you have written with the class as a whole.

Part of being human is to connect with the people around us. These connections bring us both pleasure and pain. They make us aware of our potential for feeling and giving as well as our limitations.

Theme 3

Affecting Someone Else's Life

Readings

"Acts of Charity Spring from Rock of Honesty"
BY WILLIAM ROBBINS

"Thank You, M'am"
BY LANGSTON HUGHES

"Getting Involved"
BY ANNA QUINDLEN

"I Wanted to Know Why"
BY JONATHAN AMES

"Mothers with AIDS: A Love Story"
BY PERRI KLASS

"Another Kind of Sex Ed"
BY SHARON A. SHEEHAN

"The Locker Room"
BY SUSAN RICHARDS SHREVE

In "Acts of Charity Spring from Rock of Honesty," William Robbins tells how one woman's act of honesty and courage enabled her to make her own dream come true.

"Thank You, M'am," by Langston Hughes, is also about the effect of a woman's honesty and courage, in this case about their effect on a young boy.

Anna Quindlen's essay "Getting Involved" asks when one should get involved and when one should stay within the safety of home and private world. As Quindlen notes, making connections can lead to problems.

This relationship is also illustrated in Jonathan Ames's story "I Wanted to Know Why," which shows a young boy trying to understand the suicide of an admired older schoolmate.

Perri Klass's "Mothers with AIDS: A Love Story" provides information about AIDS while exploring the relationships among sick mothers, their sick babies, and the doctors who treat them.

The complexities of living in today's world of AIDS and other sexually related diseases lead directly to Sharon A. Sheehan's essay "Another Kind of Sex Ed." Sheehan challenges the common notion that sex education should be about birth control and condoms; instead, she believes, sex education should focus on love and commitment.

Finally, "The Locker Room," by Susan Richards Shreve, tells a story about how strangers sometimes connect and help each other in unexpected ways.

Making Discoveries

In Your Journal

Write in your journal about an incident you experienced or saw on television, in the movies, or read about that was an example of a positive way in which someone can affect the life of another person outside the family. Describe why this incident stands out in your memory. Include as many details as you can that help you recall the incident.

With a Classmate

Talk to your classmate about the incidents you each chose. Explain why you chose these incidents. What do the incidents have in common?

With Your Class

Share some of the incidents you have selected and discussed with each other. What do the particular incidents have in common? On what elements did your classmates focus when they made their choices? List these elements. What does this list tell you about the values held by the people in your class?

> **EXPLORING YOUR IDEAS**
>
> Think about a time in your life when you found something and returned it to someone, or when you lost something and someone returned it to you. Write about the experience and the way you felt. Include as many details as you can remember to help you recall your experience.

Acts of Charity Spring from Rock of Honesty

WILLIAM ROBBINS

William Robbins published this article in *The New York Times* of December 16, 1990. It tells about how the honesty of one woman changed her life and the life of her family.

1. To many people this would have seemed like a huge return on a tiny investment. To people in Kansas City it has turned out to be a great Christmas story. And for Rosemary Pritchett, a homeless mother, it has become the most wondrous of object lessons for her children about doing the right thing.

2. At the center of it are Ms. Pritchett, a nurse named Cheryl Wood, and a paycheck that Mrs. Wood lost and Ms. Pritchett found. Like ripples from a stone tossed into a pond, the results spread from there.

3. As Ms. Pritchett recounts it, the case began about a month ago, on a day she and her three children, Jeremiah, 13 years old, Natasha, 8, and Stephanie, 7, had spent praying.

4. Since it was a weekday, the children were in school. "I told them to keep praying anyway," she said.

5. They were praying that a bid she had made on a rundown and abandoned

house owned by Jackson County, which includes Kansas City, might be accepted. Her bid, she explained, was all she had in the world, $1,200 saved from the Social Security disability checks she receives monthly.

It was on the day she waited and prayed, Ms. Pritchett said, that she found on a windswept street a piece of paper with Mrs. Wood's name on it. She saw that it was a paycheck for $400 from an Independence hospital with Mrs. Wood's address on it.

"Sure, I know unscrupulous people who could have got it cashed," she said. "But that thought never crossed my mind."

Ms. Pritchett combed two pages of telephone listings under the name "Wood" until she found the address matching the one on the check. The listing was under the name of Mrs. Wood's husband, Derek.

Ms. Pritchett called and spoke to Mrs. Wood. The director of the shelter where the family now sleeps came on the line to give Mrs. Wood directions to come and pick up her check. It was only then that Mrs. Wood learned the circumstances of Ms. Pritchett and her children.

Mrs. Wood came to retrieve her check and offered Ms. Pritchett a reward. All Ms. Pritchett wanted, she said, was a note of thanks that she could show to her children. "I wanted the children to know that when you find something, somebody lost it," she said. She accepted $25 only when Mrs. Wood placed it on the ground and threatened to walk away.

The next day Ms. Pritchett learned that her bid on the house had been accepted. But what she found was more than she had bargained for. The house was little more than a shell. Walls were crumbling, vandals had ripped out wiring and plumbing and sewer pipes had frozen and burst. And the foundation was weak.

A few days later Mrs. Wood, visiting the site to offer help, found her new friends in circumstances she found appalling. With only a hammer and a screwdriver, Ms. Pritchett and her children were attacking a wall of crumbling plaster.

Ignoring the warning of her husband, a lawyer, that she was tackling a mission that could break her heart, Mrs. Wood began working her way through the Yellow Pages, calling contractors, suppliers, and craftsmen.

One of the first she called was a fellow member of her church, a remodeling contractor named Charles Copeland who, without charge, became the supervisor. Another was the A. B. May electrical company. The Neenan plumbing company offered a water heater. Jim Hatfield, a construction supplier, built windows and provided other fixtures. Mrs. Wood's uncle, a retired maintenance engineer, began installing them.

"It just looked hopeless," Mr. Copeland said, recalling his initial inspection. When all is done, others estimate, the value of the work will be about $30,000.

After newspaper and television reports about the lost check and Mrs. Wood's efforts to help Ms. Pritchett, the project took on a life of its own. Carl Dunahoo, a plumbing and heating contractor, and his supplier are splitting the cost of plumbing installation and fixtures. Mr. Dunahoo called on a relative, Gomer Krieger, a remodeling and hauling contractor, who has been removing construction debris. He pays a fee of $42 for each load of trash he dumps.

As she stood surrounded by the swirl of work and workmen, Ms. Pritchett was smiling, but she still seemed stunned. "I just gave Cheryl back the money that was hers," she said. "It was no big deal." ■

DISCUSSING THE SELECTION

1. In the first paragraph, the following phrases occur:

    "a huge return on a tiny investment"
    "a great Christmas story"
    "the most wondrous of object lessons"
    "doing the right thing"

    What do these phrases make the reader anticipate the rest of the story will be about? After reading the story, which of these phrases do you think sums up the essence of the experience? Using the details of the story, explain your choice.

2. Why did Rosemary Pritchett prefer getting a letter of thanks rather than a gift of money in repayment for returning the check?

3. What specific steps did Cheryl Wood take to change the Pritchett family's life?

4. What did Rosemary Pritchett gain from meeting Cheryl Wood? What did Cheryl Wood gain from meeting Rosemary Pritchett?

THINKING CRITICALLY

1. Do you know any person who would behave as Rosemary Pritchett did? Tell the story of this person to the class so they will understand why you admire this person.

2. Why do you think the various crafts and contracting people volunteered their skills, time, and effort to help the Pritchett family?

3. What skill(s) do you have that would be useful in helping someone restore a building or apartment? How did you learn your skills?

FOCUSING ON THE WRITING

Writing a Step-by-Step Process Essay

A step-by-step process essay is used to teach or explain the process for doing something. Before you start to write, break down the whole process into individual simple steps. Make notes about these. Ask yourself the following questions:

What is the process? Why does someone need to know how to do it?

Do I need to prepare in any way before starting to do this? What is the first actual step that I must take?

What do I have to know to be able to do it? Are special tools or equipment needed?

> Is a particular location advantageous? Is a special type of clothing necessary?
>
> What precisely is the first step? How should it feel? What step follows this one? and the next, until the end? What mistakes should I be careful to avoid?
>
> How will I know when I have completed the task, and what will it be like when it is done correctly?
>
> What have I gained by learning to do this?

1. Although this article is not a process essay, it shows the steps necessary to buy a house owned by the county. Reread the article with a partner, listing the steps. Discuss the order in which the steps should be taken. Add any basic steps that are not mentioned in the article. Why do you think the author included these steps?

2. Even if an article, story, or book may seem to be about several people, one person is often the main focus. Reread the article, and decide if there is one main focus in this article. If there is, who is it? If not, explain how you came to this conclusion. What in the article influenced your decision?

3. Reread the concluding paragraph. What is its function in this article? How might you write a new conclusion that would make readers feel they should help others? or that they should be honest? or that working together is a means to end discrimination and prejudice? Read the various conclusions written in your class, and decide which you prefer and why.

CREATING YOUR TEXT

1. Write an essay in which you teach someone, step by step, how to paint a room, fix a toilet, put down flooring, plaster a ceiling, or do any other household job necessary to restore or build a house or apartment.

2. Write an essay in which you teach someone, step by step, how to find and rent or buy an apartment or house.

3. Write an essay in which you teach someone, step by step, how to personalize a dormitory room and make it feel like home.

4. Write an essay in which you teach someone, step by step, how to apply for your college.

REVISING YOUR TEXT

Share your draft with a partner. Find someone in your class who has no experience with the skill you are teaching in your essay. Together, discuss the order of the steps. Make sure you have not left out any part of the process. At any point in your essay, if your partner is confused, mark the page and reread it, trying to discover if you have left out a step or assumed your reader would know how to do this part of the process. Rewrite, keeping in mind all your partner's comments, and share the second draft.

EXPLORING YOUR IDEAS

Have you ever done anything that had an unexpected effect on someone else? Or have you ever done anything wrong and gotten caught and embarrassed, or even worse? Write in your journal about your experience, the unexpected behavior, and the way you handled the situation. What did you learn about yourself from this experience?

Thank You, M'am

LANGSTON HUGHES

Langston Hughes was born in Joplin, Missouri, in 1902. He studied at Columbia University and Lincoln University. During his literary career, which spanned some forty years, he wrote poetry, fiction, drama, and a two-volume autobiography, *The Big Sea* and *I Wonder as I Wander*.

1. She was a large woman with a large purse that had everything in it but hammer and nails. It had a long strap and she carried it slung across her shoulder. It was about eleven o'clock at night, and she was walking alone, when a boy ran up behind her and tried to snatch her purse. The strap broke with the single tug the boy gave it from behind. But the boy's weight, and the weight of the purse combined caused him to lose his balance so, instead of taking off full blast as he had hoped, the boy fell on his back on the sidewalk, and his legs flew up. The large woman simply turned around and kicked him right square in his blue jeaned sitter. Then she reached down, picked the boy up by his shirt front, and shook him until his teeth rattled.

2. After that the woman said, "Pick up my pocketbook, boy, and give it here."

She still held him. But she bent down enough to permit him to stoop and pick up her purse. Then she said, "Now ain't you ashamed of yourself?"

Firmly gripped by his shirt front, the boy said, "Yes'm."

The woman said, "What did you want to do it for?"

The boy said, "I didn't aim to."

She said, "You a lie!"

By that time two or three people passed, stopped, turned to look, and some stood watching.

"If I turn you loose, will you run?" asked the woman.

"Yes'm," said the boy.

"Then I won't turn you loose," said the woman. She did not release him.

"I'm very sorry, lady, I'm sorry," whispered the boy.

"Um-hum! And your face is dirty. I got a great mind to wash your face for you. Ain't you got nobody home to tell you to wash your face?"

"No'm," said the boy.

"Then it will get washed this evening," said the large woman starting up the street, dragging the frightened boy behind her.

He looked as if he were fourteen or fifteen, frail and willow-wild, in tennis shoes and blue jeans.

The woman said, "You ought to be my son. I would teach you right from wrong. Least I can do right now is to wash your face. Are you hungry?"

"No'm," said the being-dragged boy. "I just want you to turn me loose."

"Was I bothering *you* when I turned that corner?" asked the woman.

"No'm."

"But you put yourself in contact with *me*," said the woman. "If you think that that contact is not going to last awhile, you got another thought coming. When I get through with you, sir, you are going to remember Mrs. Luella Bates Washington Jones."

Sweat popped out on the boy's face and he began to struggle. Mrs. Jones stopped, jerked him around in front of her, put a half-nelson about his neck, and continued to drag him up the street. When she got to her door, she dragged the boy inside, down a hall, and into a large kitchenette-furnished room at the rear of the house. She switched on the light and left the door open. The boy could hear other roomers laughing and talking in the large house. Some of their doors were open, too, so he knew he and the woman were not alone. The woman still had him by the neck in the middle of her room.

She said, "What is your name?"

"Roger," answered the boy.

"Then, Roger, you go to that sink and wash your face," said the woman, whereupon she turned him loose—at last. Roger looked at the door—looked at the woman—looked at the door—*and went to the sink.*

"Let the water run until it gets warm," she said. "Here's a clean towel."

"You gonna take me to jail?" asked the boy, bending over the sink.

"Not with that face, I would not take you nowhere," said the woman. "Here I am trying to get home to cook me a bite to eat and you snatch my pocketbook! Maybe you ain't been to your supper either, late as it be. Have you?"

"There's nobody home at my house," said the boy.

"Then we'll eat," said the woman. "I believe you're hungry—or been hungry—to try to snatch my pocketbook."

"I wanted a pair of blue suede shoes," said the boy.

"Well, you didn't have to snatch *my* pocketbook to get some suede shoes," said Mrs. Luella Bates Washington Jones. "You could of asked me."

"M'am?"

The water dripping from his face, the boy looked at her. There was a long pause. A very long pause. After he had dried his face and not knowing what else to do dried it again, the boy turned around, wondering what next. The door was open. He could make a dash for it down the hall. He could run, run, run, run, *run!*

The woman was sitting on the day-bed. After awhile she said, "I were young once and I wanted things I could not get."

There was another long pause. The boy's mouth opened. Then he frowned, but not knowing he frowned.

The woman said, "Um-hum! You thought I *was going to say but*, didn't you? You thought I was going to say, *but I didn't snatch people's pocketbooks.* Well, I wasn't going to say that." Pause. Silence. "I have done things, too, which I would not tell you, son—neither tell God, if he didn't already know. So you set down while I fix us something to eat. You might run that comb through your hair so you will look presentable."

In another corner of the room behind a screen was a gas plate and an icebox. Mrs. Jones got up and went behind the screen. The woman did not watch the boy to see if he was going to run now, nor did she watch her purse which she left behind her on the day-bed. But the boy took care to sit on the far side of

Hughes *Thank You, M'am*

the room where he thought she could easily see him out of the corner of her eye, if she wanted to. He did not trust the woman *not* to trust him. And he did not want to be mistrusted now.

"Do you need somebody to go to the store," asked the boy, "maybe to get some milk or something?"

"Don't believe I do," said the woman, "unless you just want sweet milk yourself. I was going to make cocoa out of this canned milk I got here."

"That will be fine," said the boy.

She heated some lima beans and ham she had in the icebox, made the cocoa, and set the table. The woman did not ask the boy anything about where he lived, or his folks, or anything else that would embarrass him. Instead, as they ate, she told him about her job in a hotel beauty-shop that stayed open late, what the work was like, and how all kinds of women came in and out, blondes, red-heads, and Spanish. Then she cut him a half of her ten-cent cake.

"Eat some more, son," she said.

When they were finished eating she got up and said, "Now, here, take this ten dollars and buy yourself some blue suede shoes. And next time, do not make the mistake of latching onto *my* pocketbook *nor nobody else's*—because shoes come by devilish like that will burn your feet. I got to get my rest now. But I wish you would behave yourself, son, from here on in."

She led him down the hall to the front door and opened it. "Goodnight! Behave yourself, boy!" she said, looking out into the street.

The boy wanted to say something else other than, "Thank you, m'am," to Mrs. Luella Bates Washington Jones, but he couldn't do so as he turned at the barren stoop and looked back at the large woman in the door. He barely managed to say, "Thank you," before she shut the door. And he never saw her again. ■

DISCUSSING THE SELECTION

1. Before you discuss the story with your class, write for five minutes about it. What do you remember about the individual characters in the story? What incidents from the story stand out in your mind? What did you learn from reading this story?

2. What specific actions does Mrs. Jones take to convince Roger that she is in control of the situation?

3. Why does Mrs. Jones bring Roger to her home?

4. Why doesn't Roger run away when he has the opportunity?

5. Why does she give him money?

THINKING CRITICALLY

1. What does Mrs. Jones feel about Roger? What does he feel about her? Support your opinion with evidence from the story.

2. Do you think Mrs. Jones made a difference in Roger's life? Why or why not?

3. Did Mrs. Jones take the right action? Why or why not?

4. Have you ever gotten involved in a stranger's life? If so, describe the experience to the class. Looking back on the experience, do you think you did the right thing?

FOCUSING ON THE WRITING

Dialogue Writing

When you write a story and use dialogue, make sure to start a new paragraph each time you switch from one speaker to another one.

"If I turn you loose, will you run?" asked the woman.
"Yes'm," said the boy.
"Then I won't turn you loose," said the woman. She did not release him.
"Lady, I'm sorry," whispered the boy.

> Quotation marks indicate the exact words that a speaker said. In this example, notice where the commas, question mark, and capital letters are placed.

1. Reread the dialogue in the Hughes story. What do you learn about the characters by the way they speak? Look at the dialogue in another story in this book. What does it tell you about the characters?

2. What differences do you notice in language among the descriptive paragraphs, the spoken dialogue in the Hughes story, and any other story you have looked at? How do you explain these differences?

3. Reread the first paragraph of the story. Write down the words and phrases that describe Mrs. Luella Bates Washington Jones. What impression does Hughes want the reader to have of her? What specific words and phrases in the description support your answer?

4. Reread paragraphs 1–16 of the story. Write down the words and phrases that describe the boy. What impression does Hughes want the reader to have of him? What specific words and phrases in the description support your answer?

5. Reread from paragraph 22 to the end of the story, focusing on Mrs. Jones's lifestyle. What does Hughes want his readers to know about Mrs. Jones—about her home, her job, for example? What specific descriptive words and phrases in the story support your answer?

CREATING YOUR TEXT

1. Write a story in which an older person and a younger person meet for the first time in an unexpected way. As you write the dialogue spoken between the two people, show differences in the way the two people speak—think about their educational backgrounds, their experiences, the people they usually talk with, and their feelings for each other.

2. Write a story about someone who tries to help someone else, but the person is resisting that help (reread the Hughes story for ideas). As you write the dialogue spoken between the two people, keep in mind their voices and the way they communicate their ideas and feelings to each other.

3. Write a story about someone who is learning to trust someone—a teacher and a student, a patient and a doctor or dentist, a babysitter and a child, for example. As you write the dialogue spoken between the two people involved, keep their individual voices in mind.

REVISING YOUR TEXT

When you finish writing your draft, read the revision questions for writing a story on pages 13–14. Go over these with a partner in your class, reading the dialogue out loud. Decide together if it sounds as if real people were talking. Decide what changes you should make to improve your second draft, which you will share with other members of your class.

Read the dialogue aloud with a classmate. Pay attention to whether each character has his or her own voice, that is, sounds unique and individual. Make sure the dialogue has a purpose, that it tells the reader something about the characters that cannot be told in the narration itself.

EXPLORING YOUR IDEAS

Write the word *involved*, and then write the words *family, friends, school, community,* and *strangers*. Think about how involved you are in the lives of the people around you. When a member of your family has a problem, do you get involved? Does it matter which family member it is? How about when a friend has a problem? or when a stranger asks for help? Write in your journal about how you decide whom to help and what to do.

Getting Involved

ANNA QUINDLEN

This essay appears in *Living Out Loud* (1988), a book of Anna Quindlen's "Life in the 30's" newspaper columns that were originally published in *The New York Times* from 1986 to 1988. According to Quindlen, "I was permitted—and permitted myself—to write a column, not about my answers, but about my questions. Never did I make as much sense of my life as I did then, for it was inevitable that as a writer I would find out most clearly what I thought, and what I only thought I thought, when I saw it written down."

1   It was a summer night when I heard the running footsteps behind me. I ran, too, and slipped into the hallway of my building, a locked door, a pane of glass insulating me from the outside. The woman was only a few steps behind me. Her face on the other side of the glass was black with mascara mixed with tears. She said someone had tried to rape her, and that she thought he was following close behind.

It occurred to me afterward that everyone should be allowed more than a minute to suddenly discover what sort of person they are. That was all it took for me to play out the possibilities: a gang of thieves who used a seemingly distraught woman as their entrée, an unbalanced street person who would turn on me in the safe confinement of my own home. Or a rape victim.

I opened the door.

She had a cup of tea, refused to call the police, washed her face, apologized, and finally, after an hour, went home in a cab. I was left with the teacup, the blackened tissues, and an unbearable sense that the rapist had watched her enter and was now lying in wait for me. Each time I thought of the woman, I had a heavy, deep feeling in my chest that I finally recognized as rage—not at her pursuer, but at her.

I hadn't thought of that night in some ten years until lately, when I have wondered again about the responsibilities of one human being towards others of the species. There are two women that have made me consider this: Cheryl Pierson and Hedda Nussbaum. Both of their cases have made me think of another, too—that of Kitty Genovese.

Miss Pierson went to jail, after she paid a high school classmate to kill her father because, she said, her father would not keep his hands off her, because he sometimes had sexual intercourse with her two and three times a day. Miss Nussbaum went to jail, too, accused with her lover of beating their six-year-old adopted daughter to death. In photographs taken at the time of her arraignment, she looks stunned, but perhaps that is simply a function of her face, the face of an aging prizefighter who has gone back for the TKO many times too many. Clearly, it was not only the little girl who was beaten.

Two horrible secrets. But, of course, people knew. They always do. When Miss Pierson first alleged that her father had molested her, she said that she had been afraid to tell anyone. And then one friend, neighbor, relative after another appeared in court to say that they suspected, that they had watched the man grab his daughter's body, make dirty comments about it. But nothing was really done until a boy Cheryl Pierson sat next to in homeroom shot Mr. Pierson in the driveway of the Pierson house.

The horror show in Miss Nussbaum's apartment was an open secret, too. Neighbors heard screams and shouts and the unmistakable sound of something hitting a human being, hard, even through the thick walls of an old building. Some of them saw bruises on the little girl. The difference between this and the Pierson case was that some of them did something. Some of them sought help from police and social service agencies for the people on the other side of the wall. But nothing really was done until the morning when Hedda Nussbaum and Joel Steinberg were taken into custody, their adopted son taken to a foster home, and their little girl taken to the hospital, where she was pronounced brain dead.

And so to Kitty Genovese, twenty-three years dead. She was a national symbol. She was knifed to death and her neighbors listened and watched and, the modern parable went, did nothing. At the time there were two reactions to the story: that it could not have happened, and that, if it did, it could only have happened in New York City.

But it doesn't only happen in New York, and it happens all the time. We have a national character that helps it along. The rugged individualists who take care of themselves, the independent men and women who prize the freedom to manage their lives without outside interference: these are the essential Americans. We want a police force that respects the rights of individuals, the same police force that will not take a man into custody, even if his wife's face looks like chopped meat, if she insists she fell in the bathroom.

But the dark side to independence is isolation, and the dark side to managing your own life a belief that it must be perfectly managed. "Dirty laundry," we call our problems, and "Don't trouble trouble," we say. There are countries in which the answer to "How are you?" is often "Not so good." Here the answer is almost always "Fine." There are cultures in which family members get together and tell you what you are doing wrong and how to live your life. I prefer one in which everyone minds their own business—at least until that moment when I am yelling "Help!"

So sometimes the victims feel that it is impossible or unseemly to pass their problems on to another, that in the midst of self-reliance they would be blamed for having pain, or sharing it. Sometimes the bystanders feel that if there was real trouble, the victims would do something about it, that the Cheryl Piersons and the Hedda Nussbaums would call hot lines and find therapists, that when the authorities have been notified there is not much more they can be expected to do. In retrospect, of course, it is never enough. The storm breaks, the man is murdered, the child beaten to death, and people realize that, in some sense, they have been watching it all through their curtains. Life as spectator sport.

That's why I was so angry that night, when one of the players demanded with her streaked cheeks and her sobs that I come down out of the bleachers and help her out. I was taking care of my own life and I had no interest in being implicated in anyone else's. How dare a stranger pass on her vulnerability. There was nothing I could do anyway. There was no way I could help. But at least I opened the door. If I had known then what I know now, I probably wouldn't have. I would have gone upstairs and called the police, which seems a sensible, no-risk solution. Except that when I came back down she might not have been there. Perhaps she would have been somewhere with a knife at her throat. On the other hand, I would have made the right decision—for me. And I could always say I tried. ■

DISCUSSING THE SELECTION

1. In paragraph 4, Quindlen writes that she felt rage "not at her pursuer, but at her," at the victim. Using the article to support your ideas, how do you explain this attitude?

2. Quindlen defines the rugged individualist in paragraphs 10 and 11. What characteristics does she list to define this type of person? What problems does such a person face in today's world?

3. What does "life as spectator sport" mean in the context of this essay? Is Quindlen critical or supportive of life lived this way? Explain Quindlen's attitude about people who live this way, supporting your ideas with evidence from her article.

4. Quindlen writes that all people "should be allowed more than a minute to suddenly discover what sort of person they are." In this experience, what does Quindlen discover about herself?

5. In the story of Rosemary Pritchett and Cheryl Wood (see page 146), each woman has a similar moment of self-discovery. What are the moments in that story? What did Pritchett and Wood find out about themselves? What

did the two women gain from getting involved with each other? Compare Quindlen's experience to that of Pritchett and Wood.

THINKING CRITICALLY

1. Quindlen wrote about a personal moment when she suddenly learned something about herself because someone needed her help. Have you ever had such a moment? If so, what did you find out about yourself?

2. Looking at the characteristics you identified in the previous question, think about the author herself. What in this essay convinces you that Quindlen is or is not "a rugged individualist"? What people do you know who fit this definition?

3. Do you think that people should call the police or interfere in some way when they see someone abusing someone else? Do you react differently if the person being abused is a child, a woman, a man, a sick or old person, or an animal? Explain your reasons for responding differently.

FOCUSING ON THE WRITING

Writing a Definition Essay

The purpose of the definition essay is to explain a term or concept. This type of essay is meant to be an exploration of a complex term or concept to help the writer and the readers understand it better.

Some writers begin this type of essay with a question such as "What is a _____ ?" After stating what is to be defined, the writer explains the special characteristics of the term or concept. He or she explores some of the following: Why is it different from others in a similar category? What special features make it distinct and unique? Why should the readers be interested in knowing more about the term or concept?

1. What terms or concepts does Quindlen attempt to define in this essay? How does she define them? How do the stories or anecdotes she tells help develop her definitions?

2. In the introductory note to this essay, Quindlen writes, "As a writer I would find out most clearly what I thought, and what I only thought I thought, when I saw it written down." What does this mean to you? Have you ever had the experience of understanding something better by writing it down?

3. In what paragraph in this article is the main idea or thesis statement located? Explain why you think this is the main idea of the essay.

4. In paragraph 10, Quindlen writes, "We have a national character that helps it along." To what does "it" refer? How did you know?

5. Quindlen refers to three news stories in this article. What is the purpose of using these news stories and not just telling stories that she knows from her own experience? Copy down the information revealed about the Pierson, Nussbaum, and Genovese stories. Decide why she put them in this order. How much information does she reveal about each news story? As a reader, did you want to know more? Why do you think writers sometimes refer to news events to support their main points?

CREATING YOUR TEXT

1. Reread your journal entry (see page 159) in which you wrote about the word *involved*. Under your first entry, write the phrase "getting involved" in your journal. This time, after reading the Quindlen article and discussing

it with your class, write about what these words mean to you. After writing for about five minutes, read your two entries, paying attention to any differences in your thinking. Think about what you learned from reading the article and discussing it with your class.

2. Write an essay describing two incidents in which someone needed your help—one in which you decided to do something, and one in which you decided not to get involved. After you have described the incidents and your decisions, write a concluding paragraph explaining why you made each decision and what your reaction has taught you about yourself.

3. Write an essay in which you explain the responsibility of one human being to another. Refer to two or three news stories (or any selections you have read in this book) in your essay. Think about your opinion on this subject before you begin to write.

   Make a list of several possible stories to which you might refer in your essay. Discuss these with a classmate to help you decide which are the most appropriate. Reread paragraphs 5–9 in the Quindlen article to see how she uses these sources in her writing. In your conclusion, state your main point about the responsibility one person should have toward another.

4. Write an essay discussing the following quote from the Quindlen article: "The rugged individualists who take care of themselves, the independent men and women who prize the freedom to manage their lives without outside interference: these are the essential Americans."

   Write about whether or not you agree with Quindlen's definition of the "essential American." Give examples of people you know or events you have seen that illustrate the American character, bad or good.

REVISING YOUR TEXT

When you finish your first draft, with a classmate, read the revision questions for an essay on page 11. In addition, discuss the following questions in relation to the draft:

What term or concept is the essay about?

In defining the term, did you explain why this term is different from or similar to others in the same category? For example, compare the essential American with the unique American; compare when to get involved with when to walk away from a situation.

Did you include special features that make your concept unique and distinct?

Does the definition match the examples or illustrations included in the draft?

Did you make it clear why the reader should be interested in knowing more about this term or concept?

After you have discussed these questions, write your second draft, which you will share with the rest of the class.

ADDITIONAL PROJECT

At the library, look up and read about one of the news events described in this article. Decide if Quindlen's reference to this particular news event was appropriate. What other recent news events make you question whether or not to get involved? Share this information with your class.

Write the steps that you took to find the news events referred to in the Quindlen article. Share with your class what reference materials in your college library can help you locate news events of the past.

EXPLORING YOUR IDEAS

What does the title of this story make you think about? Write down any ideas that come to your mind. Has anything happened in your life that you want to know more about or to understand better? How can you find the answers to your questions? Write about these ideas in your journal.

I Wanted to Know Why

JONATHAN AMES

Jonathan Ames grew up in New Jersey and graduated from Princeton University in 1987. His first novel, *I Pass Like Night*, was published by William Morrow and Company. This story, written while he was in a writing program at college, won the Henfield Prize and was published in *The Henfield Prize Stories*.

I've been thinking about suicide ever since Roy Laudner killed himself. He was a handsome boy whom everyone knew and said good things about. He was president of the ecology club. And what stood out about him to me was that the handlebars on his bike were the old-fashioned type, and I didn't know why he didn't have the ten-speed handlebars like everyone else. His bike even had mud guards and an old, fat leather seat. He had curly brown hair which my sister wrote about in the poem. She said it was like a "wreath of olive leaves wrapped around your head." Her poem about Roy is still one of the most beautiful things I've ever read, it was written like a letter to him. I remember the last time I saw him he stopped with that black bike of his at my friend Ethan's driveway. We had been playing basketball. And it was a cool fall day and we talked a little while. Roy knew me because of my sister, and I pretended I didn't notice his old-fashioned handlebars. I was pretty happy after he rode away thinking what a nice guy. And I felt cool in front of my best friend Ethan that a guy in high school would talk to me. I also remember he had a catch with me once down at the rec field and didn't make me feel like a little kid. He was kind to me and I never really knew why.

And then it spread all over town that he hanged himself. My sister ran around our house screaming and crying. I stayed out of her way, and she ran into her room and slammed the door, shrieking. I wasn't sure who it was at first, and then I realized it was the guy with the bike. Slowly the facts started coming out and we all found out that he had hanged himself nude in the basement and was found by his sister. Supposedly she touched him once or twice and said, "Roy, quit fooling around," and then realized he was dead and ran out of the house. What struck me was thinking about him hanging there nude. I always have thought that must've been the first shock, seeing her brother all nude. I bet she even laughed, she was only fourteen, and I bet she's got some secret shame about seeing her brother's penis and feeling excited with him being dead. Over the years I would ask my sister to tell me all she knew about the suicide, I wanted to know every detail.

When my sister wrote the poem it was about how Roy might've loved her and she had loved someone else, but now that he was dead she knew she loved him, only it was too late to say "I love you." So she felt, like everybody did in their own way, that it was her fault, but it wasn't. The rumor was that he wanted to go to college, but his parents couldn't afford it. And that seemed to explain why he had the old-fashioned handlebars. So one day Roy stayed home sick from school.

I tried to imagine him walking around his house naked, carrying that rope. What was he thinking, was he crying, when he threw it over the beam and went swinging down, oh Roy, why? I asked my sister if he left a note and she didn't think he did. My parents said things like, "See? Parents should never hesitate to give to their children." Somehow when things like that happen my parents start feeling all high and mighty because my sister and I haven't killed ourselves. I hate it when they act like that.

At the end of the school year the yearbook came out. And we all skimmed through it looking for pictures of Roy. And sure enough, there he was sitting in the stands of a football game and it seemed to me his face stood out above all the rest. He was in a large crowd and everyone was shouting and smiling, except for Roy who looked so quiet and erect. And I thought, was he thinking about killing himself at that very moment? There was another one of him in the stands and it had the same eerie feeling, you knew he was dead now. The yearbook was dedicated to him, he was the only one who had died, and it was at this time that I began to fantasize about my own suicide. Usually at night I'd put myself to sleep wondering if (and hoping) the whole town would cry for me the way they did for him. I even experimented in front of the mirror with a towel around my neck, but I didn't know how to tie it right (my father has always told me I'm no good with my hands), and I have never learned. I had only talked to Roy Laudner twice in my life, but I started mourning for him. My mother and sister didn't know it, but I'd take out the yearbook and look at him in those stands alone, and I'd look at his senior picture in his tie, and I'd read my sister's beautiful poem, and I'd cry for him. It was my secret that I missed him.

In eighth grade a few years after it happened, my teacher started talking about suicide and she brought up Roy. She said, "You never know why someone might kill himself, but most likely it is when he has a problem he can't talk about. When Roy Laudner killed himself a few years ago," and then my ears pricked up, she was talking about my Roy Laudner, how dare she say his name out loud, I was hating her, "they found in his dresser drawer that he had tied all his socks in knots." I wanted to scream, how did you know that? How can you tell everyone Roy's secrets? By this time I had thought so much about Roy Laudner's suicide, had played it over so many times in my head, that I almost felt I had walked down his basement stairs with him, looked at his naked body, watched him tie the rope (he was an Eagle Scout), and stared at him swaying and swinging, just like his sister. I just didn't want to think of Roy tying his socks in knots and the teacher had spoken about him as if he were nobody, and like everybody she blamed the parents for not seeing their son's problem.

The following year my sister started going out with Roy's younger brother, Paul, who looked just like Roy, the same tight curly hair, handsome face, and that smile that made you feel like you were friends. And so one day I went over to the Laudner house with my sister and I met the whole family. Roy's sister, the one who found him, was pretty and I had a lot of questions I wanted to ask her, but I couldn't. And you could see Roy in her face and I liked her, but she was older than me. I guess I liked her the same way my sister liked Paul. The two girls went to talk and Paul took me to the basement down the old dirty wooden stairs to show me a model he was working on. And I tried to look at the rafters without him noticing and figure out which one, and how did Roy do it (with a ladder maybe?), and then I saw his black bike old and lost in the corner with tools and broken furniture. I remembered Roy riding it, his arms bent to the handles, and then I wondered who had cut him down, who had held his dead naked body? And my mind would not stop and I never wanted to leave there, I wanted to figure it all out. I felt somehow that if I stayed there forever, I could watch it all happen again and I would know. But then Mrs. Laudner called us upstairs for dinner and I looked back at the basement to remember exactly how it was and to imagine Roy hanging above all the clutter.

When everyone was at the table I looked at the parents trying to see their pain and loss which I thought must be so evident (my parents had said they would not go on living if it was them), but I could see nothing in their faces. Yet I knew it was there surrounding all of us. I excused myself to go to the bathroom, but instead went to Roy's room which was also down the hall. My sister had pointed it out earlier and had whispered that it had been left untouched since he died. The door was open a crack and I went in. The whole room was neat and the bed was perfectly made. I saw a pair of sneakers by the closet and his jeans hanging over his desk chair. And a science book was open, he must have been studying before he died. I wished that I would find a note that no one else had seen and then I would know why, but it wasn't there of course, and I stepped out growing too scared to continue and made sure to shut the door the same amount it had been open. I went to the bathroom to flush the toilet and returned to the dining room. I was thirsty from my adventure and I asked Paul, "Roy, could you pass the milk?" Everyone stopped talking, I had evoked his name. I stared down at my plate unable to move and I was saying to myself over and over again so that God would hear, "I'm sorry, I'm sorry." and I wished that I were dead. ■

DISCUSSING THE SELECTION

1. In the first paragraph, the narrator describes Roy as "a nice guy." What specific words or incidents in the story communicate that Roy is a nice guy?

2. What indications do you have that the narrator perceives Roy as being from a different economic class? What evidence does Ames provide that Roy's parents have different values from those of the narrator?

3. What does the reader know about the narrator by the end of the story? Choose three words from the following list that best describe the narrator:

immature	intelligent	sensitive
depressed	lonely	curious
friendly	happy	imaginative

Explain why you chose these words, using specific incidents in the story as evidence of the narrator's personality.

4. Why did Roy Laudner's death make such a difference in the narrator's life? What evidence do you have in the story that Roy's death affected other members of the narrator's family too?

THINKING CRITICALLY

1. Ames won the Henfield Prize, a literary prize, for this short story. What qualities do you think the reviewers were looking for when they chose this short story?

2. Have you ever lost anyone who was important to you? How did you feel? What did you do that helped you cope with the loss?

3. Why do you think suicide is such a big problem among teenagers in our society today?

4. Writers often deal with their personal difficulties by writing about them in a story or essay form. Have you ever written about your feelings as a way of understanding a difficult circumstance better? What stories, books, or poems have you read that dealt with a similar subject? What differences did you notice in the ways the writers dealt with their subjects?

FOCUSING ON THE WRITING

1. Ames uses many run-on sentences throughout this story. Locate some of them, and discuss what effect they have on you as a reader. Why do you think he included these run-on sentences? What mood do they create for his readers? *magative (another idea)*

2. The first sentence in this story is "I've been thinking about suicide ever since Roy Laudner killed himself." From whose point of view is the story being told? (See page 97 for a discussion about point of view and types of narrators.) Reread the rest of the story. What type of narrator is telling the story?

3. Reread the descriptions of the Laudners' basement and of Roy's bedroom. In these two examples, Ames shows rather than tells his readers about feelings. What do these descriptive details reveal about how the Laudner family has responded to Roy's suicide?

CREATING YOUR TEXT

1. Write the story of an event that had a profound effect on your development. Tell the details, and explain why this event had such an effect on you. Tell your reader what you learned from this experience.

2. Have you ever lost anyone or anything that had special meaning to you? Write the story of this experience, and then explain why the loss of this person or thing meant so much to you. What did you learn from your experience?

3. Suicide is one of the major causes of death among young people under the age of twenty-one. This story makes it clear that suicide hurts many

people who know and care about an individual. Imagine that a friend told you he or she was thinking about suicide. Write the story of your encounter and what advice you would give to your friend.

4. Adults do not always have the answers for troubled young people. In an essay, explain the types of difficult situations young people face and what family members, teachers, and advisers can do to help young people deal with such problems in a healthy, productive way.

REVISING YOUR TEXT

Review the first draft of your writing on your own or with a partner, by going over the revision questions on page 11 or 12 if you have written an essay or on page 13 or 14 if you have written a story. Think about the following before you write your second draft:

What is the most important point you want your readers to get from reading your essay? How do you make that point stand out in your draft?
How do you distinguish between the people you describe so each one seems unique and real to your readers?
Do your examples or illustrations support your main idea?
Does your conclusion tie together your ideas or reinforce your main idea?

Keeping these questions in mind, rewrite your second draft. Share this second draft with your class.

EXPLORING YOUR IDEAS

We all have learned about the HIV virus and the AIDS disease from various sources. Before you read this article, write about what you already know about the virus and disease. Some questions to think about as you write include: How do people get this illness? How can people protect themselves from the illness? What causes babies to get this illness? What happens to them?

Mothers with AIDS: A Love Story

PERRI KLASS

Perri Klass is a pediatrician practicing in Boston. She writes essays on health issues and is the author of a novel, *Other Women's Children*. This article originally appeared in *The New York Times* in November 1990.

When my daughter was 4 months old, I stuck myself with a needle. Fortunately, it was a clean needle. I was starting an IV on a baby, and after several unsuccessful attempts I had finally threaded a tiny plastic catheter into a twisty little hand vein. I reached for a fresh syringe, full of sterile saline, trying to keep the catheter steady, and when I tried to unscrew the needle attached to the new syringe, I handled it clumsily and felt a small but real prick through the rubber gloves I was wearing into my thumb.

Reasonably enough, I didn't worry too much about it at the time. True, the baby had AIDS, but you don't transmit the HIV virus by sticking yourself with a clean needle when there's an AIDS patient in the room. I started to get paranoid in the bleary hours of the morning, when I found myself, as usual sitting in my rocking chair and nursing my daughter. What if somehow the virus had gotten into that tiny hole made in my skin by that sterile needle? I was looking down at my daughter's head, as she suckled and snorted with that avid middle-of-the-night concentration, and I was insanely terrified that my breast milk was contaminated.

I think that if I hadn't been nursing I would have taken this needle stick as a warning and learned the appropriate lesson about being more careful. But the images that played over and over in my brain had nothing to do with fears about my own health. What I kept imagining, in melodramatic Technicolor, was that suddenly, instead of nurturing and nourishing my baby girl, I might be poisoning her, infecting her, betraying her.

The baby, two weeks out of the nursery, still looks newborn. His mother only found that she was HIV-positive six months into the pregnancy, and confides now that if she had known sooner she probably would have had an abortion: "I mean, he didn't ask to be born. It isn't fair to him, really." But there's reason to hope that he'll escape infection; only about 30 percent of the children born to HIV-infected women acquire the virus in utero. Unfortunately, it isn't possible to determine definitively that a child is not infected until he or she is over a year old, subjecting parents to a difficult limbo of watching and waiting—and a definite positive may end that waiting at any point.

An elaborate car seat is parked in the corner of the examining room; this is a baby whose mother is determined to protect him. She will never leave him unattended in the bathtub, never fasten his pacifier around his neck on a string, never take any of the risks that other parents sometimes take. She will do anything to keep her baby safe, because she is terrified that he is already in danger.

"There's just one thing," she says. "His nails are so long." Indeed, like many newborns, the baby has nails that have grown past his fingertips, tiny, almost transparent curves. "I'm afraid to cut them, and in the nursery they told me to just bite them off."

I nod. It's common advice, since scissors look so large and sharp next to tiny baby fingers.

"But I don't want to bite his nails—I heard the virus might be in my saliva, and what if I bite him by mistake? I couldn't stand it if I thought he was O.K. and then he got infected from me."

I tried to reassure her that this was a highly unlikely, if not impossible, way for the virus to be transmitted. I suggested that she buy an infant nail clipper and trim his nails while he slept. I reminded her that it was O.K. to kiss and cuddle her baby. But I could not take away the power of her fear, of her sense that she is herself the source of the shadow hanging over her infant.

Another mother, another infant, the same clinic.

"Did you ever nurse the baby?"

"No, they told me not to."

"Good," I say. The current understanding is that breast milk can transmit HIV, so babies who escape infection in the womb could contract it from their mothers after birth. And so, instead of passing out the usual pediatric message (breast-feeding is best), I am saying, good, your child has never tasted your milk.

And yet, what a message for a mother to live with: you are dangerous to your child. For that matter, what a message for a pregnant woman. Even if she eats right and stops smoking, even if she stays away from drugs and sees her doctor regularly, she has to live with the fear that along with oxygen, calories, and protein her body may be sending through those complex blood-rich interconnections a virus that will one day make her child sicken, and even die.

Pregnancy, childbirth, nursing. For many women, there is a certain unvoiced smug delight in these biological extravaganzas, in watching our bodies perform their most extreme functions. See how I expand to carry a baby, see how I contract to give birth, see how I produce the food my baby needs—look, look, look at this remarkable baby! Along with everything else that the HIV virus steals from its victims, it leaches out this unadulterated pride. Infected mothers love their babies, love them maybe as only people can who feel with real force the possibility of loss. But the biological bond has been usurped,* so that the protection and nourishment of one body by the other has to be seen also as the route of infection.

*usurped: taken and held in possession by force or without right.

It's analogous* in some ways to what this virus has done to one of the other sources of great joy that our bodies have to offer us. I spent my formative years in the casual-sex-can-be-fun era, and I despise pundits[†] who piously conclude that the good thing about AIDS is the return to sex with commitment. There is no good thing about AIDS, and commitment through fear of contagion is nothing to write home about. This microscopic virus has cast its shadow over lovemaking, both past and present, has made the "sexual history" a source of danger and doubt for many people, rather than a source of pride and embarrassment. In a certain sense, the virus has quite literally poisoned intimacy and love.

And yet, of course, sit in the clinic and watch a mother with her baby, and mostly intimacy and love are what you will see. The baby, almost a year old, has just started walking and is making her way unsteadily down the hall; the mother follows, ready to serve as a safety net. Doctors and nurses and social workers ooh and ah over the ruffled dress, the gleaming white baby shoes. Afterward, in the examining room, the mother confides that she is pregnant again. She's a little defensive—she didn't plan this, she volunteers. She knows this new baby might be infected. But still, look at the 1-year-old, so big and healthy. Surely when all the watching and waiting is over that child will turn out not to have the virus. And she just has a feeling, she confides, that this new baby will be O.K.

I recognize the courage, and the desperate optimism, and that most comforting emotional defense, denial. The magnitude of this infection necessitates a mental defense that may have been too strong for her own good. What could happen is too terrible to contemplate, so she will not contemplate it.

From the doctor's point of view, of course, it's all wrong. She should have been using condoms; unprotected intercourse puts her partners at risk. And it's possible that pregnancy will have an adverse effect on her own health (and shorten the time she has to care for her family)—and there's at least a 30 percent chance that she'll have a baby who's infected. She repeats: I just know this baby will be O.K. And the doctor answers: I hope you're right. ■

*analogous: similar or comparable.
[†]pundits: learned people.

DISCUSSING THE SELECTION

1. Before you discuss this selection, write down for three minutes, in your journal, what you can remember from reading the selection. What stands out in your memory? What information in the article surprised or upset you? What overall feeling did you have after reading the article? After writing about the article, discuss your answers to these questions with your classmates.

2. What does Klass think mothers with AIDS need to know about taking care of their newborns or small children?

3. What does Klass want the general population to know about how the virus can be transmitted?

4. Klass believes that infected mothers love their babies, "but the biological bond has been usurped." What does this phrase mean? What specific actions should mothers take to reinforce the biological bond with their babies?

THINKING CRITICALLY

1. What is the difference between being HIV-positive and having AIDS? If you do not know the answer, how can you find this out?

2. What are the main ways in which people become HIV-positive? According to present knowledge, how can people prevent contracting this virus?

3. How do you explain the fact that Klass does not discuss the responsibility or involvement of fathers in this article? Should she have included fathers? What should their involvement be?

4. Should there be more laws to protect health care workers? more laws to protect health care users? If so, explain what types of laws you would like to see passed. Explain your reasons. If not, explain why you do not think laws are necessary.

FOCUSING ON THE WRITING

Telling Facts from Opinions

Writers use facts and opinions to support their main ideas or points. A factual statement is based on evidence that can be verified or proved. Writers may include the source of their factual information if it is derived from a written source or from an observation or experiment. Some facts are common knowledge, such as the fact that the sun rises in the east and sets in the west.

Opinions are based on feelings, ideas, or attitudes. Some opinions are also commonly accepted knowledge, such as the opinion that mothers love their babies.

1. What specific facts does Klass include in this article? What opinions does she include to support her point of view?

2. In paragraph 4, Klass shifts the focus in her article. What difference in tone and type of narration, or storytelling, do you now find? Why does she make a change at this point?

3. In paragraph 16, there is another shift in focus. What difference do you find here? What point is Klass trying to make that makes her shift her focus?

4. What is Klass's point of view about the mother mentioned in the last three

paragraphs? What specific words or phrases in the article support your explanation?

CREATING YOUR TEXT

1. Write an essay in which you tell the story of someone you know or have read about who has AIDS. Explain any ways in which the person's life has been altered. Has the society done enough to provide care and support for this person? If not, what responsibility should society take on?

2. Recent statistics suggest that although many young people are educated about AIDS in school, many still have more than one sexual partner and often do not use condoms. Write an essay in which you convince your peers that people must be cautious and use condoms.

3. In many school districts around the country, there is disagreement about how much students should learn about sexually transmitted diseases such as AIDS and when this education should begin. Write an essay in which you explain if and when children should begin to learn about diseases such as AIDS. What should they be taught at different ages? Reread your journal entry and reflect on the class discussion; then base your ideas on your experience, observations, readings, and discussions.

4. In some parts of the United States, laws require HIV-positive patients to inform their doctors about the diagnosis. In some places, people are required to inform their co-workers. Write an essay taking a position about whether or not HIV-positive people should have to inform the health care workers who care for them, and whether or not they should have to inform their co-workers. Explain your point of view based on the Klass article, your discussions, and your observations.

5. Should people be required by law to inform their sexual partners that they are HIV-positive? Write an essay in which you take a position on this issue. Explain your position using examples and factual information.

REVISING YOUR TEXT

When you have completed your first draft, share it with a partner. Read it together to determine the strongest parts and the parts of the essay that need improvement. Review the essay again, going over the revision questions on page 11.

Notice where you have relied on facts and where you have relied on opinions to support your point of view. Do you need to explain the source of your facts? Decide if your opinions are enough to support your point of view. Rewrite your draft, keeping in mind the suggestions made from both processes. Share your second draft with your class.

ADDITIONAL PROJECT

Find out the facts about AIDS. What can college students do to help others cope with this sickness? What is being done in your community to educate people and to help ill people? What role can your class play in improving understanding about AIDS?

> **EXPLORING YOUR IDEAS**
>
> Think about any couple you know who has had a successful love relationship for ten, twenty, thirty, or forty years. Choose one of these relationships and describe it in your journal. How long have the partners been together? What do you know about their lives together? How have they resolved their differences? How do you think they maintain their love? What questions do you have about their relationship?

Another Kind of Sex Ed

SHARON A. SHEEHAN

Sharon Sheehan, who lives in California, wrote this article, which appeared in *Newsweek* in July 1992. She has worked with young people in California regarding sexually related issues for many years. She is concerned that young people may be getting the wrong message about sex and love.

1 Our local newspaper ran an essay recently by the president of the Youth Council. It explained its vote favoring condom machines in high schools. He said that students should be able to get the prophylactics in the school bathroom because they fear personal embarrassment at the checkout counter of the local drugstore.

2 Could it be that many teenagers would rather take their chances with AIDS than run the risk of embarrassment? And what about the risk of pregnancy?

3 Family-planning workers have observed that many teenage girls cannot bring themselves to march into a clinic and declare that they are planning to

lose their virginity. It's too embarrassing. Running the risk of pregnancy is preferable.

After earning a graduate degree in public health, I was employed by the State of California to help solve the problem of teenage pregnancy by educating teenagers about birth control. The fundamental origin of the problem—the premarital sexual activity of teenagers—was accepted as a given. The Planned Parenthood professional assigned to train me pointed out that the real solution to this problem was to eradicate the sense of shame associated with premarital sex.

I was stunned. But the logic was obvious: teenage pregnancy is a problem. Birth control is the solution. Shame is the barrier to applying the solution. Therefore eliminate shame in order to solve the problem. But taking a young person's sense of modesty and giving back a pill or a condom wasn't what anyone would call a fair trade.

Nonetheless, for the next several months I proceeded to talk to hundreds of teenagers about various methods of birth control. But I was never convinced that I was genuinely helping them.

Professionally, I succumbed to the obligatory gag rule: don't say anything that could arouse the sense of shame. In practice, then, I was compelled to imply that all sexual choices were morally neutral. Thus everything that I had learned from my parents' marriage and my own marriage was off-limits. Everything I believed about how human beings form meaningful and lasting relationships was not only irrelevant but counterproductive.

The new sexual ideology protected teenagers from shame by saying, "If you feel like you are ready, then it's OK." Ready for what? Ready to build a life together? Ready for conquest? Ready to feel like a slut? Ready to bring a new life into the world? Shame is a powerful word that explodes in many directions. There is a cruel, destructive side to shame. Controlling people by shaming them into self-loathing or compliance, for example. But shame also protects us. It prevents us from treating others in a despicable fashion. And it protects "the sanctity of our unfinished or unready selves."

In his book, "The Meaning of Persons," Paul Tournier reflects on a young person's innate sense of modesty: "The appearance of this sense of shame is, in fact, the sign of the birth of a person. And later the supreme affirmation of the person, the great engagement of life, will be marked by the handing over of the secret, the gift of the self, the disappearance of shame."

Recently, I returned to the high-school campus to talk with students about how they see themselves and what they hope for. Many were offended by the adult assumption that most teens are sexually active. One girl was so uncomfortable that she went to her teacher in Living Skills class to explain that she was not sleeping with her boyfriend. "It's like the adult world invading our world," another girl commented.

Yet they are embarrassed to ask the questions they care about most. "What should I look for in a guy?" "How do I know if it's morally right?" "How will I feel afterward?"

Behind their "correct," value-free facade lurks a deep sense of loss. They lament the lack of guidelines and moral structure. One girl described it this way: "It used to be that people got married and then they had sex. Then when the baby came there was a place all prepared for it. Now technology has taken away the worry of having children. That leaves sex to float around in everyone's life when there's no guy who's going to stick around."

"It used to be that kids wouldn't want to disappoint themselves or each other," a boy remarked. "I think it's really lonely," said another. "It's sad."

It's as if the gap between sex and marriage had opened up a huge empty hole in which there were "no real sure thing." A loving relationship that lasts. Hasn't that always been the goal and bottom line? Isn't the real C word for sex education commitment, not condoms?

It's time to give the thousands of couples in this country who have been happily married 20, 30, 40, 50 years equal access to sex-education classrooms. One boy told me, "I'd like to hear more stories . . . how they met . . . how they kept the love alive." If you have built a marriage and family the "old-fashioned" way, go to a classroom and tell your story. Share the wisdom gained by keeping the promises of your youth. Let them ask the questions they care about the most.

In coming face to face with other human beings, how much do we value the self that we glimpse through their eyes, that flutters past in a gesture or a smile? Sex education is about nothing less than how and when we hand over this astonishing gift of the self. The goal is that we can love and trust and believe enough to commit our whole self and our whole future. ■

DISCUSSING THE SELECTION

1. What does the title "Another Kind of Sex Ed" mean?

2. What aspect of sex education for young people is Sheehan concerned about and opposed to? Why?

3. Is Sheehan opposed to students learning about condoms and birth control? Support your answer with evidence from the article.

4. According to Sheehan, what changed her mind about what young people should learn about sex from family planning experts?

5. What do you think her attitude toward sex on the first date would be? Support your answer with evidence from the article.

6. In the article on page 174, Perri Klass writes about her attitude toward sex and commitment. Reread that selection, and discuss the attitudes of the two authors.

THINKING CRITICALLY

1. In the article, Sheehan writes that young people miss the "guidelines and moral structure" if adults do not discuss such things when they discuss sex. Explain why you agree or disagree with her about this issue.

2. How do you feel about Sheehan's use of the word "slut" in paragraph 8? Is this term evidence of a double standard?

3. Explain why you think sex education classes should or should not include more information about "commitment."

4. Explain why sex education classes should or should not include more stories about couples who have had long-term successful relationships.

5. Do you think that Sheehan is "old-fashioned" in her attitudes toward sex and relationships in today's world? Explain your answer by discussing your experiences and observations of the world around you.

FOCUSING ON THE WRITING

Writing a Comparison-and-Contrast Essay

When writers compare, they look for *similarities*. When they contrast, they look for *differences*.

Comparison-and-contrast essays follow two general patterns of organization. In the first method, writers present all the information about one subject and then all the information about the other. They conclude with an analysis containing their final comparisons and contrasts.

In the second method, writers compare and contrast both subjects throughout the essay topic by topic. They also conclude with an analysis that acts as a final summary.

Terms often used when comparing are *also, as . . . as, as well as,* and *too*. Terms often used when contrasting are *but, however, nevertheless, not as . . . as,* and *in contrast*.

1. Sheehan compares and contrasts two types of sex education. What are the two types? What examples does she give to illustrate each of them? Which does she prefer? What specific words or phrases in her article tell you her point of view? How does she organize her comparison-and-contrast essay?

2. In writing this article, Sheehan included many questions. List those questions. Which (if any) are answered in the selection? What was the purpose of including the questions in the article?

3. Sheehan includes a quote from another writer in her article. Reread the quotation, and rewrite it in your own words. Why do you think she included the quotation in her essay instead of paraphrasing it into her own words?

4. In the article, Sheehan refers to the "gift of the self" without ever actually defining what she means. What specific words or phrases in the article help you understand what this phrase means to her?

CREATING YOUR TEXT

1. Write an essay in which you compare and contrast the sexual attitudes of young people you know or have read about. Explain your own point of view and the evidence or observations on which it is based.

2. Sheehan believes that sex education should stress commitment, not condoms and birth control. Write an essay in which you agree or disagree with her position. Support your point of view with your experiences, observations, and readings.

3. Reread your journal entry, and then write an essay describing a long-term relationship (ten years or more) of any two people whose relationship you admire. To conclude your essay, explain why you have chosen the couple and what you have learned about relationships from knowing them.

4. Write an essay in which you describe a relationship of any two people that did not last or that you think is in trouble. Think about the reasons why the two people do not or cannot get along. To conclude your essay, explain why you have decided to focus on this couple and what you have learned about relationships from knowing them.

5. In some schools and family planning clinics, students are taught about preventing AIDS by making sex safe. Others, instead of teaching safe sex, stress "no sex" or abstinence as the only sure way to prevent AIDS. Write

an essay in which you discuss the way you think people should be taught to prevent AIDS. Support your point of view with evidence from your experience, observations, and readings.

6. In the United States today, it is estimated that one-third of all women and one-sixth of all men will be raped or sexually molested in their lifetime. In an essay, explain the role that sex education in schools, religious institutions, and in community settings should play in dealing with rape and sexual molestation.

REVISING YOUR TEXT

When you finish your first draft, on your own or with a classmate, read the revision questions on page 11 or 12 and examine the places in which your draft succeeds and where it can be improved. Write your second draft to share with the class.

In addition, think about the following questions:

Did you include any quotations in your writing? If so, what did they add to your essay? Could you have paraphrased instead? Did you identify your source?

Did you include any questions in your writing? If so, what did they add to your draft? Did you answer them in your writing, or were they meant to be "rhetorical" or unanswered questions?

Did you compare and/or contrast? How did you present this information? Did it make your point of view clearer and stronger?

EXPLORING YOUR IDEAS

Write a description of a person whom you see frequently but whose name you do not know. The person could be someone in your school, your neighborhood, or someone you see on the bus or at parties. Think about the person. Make a guess about the life of the person based on your impression of him or her over time.

The Locker Room

SUSAN RICHARDS SHREVE

Susan Richards Shreve lives in Washington, D.C., and teaches at George Mason University. She writes essays for the "MacNeil/Lehrer NewsHour." She has written several novels, including *A Fortunate Madness, A Woman Like That,* and *Daughters of the New World.* This story was published in *The Sound of Writing: America's Short Story Magazine of the Air.*

In the morning early, I swim in the Olympic-size pool underneath the basketball court of a boys' Episcopal school. Back and forth in the turquoise dawn, keeping to the left of the black line, careful not to crash into the wall. Half a mile, predictably, and then the locker room. This morning is no different.

The locker is like a men's locker room, without privacy—a tile room with showers lined up against one wall. You will rub against the flesh of the woman next to you unless you are centered neatly under the spray from your own nozzle. That's how familial and democratic this locker room is, with women I have seen every day for ten years first off in the morning before coffee and the newspaper, more regular than my husband or my mother.

I don't know their names. I probably wouldn't recognize them on the street. Many of them are older than I am and have been swimming much longer than this sport has been popular. They swim for survival because they have lost a breast or have had back surgery or arthritis. One has a pin in her hip and walks with a walker. Another has had heart attacks.

What is striking about older women, I have noticed, is that the flesh on the torso remains supple in spite of the assaults of age on the face, the slackening of the skin on the arms and legs. I did not know this about women until I started to swim here. In fact I knew very little about nakedness.

When I was a girl, especially in junior high school, I never dressed in the locker room. I stood on the toilet behind the locked cubicle door and only exposed my breasts to the empty space for half a minute between changing from school clothes to gym clothes and back.

So this locker room has been a liberation for me. To stand naked, one in a line of naked women, to know them intimately without knowing their names, has made me feel a kind of membership I never knew before.

This morning, the very tall woman with white hair to her waist is back. "Rapunzel," I call her to my husband. She is fair and freckled, with one small breast, a long incision crosswise on her belly, and high hips. She comes into the shower just after me, takes off her suit slow motion, lets her hair fall out of the white old-fashioned rubber cap. Everyone is glad to see her.

"Hello," I say. "We missed you."

"Thank you," she says. She has a certain dignity that commands a room in spite of the lopsided oddness of her figure.

"Were you on holiday?" the sweet-faced round woman who keeps her walker just in front of her while she showers asks.

"No," the Rapunzel woman says. "There was of course no way for you to know." She turns the shower to hot and stands facing out, underneath the nozzle, her eyes closed, her head tilted back. "My younger child died."

We are stunned. The soft round woman takes hold of her walker, forgetting to rinse the shampoo out of her hair. Weak-kneed, as though this news is personal, I sit on the wooden bench next to Abigail, the one woman whose name we all know because she is southern and gregarious and insists we know her name.

"Oh, my God," Abigail says. "How awful. This is such terrible news." She seems to be the only one among us to whom language comes as easily as living.

"She was ill for a very long time," the Rapunzel woman says. "I didn't tell you because I didn't want to believe it was true."

She pours Flex shampoo into the palm of her hand, lathers it quickly, washing and rinsing her hair simultaneously so her whole body is sudsy.

"I don't know what to say, dear," the woman with the walker says. "I am so sorry."

"Thank you," Rapunzel says. She turns off the shower and steps out.

I embrace her wet and slippery body. I am weeping. The woman with the walker takes her hand and kisses the fingers. Abigail steps into the room where the lockers are and tells the other women, half dressed, drying their hair, putting on stockings, tying their shoes.

"Thank you," Rapunzel says as she embraces one after another of the women. "It was only bad in the last weeks." She combs out her long white hair, puts on gray wool slacks and a turtleneck. I notice that she doesn't once look in the mirror at herself.

"Suddenly she got much worse." She puts on a wool cap over her wet hair and a down ski jacket.

"Thank you all very much." Shyly, she blows a kiss toward the rest of us dressing. Just as she is about to leave, she says, as if in answer to a question, "Her name was Caroline Marie."

After the door closes, the woman with the walker, bundled for winter, shakes her head.

"I would send flowers if I knew where." She touches my cheek. "Goodbye, dear."

"Goodbye," I say.

"Goodbye," she says to the others.

I put my hood up, tie the laces of my heavy boots.

"Goodbye," I call, opening the door to the cold. "See you tomorrow," I say, flooded unaccountably with gratitude. "See you tomorrow."

Outside, it has begun to snow—a thin gray city snow, falling in sheets at an angle to the earth, obscuring the people on the sidewalk hurrying to work. But I am suddenly lifted out of the darkness of a winter dawn. ■

DISCUSSING THE SELECTION

1. In what setting or place does this story occur? What is the purpose of setting this story in this place? What happens here that would not occur in another setting?

2. Shreve describes several of the swimmers. What do you recall from these descriptions that makes each woman stand out as an individual?

3. In the fairy tale by that name, Rapunzel is a young woman with long, long hair, who is imprisoned in a high tower. In order to get to her room, a visitor must call, "Rapunzel, Rapunzel, let down your hair." The visitor then climbs her hair. What physical characteristic does the character called Rapunzel in the Shreve story have that makes her name appropriate? What other meaning does the phrase "let down your hair" have that also applies to this story? Rapunzel is a prisoner in the fairy tale. In what way is Rapunzel a prisoner in this story?

4. Shreve describes the relationships of the women as distant. They do not know each other's names, and they probably would not recognize each other on the street. What happens in the story that changes their relationships? What is the significance of the women saying, "See you tomorrow," at the end of the story?

THINKING CRITICALLY

1. Why do you think the younger woman cries and embraces the older woman? Have you ever had an experience in which you felt close to a virtual stranger? Describe your experience.

Shreve *The Locker Room*

2. What in the story tells you the younger woman's attitude toward herself? What in the story tells you about her attitude toward older women? What makes you think her attitudes have changed during the ten years she has been swimming in the pool?

3. Is there any sport or athletic activity that is especially meaningful to you? Tell the class what it is and why it makes a difference in your life.

FOCUSING ON THE WRITING

1. Make a list of the words Shreve uses to describe the pool and the locker room. What feelings do you get from these descriptive words?

2. In the first paragraph, Shreve writes, "in the morning early," rather than "in the early morning." In the next line, she writes, "in the turquoise dawn," instead of "in the turquoise water of the pool." In her descriptions, she avoids obvious wording and instead creates a unique vision of the world through her words. What other examples of this can you find in the story? As a reader, what is your response to these unique descriptions?

3. The term "point of view" refers to the angle of the narrator or storyteller as a story is told (see page 97 for more information about this term). From what point of view is this story told? What type of narrator is found in this story? If you could read this same story from another point of view, whose point of view would you like to know and why?

4. What tense does Shreve use in paragraph 1? What is the reason for using this tense? In paragraph 5, Shreve shifts to a different tense. What is the reason for the shift?

CREATING YOUR TEXT

1. Write a description of a place you know well. In your introduction, explain why you want your reader to experience this place. In your conclusion, tell your reader what the most important reasons are for knowing about this place.

2. Write a description of a place that you have only been to once or twice but that remains in your memory.

3. Imagine that you are entering a contest in which you will win a trip to a place you have always wanted to visit. Write a description of that place, relying on what you know through movies or photographs. Convince your readers that you should win the tickets to visit the place.

4. Our contacts with strangers may be powerful and important in our learning to understand human nature. In an essay, explain the preceding statement based on your own observations and experiences.

REVISING YOUR TEXT

Review your first draft by rereading it with a partner while looking at the revision questions on page 11. Ask your classmate what you should add to enable him or her to "see" the place through your description. Reread Shreve's story, noticing her use of unique descriptive phrases. Try to create some of your own that describe the place as only you can see it.

EXPANDING YOUR IDEAS

Collaborative Writing Projects

1. As part of a small group, decide on an issue related to HIV or AIDS information about which you would like to know more. Together, construct a question to research as a group. Present the questions to your class, and discuss what kind of project—research, writing an article, a play, or so forth—is the best way for the groups to get answers to their questions and to share the information with the class. Decide which members of the group will have which responsibilities in completing the project. Do the research or outside work, and present the results of your project to the class.

    In addition, as a group, write a short paper revealing what you have read and what you have discovered by working together in a group.

2. As a small-group project, talk about friendship to people in your class and in other classes in the school. Make a list of topics that you would like to know more about in relation to friendship. Some questions might include

    How long have you been friends?
    What happens when a difficulty occurs in your relationship? How do you resolve it?
    How do you make friends outside of college?
    How do you maintain friends from high school when you go to college?

    Add your own questions about issues that interest you in relation to friendship.

    Make sure the person with whom you would like to talk is willing to meet with one or two students to discuss the project. If the person is willing, make an appointment to get together. Then use the questions you have developed to begin your discussion or interview. Find out if the person will let you audiotape as you talk. If not, someone in the group should take notes. In any case, someone in the group should transcribe the discussion to share with the others. Then, as a group, write about the discussion and the experience of meeting with the person. Together, write about what you have learned about friendship. Share your writing with the person with whom you had the discussion.

Entering school is a step into the public world of our society. In school, we develop the abilities that enable us to take control of our lives and make decisions about our future.

Theme 4

Changing Through Learning

Readings

"The Sanctuary of School"
BY LYNDA BARRY

"The Unwritten American Bargain"
BY COLIN L. POWELL

"Annie John"
BY JAMAICA KINCAID

"The Physician Who Healed Himself First"
BY LINDA KRAMER

"West Real"
BY ALBERTO ALVARO RÍOS

"Reading to Know"
BY RICHARD RODRIGUEZ

"It's Such a Pleasure to Learn"
BY WALLACE TERRY

In "The Sanctuary of School," Lynda Barry contrasts her warm supportive experience in school with her troubled home.

Colin L. Powell's essay "The Unwritten American Bargain" inspires students to believe in the power of higher education to change the future.

Jamaica Kincaid, in a story from her novel *Annie John*, describes the feelings of a confident, successful student during her first day in a new school.

In "The Physician Who Healed Himself First," Linda Kramer tells about how education was a salvation for pediatric surgeon, Ben Carson.

Although he agrees with the idea that education is necessary for success in life, Alberto Alvaro Ríos uses his essay "West Real" to explore the question of why his bilingualism was not valued in his early education.

Richard Rodriguez, in "Reading to Know," describes his reading program and the way that reading opened the door to knowledge for him.

In "It's Such a Pleasure to Learn," Wallace Terry introduces his readers to 100-year-old John Morton-Finney, a man with eleven college degrees, who taught school until the age of eighty-one, and who is still practicing law.

Making Discoveries

In Your Journal

Write in your journal about a person who made a major change in his or her life because of school or formal education. The person could be someone you know, someone you have seen on television, in the movies, or read about. Describe the person before and after the change took place. Explain which aspects of the change were positive and which were negative. Decide whether the changes affected personal behavior or related to specific knowledge. Discuss the ways a person can change and grow yet still maintain family relationships and old friendships.

With a Classmate

Talk to your classmate about the person you have chosen. Explain why you selected this person. Together, discuss what you mean by negative and positive changes. Discuss how a person can change and grow and still maintain relationships with friends and family.

With Your Class

Discuss some of the individuals you have selected. What characteristics do these people share? How did they change for the better or for the worse? Discuss their strategies for maintaining connections with their friends and families while they were growing and changing.

EXPLORING YOUR IDEAS

One meaning of "sanctuary" is a place of protection. Think of a place that you see as a place of protection, a place in which you can relax, be quiet, and feel good about yourself. Write about that place in your journal. Then write about why that place is special to you.

The Sanctuary of School

LYNDA BARRY

Lynda Barry, a cartoonist and writer living in Chicago, is the author of the play *The Good Times Are Killing Me*. Her essay "The Sanctuary of School" appeared in *Education Life*, a special feature in *The New York Times*, on January 5, 1992.

1   I was 7 years old the first time I snuck out of the house in the dark. It was winter and my parents had been fighting all night. They were short on money and long on relatives who kept "temporarily" moving into our house because they had nowhere else to go.

2   My brother and I were used to giving up our bedroom. We slept on the couch, something we actually liked because it put us that much closer to the light of our lives, our television.

3   At night when everyone was asleep, we lay on our pillows watching it with the sound off. We watched Steve Allen's mouth moving. We watched Johnny Carson's mouth moving. We watched movies filled with gangsters shooting machine guns into packed rooms, dying soldiers hurling a last grenade and beautiful women crying at windows. Then the sign-off finally came and we tried to sleep.

4   The morning I snuck out, I woke up filled with a panic about needing to

get to school. The sun wasn't quite up yet but my anxiety was so fierce that I just got dressed, walked quietly across the kitchen, and let myself out the back door.

It was quiet outside. Stars were still out. Nothing moved and no one was in the street. It was as if someone had turned the sound off on the world.

I walked the alley, breaking thin ice over the puddles with my shoes. I didn't know why I was walking to school in the dark. I didn't think about it. All I knew was the feeling of panic, like the panic that strikes kids when they realize they are lost.

That feeling eased the moment I turned the corner and saw the dark outline of my school at the top of the hill. My school was made up of about 15 nondescript portable classrooms set down on a fenced concrete lot in a rundown Seattle neighborhood, but it had the most beautiful view of the Cascade Mountains. You could see them from anywhere on the playfield and you could see them from the windows of my classroom—Room 2.

I walked over to the monkey bars and hooked my arms around the cold metal. I stood for a long time just looking across Rainier Valley. The sky was beginning to whiten and I could hear a few birds.

In a perfect world my absence at home would not have gone unnoticed. I would have had two parents in a panic to locate me, instead of two parents in a panic to locate an answer to the hard question of survival during a deep financial and emotional crisis.

But in an overcrowded and unhappy home, it's incredibly easy for any child to slip away. The high levels of frustration, depression, and anger in my house made my brother and me invisible. We were children with the sound turned off. And for us, as for the steadily increasing number of neglected children in this country, the only place where we could count on being noticed was at school.

"Hey there, young lady. Did you forget to go home last night?" It was Mr. Gunderson, our janitor, whom we all loved. He was nice and he was funny and he was old with white hair, thick glasses, and an unbelievable number of keys. I could hear them jingling as he walked across the playfield. I felt incredibly happy to see him.

He let me push his wheeled garbage can between the different portables as he unlocked each room. He let me turn on the lights and raise the window shades and I saw my school slowly come to life. I saw Mrs. Holman, our school secretary, walk into the office without her orange lipstick on yet. She waved.

I saw the fifth-grade teacher, Mr. Cunningham, walking under the breezeway eating a hard roll. He waved.

And I saw my teacher, Mrs. Claire LeSane, walking toward us in a red coat and calling my name in a very happy and surprised way, and suddenly my throat got tight and my eyes stung and I ran toward her crying. It was something that surprised both of us.

It's only thinking about it now, 28 years later, that I realize I was crying from relief. I was with my teacher, and in a while I was going to sit at my desk, with my crayons and pencils and books and classmates all around me, and for the next six hours I was going to enjoy a thoroughly secure, warm, and stable world. It was a world I absolutely relied on. Without it, I don't know where I would have gone that morning.

Mrs. LeSane asked me what was wrong and when I said "Nothing," she seemingly left it at that. But she asked me if I would carry her purse for her, an honor above all honors, and she asked if I wanted to come into Room 2 early and paint.

She believed in the natural healing power of painting and drawing for troubled children. In the back of her room there was always a drawing table and an easel with plenty of supplies, and sometimes during the day she would come up to you for what seemed like no good reason and quietly ask if you wanted to go to the back table and "make some pictures for Mrs. LeSane." We all had a chance at it—to sit apart from the class for a while to paint, draw, and silently work out impossible problems on 11 × 17 sheets of newsprint.

Drawing came to mean everything to me. At the back table in Room 2, I learned to build myself a life preserver that I could carry into my home.

We all know that a good education system saves lives, but the people of this country are still told that cutting the budget for public schools is necessary, that poor salaries for teachers are all we can manage and that art, music, and all creative activities must be the first to go when times are lean.

Before- and after-school programs are cut and we are told that public schools were not made for baby-sitting children. If parents are neglectful temporarily or permanently, for whatever reason, it's certainly sad, but their unlucky children must fend for themselves. Or slip through the cracks. Or wander in a dark night alone.

We are told in a thousand ways that not only are public schools not important, but that the children who attend them, the children who need them most, are not important either. We leave them to learn from the blind eye of television, or to the mercy of "a thousand points of light" that can be as far away as the stars.

I was lucky. I had Mrs. LeSane. I had Mr. Gunderson. I had an abundance of art supplies. And I had a particular brand of neglect in my home that allowed me to slip away and get to them. But what about the rest of the kids who weren't as lucky? What happened to them?

By the time the bell rang that morning I had finished my drawing and Mrs. LeSane pinned it up on the special bulletin board she reserved for drawings from the back table. It was the same picture I always drew—a sun in the corner of a blue sky over a nice house with flowers all around it.

Mrs. LeSane asked us to please stand, face the flag, place our right hands over our hearts and say the Pledge of Allegiance. Children across the country do it faithfully. I wonder now when the country will face its children and say a pledge right back. ■

DISCUSSING THE SELECTION

1. What role does television play in the lives of Barry and her brother?

2. Why does she go off to school before dawn? What about school makes it feel like a sanctuary to the child?

3. What does Barry mean by saying, "We were children with the sound turned off"? What family problems cause her parents to neglect their children? What is the difference between neglect and abuse?

4. How does Mr. Gunderson make the child feel welcome?

5. How does the reader know that Mrs. LeSane is aware that there are problems in Barry's home? What does Mrs. LeSane do to deal with the child's problems?

THINKING CRITICALLY

1. In your experience, has school ever felt like a sanctuary from problems or difficulties? Explain your answer to the class.

2. Explain why you agree or disagree with Barry that our society behaves as though public schools were not important and "that the children who attend them, the children who need them most, are not important either."

3. If you were able to redesign one aspect of public schooling in the United States, what would you change about it and why?

4. Do teachers, administrators, and other school workers have a responsibility to interfere when they suspect a problem in the home such as the one described in Barry's essay? What if they suspect physical abuse of a child?

FOCUSING ON THE WRITING

Chronological Order

Many writers arrange their ideas in chronological or time order, the order in which they happened. Many narratives, stories of personal experiences, summaries, and descriptions of historical events are arranged in chronological order so the readers can follow the experience from the beginning to the end.

Some words used to arrange events in chronological order are *first, second, third, next, then, before, after, initially, later, eventually,* and *finally.*

1. Reread the essay, underlining Barry's references to time. Her essay is developed through chronological or time connections. What specific time words do you find in the essay? Notice how she moves the reader through time from the night to the light of day. What other references to time do you find in this essay?

2. What is the symbolic meaning of going from dark to light? How does this meaning fit with the meaning of Barry's essay?

3. Barry tells a specific story about herself to make a general point about public education in our society. Where in the essay does she write her main idea or thesis statement? What is the main idea or thesis?

4. Rewrite the introduction, and move the thesis statement to the beginning of the essay. What effect does this have on your reading? In which place do you prefer the author to make her main point? Why?

5. In the conclusion, Barry combines her specific story with her general thesis. What does Barry want the country to do for its children? On page 31 the purposes of the conclusion are explained. What is the purpose of this conclusion?

CREATING YOUR TEXT

1. Write an essay in which you describe a teacher who made a difference in your life. Reread the Barry essay as a model for taking a specific incident and expanding it to a general idea about education and teachers.

2. Should education in the United States be free through college? Or should students have to pay for their own higher education? Write an essay in which you explain what you think about this subject. Support your point of view with your experience, observations, or readings.

3. Recent studies of schools in poor neighborhoods have shown that some

do not have laboratory equipment, computers, books, or art material. Some do not have enough desks or even enough heat in the winter. No matter how good the teachers are, such schools will not succeed if they do not get the money to provide more to their students. Write an essay in which you explain the value of having good facilities for improving learning. Use your own observations, experiences, and readings to support your viewpoint.

4. "It is time for the United States to face its children and pledge its allegiance to them and to their learning." Write an essay explaining what this statement means to you. In specific terms, describe what steps the United States should take to show its commitment to education.

REVISING YOUR TEXT

When you finish your first draft, read the revision questions on page 11 with a partner. Decide together which changes you should make to improve your second draft. Write the second draft, and share it with your class.

If you have included a narrative of a specific event in your essay, reread it examining the time ordering of the event. Does it begin at the beginning and clearly move the reader to the conclusion of the event? Do you accurately use time words and phrases to help the reader follow the time shifts?

EXPLORING YOUR IDEAS

"My parents expected me to go to college—they expected me to do better than they had done." Write about this sentence and what it means to you as a student today.

The Unwritten American Bargain

COLIN L. POWELL

Gen. Colin L. Powell is the chairman of the Joint Chiefs of Staff, the U.S. Department of Defense. This article appeared in *The American School Board Journal* in February 1991.

I graduated from Morris High School on Boston Road in the Bronx when I was 16. My parents expected me to go to college—they expected me to do better than they had done. And I valued my parents' opinion so highly that there was no question in my mind. I was going to college. And where to go to college was not an issue either. I was accepted at New York University and at the City College of New York. But NYU cost $750 a year and CCNY cost $10—no contest for a poor boy from the South Bronx.

I didn't do exceptionally well at CCNY—or at least, I didn't think so at the time. I passed with straight C's and graduated only because of my superior grades in ROTC, the Reserve Officer Training Corps. It took me four and one-half years, one summer session and a change of academic major—plus straight A's in ROTC—but I did graduate.

My CCNY graduating class went off in a thousand and one directions, as do all classes. Many people went the same way I did, into the Army. The Army was exciting: It promised adventure, it was a way to serve and most of all it was a job. For me, it turned out to be a maturing process also.

Between the ages of 16 and 33, something happened to me because later, when I went to George Washington University and got my Master's degree, I made an A in every course except one, in which I made a B. I believe the difference was a matter of growing up, the sense of responsibility the Army had given me, a few years of war and perhaps a wife and two children.

But I believe it was also the foundation I had gotten at CCNY. In fact, soon after entering the Army, I discovered how important CCNY had been. I was serving with West Pointers and with other ROTC graduates who had the benefit of having attended some fairly prestigious universities. But I found out that the education my fellow ROTC cadets and I had received at CCNY was a great one, notwithstanding my own failure to drink as deeply from it as I might have. In terms of our ability to write, to express ourselves, to reflect the skills and mental disciplines of a liberal arts education, to be knowledgeable of our culture and our values, to know our history, we were equal to our contemporaries from any school in the nation. And for that I must thank the institution—the teachers and faculty of the City College. And also the entire public school system of the City of New York—including Public Schools 20 and 39, Junior High School 52, and Morris High School.

My story is not very different from the stories of tens of thousands of other CCNY graduates who received the benefits of a great, free public education. Most of those people fit the same mold as I did—kids from working-class and immigrant families. Their parents had dreams and ambitions for their children—if not always the means to fulfill those dreams. And we lived in a city that believed in its obligation to educate its youth and to be the dream-maker for those parents.

It was sort of an unwritten but intuitively understood three-way bargain: a bargain among parents, kids, and schools. The parents were aware of it. The kids weren't so much aware but just sensed it through their parents. The schools strove to hold to it. Entire neighborhoods were buoyed* by it—how could they not be? Education was the way up.

Parents worked long hours, many of them at menial tasks. The kids were often latchkey boys and girls. There were so many "minorities" that none of us really thought of ourselves as being in a minority. An implicit trust in "the bargain" and in one another, person to person and person to institution, was undefined but nonetheless powerful, strong, and abiding. After all, it was

---

*buoyed: lifted up or raised.

America. And America meant progress. There simply was no disputing that—you could get a black eye if you tried.

Looking back, I guess if I had to say what was the most important lesson I ever learned—and that's hard because there are several—my first inclination would be to say it is the imperative* to drink very deeply at the fountain of knowledge wherever, whenever, and in whatever guise that fountain may appear.

But looking more deeply, I believe there's a more vital thing to be learned. It's the obligation we all have to keep the fountain flowing, now and for future generations. The lesson is not simply to get the most we possibly can out of every ounce of education we can get our hands on and never stop learning. That's very important, but there is more. We must ensure there is always a fountain to drink from and no obstacles to drinking.

We must ensure there is always some sort of bargain—a mutual promise concerning education—among the parents, schools, and children in our cities. This bargain is the single most important building block of our future. It will determine what America will be like in the 21st century. It will shape our future more dramatically than anything else we do.

I believe it was Henry Adams who said that the purpose of education is to increase the extent of our ignorance. That sounds a bit crazy until you give it some long, hard thought. If Adams was right, maybe that's why my teachers at CCNY and elsewhere knew someday I would be sufficiently ignorant to look back and thank them. And sufficiently ignorant to want to protect the imperfect but beautiful process that made me that way. ■

DISCUSSING THE SELECTION

1. Before you discuss the selection with your class, write for five minutes about the essay. What ideas did Powell present that stand out in your mind? What ideas confused you? What do you know about him that you did not know before you read this article?

*imperative: absolute necessity.

2. How does Powell explain the difference in the grades he received in undergraduate and in graduate school? What is "a sense of responsibility"? What helps people develop this sense of responsibility?

3. In paragraph 5, Powell lists the characteristics that establish him as an educated person. Copy them into your notebook. What do they reveal about him as a human being?

4. What is the "unwritten American bargain" to which Powell refers in this article?

THINKING CRITICALLY

1. What made you decide to go to college? Did your parents influence your decision? Did any other person influence this decision?

2. Read the characteristics of an educated person you listed in the preceding exercise (part 3). What characteristics would you add? What would you omit? Explain your reasons for your choice.

3. Can you think of any other people, besides Powell, for whom education was the way up? Is this potential as available in today's world as when Powell was growing up? Explain your answer, discussing your own experiences and those of people you have known.

FOCUSING ON THE WRITING

Writing a Persuasion Essay

Persuasive writing calls for clear organization of your ideas. Make sure you have a clear position about an issue before you begin to write.

Before you start to write your essay, make notes to help you organize your ideas. In your notes, write your main idea or belief in a strong, clear sentence. You may decide not to use this sentence in your essay, but it will help you organize your ideas.

List the reasons why you believe as you do. Think about an event or incident that influenced your feelings about this subject. List any other specific examples you will use to support your main point. Make sure you have enough examples to convince a reader.

Keep in mind the audience who will be reading your writing, and appeal to its needs and interests. Choose your words carefully to make your point. Make your conclusion powerful and to the point.

1. What is Powell's thesis statement or main idea? Where is it located in this article? Explain how you identified his main idea.

2. In paragraph 1, Powell begins to tell his personal specific story. What does he write in paragraph 6 that changes this from a personal story to a more general one? How does that affect you as a reader? Explain whether this change makes his thesis statement stronger or weaker.

3. Powell carefully connects his ideas to help his readers follow his thoughts throughout this essay. Notice the words and phrases Powell uses to connect each paragraph to the one that follows it:

What specific words connect paragraph 2 to paragraph 3?
What words connect paragraph 3 to paragraph 4?
What words connect paragraph 4 to paragraph 5?
To what does "It"—the first word in paragraph 7—refer? How do you know?

CREATING YOUR TEXT

1. "My parents expected me to go to college—they expected me to do better than they had done." Reread the journal entry you have written about this sentence. Think about the Powell article you have just read. Write an

essay in which you compare and contrast Powell's family attitude toward this statement and the attitude expressed by your family. Conclude by explaining how your family's attitude toward education has affected your educational experience.

2. Each generation to some degree redefines what it means to be a success. Write an essay in which you explain what you think it means to be a success in our world today. Use your own experiences and those of people you know to support your point of view.

3. Powell states that education is the way up in society. After having read his article and discussed this subject in class, write an essay in which you take a position on whether this is still true today. Explain your point of view by discussing your own experiences and those of people you have known.

4. Do you think that to succeed in life one must develop "a sense of responsibility," responsibility toward oneself, one's family, the community, or some cause or belief? Write an essay in which you explain your feelings about this issue and whether or not you agree with it, given your experiences or those of people around you.

REVISING YOUR TEXT

When you finish your first draft, read the revision questions on page 11, going over your paper with a partner. Decide together what changes you should make to improve your second draft. In addition, ask your partner to answer the following questions about your draft:

What is the main idea? Where is the thesis statement located in the essay? Is this the best position for the thesis statement?

What specific examples illustrate the main idea? Are any of the examples not useful in presenting the main idea?

What specific words and phrases connect the ideas from paragraph to paragraph? (Do this paragraph by paragraph, pointing out specifically how the essay is connected from beginning to end.)

Is there any part of the essay in which the ideas do not connect?

Does the conclusion tie together the main ideas of the essay? Is it powerful and exciting to read? If not, how could it be improved?

Based on the discussion with your partner, write your second draft and share it with your class.

EXPLORING YOUR IDEAS

"After peeping over my shoulder left and right, I sat down in my seat and wondered what would become of me." Think of a first day in a new school or new class. Write in your journal about that experience, including as many details as you think will create a vivid and complete picture of your experience.

Annie John

JAMAICA KINCAID

Jamaica Kincaid was born in St. John's, Antigua, in the West Indies. She is a staff writer for *The New Yorker* magazine, and her stories have also appeared in many other magazines, including *Rolling Stone* and *The Paris Review*. The following excerpt is from *Annie John* (1983), her second novel, and is about Annie's first day in a new school.

After peeping over my shoulder left and right, I sat down in my seat and wondered what would become of me. There were twenty of us in my class, and we were seated at desks arranged five in a row, four rows deep. I was at a desk in the third row, and this made me even more miserable. I hated to be seated so far away from the teacher, because I was sure I would miss something she said. But, even worse, if I was out of my teacher's sight all the time, how could she see my industriousness and quickness at learning things? And, besides, only dunces were seated so far to the rear, and I could not bear to be thought a dunce. I was now staring at the back of a shrubby-haired girl seated in the front row—the seat I most coveted,* since it was directly in front

---

*coveted: envied, longed for.

of the teacher's desk. At that moment, the girl twisted herself around, stared at me, and said, "You are Annie John? We hear you are very bright." It was a good thing Miss Nelson walked in right then, for how would it have appeared if I had replied, "Yes, that is completely true"—the very thing that was on the tip of my tongue.

As soon as Miss Nelson walked in, we came to order and stood up stiffly at our desks. She said to us, "Good morning, class," half in a way that someone must have told her was the proper way to speak to us and half in a jocular* way, as if we secretly amused her. We replied, "Good morning, Miss," in unison and in a respectful way, at the same time making a barely visible curtsy, also in unison. When she had seated herself at her desk, she said to us, "You may sit now," and we did. She opened the roll book, and as she called out our names each of us answered, "Present, Miss." As she called out our names, she kept her head bent over the book, but when she called out my name and I answered with the customary response she looked up and smiled at me and said, "Welcome, Annie." Everyone, of course, then turned and looked at me. I was sure it was because they could hear the loud racket my heart was making in my chest.

It was the first day of a new term, Miss Nelson said, so we would not be attending to any of our usual subjects; instead, we were to spend the morning in contemplation and reflection and writing something she described as an "autobiographical essay." In the afternoon, we would read aloud to each other our autobiographical essays. (I knew quite well about "autobiography" and "essay," but reflection and contemplation! A day at school spent in such a way! Of course, in most books all the good people were always contemplating and reflecting before they did anything. Perhaps in her mind's eye she could see our futures and, against all prediction, we turned out to be good people.) On hearing this, a huge sigh went up from the girls. Half the sighs were in happiness at the thought of sitting and gazing off into clear space, the other half in unhappiness at the misdeeds that would have to go unaccomplished. I joined the happy half, because I knew it would please Miss Nelson, and, my own selfish interest aside, I liked so much the way she wore her ironed hair and her long-sleeved blouse and box-pleated skirt that I wanted to please her.

The morning was uneventful enough: a girl spilled ink from her inkwell all

---

*jocular: joking, full of fun.

over her uniform; a girl broke her pen nib and then made a big to-do about replacing it; girls twisted and turned in their seats and pinched each other's bottoms; girls passed notes to each other. All this Miss Nelson must have seen and heard, but she didn't say anything—only kept reading her book: an elaborately illustrated edition of *The Tempest*, as later, passing by her desk, I saw. Midway in the morning, we were told to go out and stretch our legs and breathe some fresh air for a few minutes; when we returned, we were given glasses of cold lemonade and a slice of bun to refresh us.

As soon as the sun stood in the middle of the sky, we were sent home for lunch. The earth may have grown an inch or two larger between the time I had walked to school that morning and the time I went home to lunch, for some girls made a small space for me in their little band. But I couldn't pay much attention to them; my mind was on my new surroundings, my new teacher, what I had written in my nice new notebook with its black-all-mixed-up-with-white cover and smooth lined pages (so glad was I to get rid of my old notebooks, which had on their covers a picture of a wrinkled-up woman wearing a crown on her head and a neckful and armfuls of diamonds and pearls—their pages so coarse, as if they were made of cornmeal). I flew home. I must have eaten my food. I flew back to school. By half past one, we were sitting under a flamboyant tree in a secluded part of our schoolyard, our autobiographical essays in hand. We were about to read aloud what we had written during our morning of contemplation and reflection.

In response to Miss Nelson, each girl stood up and read her composition. One girl told of a much revered and loved aunt who now lived in England and of how much she looked forward to one day moving to England to live with her aunt; one girl told of her brother studying medicine in Canada and the life she imagined he lived there (it seemed quite odd to me); one girl told of the fright she had when she dreamed she was dead, and of the matching fright she had when she woke and found that she wasn't (everyone laughed at this, and Miss Nelson had to call us to order over and over); one girl told of how her oldest sister's best friend's cousin's best friend (it was a real rigmarole*) had gone on a Girl Guide jamboree held in Trinidad and met someone who millions of years ago had taken tea with Lady Baden-Powell;†

---

*rigmarole: nonsense.
†Lady Baden-Powell: sister of founder of Boy Scouts, with whom she co-founded Girl Guides.

one girl told of an excursion she and her father had made to Redonda, and of how they had seen some booby birds tending their chicks. Things went on in that way, all so playful, all so imaginative. I began to wonder about what I had written, for it was the opposite of playful and it was the opposite of imaginative. What I had written was heartfelt, and, except for the very end, it was all too true. The afternoon was wearing itself thin. Would my turn ever come? What should I do, finding myself in a world of new girls, a world in which I was not even near the center?

It was a while before I realized that Miss Nelson was calling on me. My turn at last to read what I had written. I got up and started to read, my voice shaky at first, but since the sound of my own voice had always been a calming potion to me, it wasn't long before I was reading in such a way that, except for the chirp of some birds, the hum of bees looking for flowers, the silvery rush-rush of the wind in the trees, the only sound to be heard was my voice as it rose and fell in sentence after sentence. ■

DISCUSSING THE SELECTION

1. What evidence does Kincaid provide to persuade her readers that Annie John is a good student who likes school?

2. What evidence convinces Annie that she will be accepted in her new school?

3. Why is Annie pleased about the assignment to reflect and contemplate? How does Annie feel about herself as a writer? What evidence in the selection influenced your answer?

4. What does Kincaid want her reader to think about schools in Trinidad? Does she approve of girls' schools? What evidence in the selection supports your responses?

THINKING CRITICALLY

1. Have you ever attended a school in which the students stood up when the teacher entered the room? Explain how this activity made you feel toward your teacher, the school, and yourself.

2. Compare your experiences of the first day(s) in a new school with those described in this story.

3. How do you feel when you have to read your writing aloud to your classmates? Describe your experiences and what you learned about yourself from it. What techniques have you developed that have made it easier for you to do this?

4. What was your most successful writing assignment in any class? Explain why the assignment was so productive for you.

FOCUSING ON THE WRITING

1. In paragraph 5, Kincaid writes, "As soon as the sun stood in the middle of the sky," instead of writing "at noon." Writers choose their words carefully to make an effect or to create a particular mood. What effect does Kincaid's words have in this sentence that "at noon" does not have? Why?

2. What is the general mood of this story? What specific words create this mood for you as a reader? Change those specific words mentioned, and reread the story. In what way is the mood of the story altered by those word changes?

CREATING YOUR TEXT

1. Reread the writing biography you wrote about yourself at the beginning of the semester. Write another essay in which you explain how your writing has changed this semester. What specific techniques have you learned that have helped you improve? What have you learned about yourself as a writer? What specific selections have you read that have influenced your feelings about yourself as a writer? Explain in detail.

2. Entering college is a challenging experience for many students. Write an essay in which you describe the process step by step (see page 149 for more information about this type of writing) for finding out about the appropriate college, filling out applications, taking tests, getting accepted into, and registering for college. Explain which steps are most important and why. What should a prospective college student keep in mind to make this process easier?

3. Write an essay in which you describe your first weeks in college—think about registration, new classes, teachers, buying books, fulfilling assignments, and so on. What advice would you give a friend who will be attending your college in the near future?

4. Write an essay in which you compare and contrast two different schools you have attended—high school and college, elementary school and high school, or any two schools in which you have been a student. Some questions to think about include: "What differences and similarities do you notice in teaching style? in student responsibilities? in feedback on papers? in amount of writing required? in relationships with your teachers? in relationships with your peers?" Overall, explain what has helped you succeed in either or both of these systems.

REVISING YOUR TEXT

After writing your first draft, read it over with a classmate looking at the revision questions on page 11. In addition, together discuss the following questions, looking at each of your drafts:

What in the introduction makes you want to read more?
Which specific words in the draft signaled to the reader that the writer was comparing and contrasting (see page 186 for information about the comparison-and-contrast essay)?
In what order did the writer present the comparisons and contrasts?
If the essay is a step-by-step description, does the writer include enough steps for the reader to understand how to follow or do the action?
What in the conclusion ties together the essay or ends it with an interesting or amusing idea?

Discuss your draft, thinking about these questions. Make notes of suggestions and questions that will help you write your second draft. Share your second draft with your class.

ADDITIONAL PROJECT

Read the rest of Kincaid's novel *Annie John*. What do you learn about Annie John from reading the novel that changes your feelings about her character? How does Kincaid use the setting or location of the novel? How does the story excerpt in this text fit into the novel as a whole? If you excerpted one part to share with the class, what part would you choose and why?

EXPLORING YOUR IDEAS

This article is about a person who despite hardships fulfilled his dream and then wrote about what he did, to help others fulfill theirs. Write in your journal about any special techniques or routines that have helped you become successful in school or in any other aspect of life. Who influenced you in developing these techniques or routines?

The Physician Who Healed Himself First

LINDA KRAMER

This article was written by Linda Kramer for a special edition of *People* magazine that honored Americans who made a difference in the lives of others. The article is about Dr. Ben Carson, a pediatric neurosurgeon, who became successful despite early problems.

Ben Carson did not have an easy childhood. When he was 8, his father abandoned the family, and he had to live in tenements in Boston and Detroit. Abysmal grades and a hair-trigger temper got him into trouble at school. At times, whites taunted and threatened him because he was black. He could easily have ended up on drugs, in prison—or in the morgue. But a funny thing happened on the way to oblivion: Ben Carson became a doctor.

Not just any kind of doctor. In 1984, at the age of 33, he became the youngest chief of pediatric neurosurgery in the United States at one of the world's most prestigious hospitals, Baltimore's Johns Hopkins. "Earlier this year I was speaking to the inmates at San Quentin prison," Carson says. "And I was talking about choices in life, and it just hit me so vividly that I could have ended up in a place like that."

A lot of parents are thankful he did not. In the seven years since he joined Johns Hopkins, Carson, now 40, has become something of a medical legend, pioneering surgical procedures that have saved hundreds of children, many previously diagnosed as hopeless. He has developed a number of new methods to help kids with brain-stem tumors or with chronic seizures caused by such diseases as Rasmussen's encephalitis.

But his most famous operation was in 1987, when he led the team of 70 doctors, nurses, and technicians that successfully separated Siamese twins joined at the back of the head. In previous operations of this type, at least one twin died or was left in a vegetative state. But in this case, both twins—Patrick and Benjamin Binder of Germany—happily survived. Carson "is more brave than controversial," says Edward Laws Jr., chief of neurosurgery at George Washington University, since his cases are "not the sort of thing everyone's got the guts and talent to take on."

Carson credits his mother, Sonya, 63, for his success. To make ends meet after her divorce, she rented out her small Detroit home and moved with her two young sons to live with relatives in a rundown area of Boston. Two years later she had saved enough money—by working as many as three domestic jobs at the same time—to return to Detroit, where she rented an apartment in an industrial section near some railroad tracks. Ben, then in the fifth grade, and his elder brother, Curtis, in the seventh, both did poorly in school. For Ben, F's were the norm; mere D's were considered a victory. "He had no hope," recalls his mother. "He just felt there was no way out, and so why should he try? He was just really at the point of no return."

Sonya decided to take action. She cut her sons' television viewing to three shows a week and ordered them to read two books every week. Leaving nothing to chance, she also insisted they submit written book reports to her. It was a major bluff on her part; she had only a third-grade education and could barely read what they turned in. But she stayed on top of her sons. And slowly her plan began to work. "Once I discovered that between the pages of those books . . . we could go anywhere and we could meet anybody and we could do anything," Carson says, "that's when it really started to hit me."

By the time he entered predominantly white Wilson Junior High, he was at the top of his class. Kids who had once teased him and called him "dummy" now asked for his help on homework. But all was not well: Carson repeatedly ran into racial prejudice. On the way to school one day, he and Curtis were confronted by a group of boys armed with sticks. "You know, you nigger kids ain't supposed to be going to Wilson Junior High," one told them. "If we ever catch you again, we're going to kill you." After that, they took a different route to school. When they joined a neighborhood football league, a group of white adults warned them to stay away—and they did. Carson's most humiliating experience, though, was in the eighth grade. His teacher publicly berated his white classmates for allowing him, a black, to win an award for outstanding student.

Such incidents only heated up Carson's already red-hot temper. "I would just fly off the handle, and the only thing that was important to me, if somebody made me mad, was to make them unhappy," he says. "If that meant hitting them with a rock or a brick or a baseball bat, that's what I wanted to do." He opened a three-inch gash in the forehead of a schoolmate who teased him, using the padlock from his locker. He broke the nose of another boy with a rock. He almost punched out his own mother for buying him a pair of pants he didn't like, but he was stopped by Curtis in the nick of time. And once, during an argument, he unsuccessfully went after Curtis with a kitchen knife.

But the worst blowup took place when he was 14. One day after school, he and a friend were listening to a transistor radio. "He had changed a radio station and I didn't want it changed," Carson remembers. "He argued with me, and I grabbed this camping knife and tried to stab him. I was totally irrational. Fortunately, he had a large, metal belt buckle under his clothing, and the knife blade struck it and broke. He fled, and I ran home and locked myself in the bathroom and just started contemplating what would have happened if he had not had that belt buckle on."

After several hours in the bathroom, he decided to fall back on a deep belief in God (he is a Seventh Day Adventist) and pray. As he explains in his 1990 autobiography, *Gifted Hands*, he walked out of the bathroom a changed person. He says that he has never had a problem with his temper again. "During those hours in the bathroom I came to realize that if people could make me angry, they could control me," he wrote. "Why should I give someone else such power over my life?"

Despite that cathartic experience, Carson still had another demon to conquer. His family had moved to a black Detroit neighborhood, and he found a new temptation: hanging out. Instead of studying, he spent his evenings playing basketball, sometimes until 11. His grades promptly dropped back to C's. "I started believing for a little while that academics weren't all that important," he says. "It was more important to be one of the guys."

Once again his mother stepped in. By this time she had learned to read better and would recite poems and proverbs about self-help. Eventually, she got through. Carson went back to getting A's and, in 1969, graduated third in his class.

That fall he entered Yale on a scholarship. Four years later he pursued a love that began when he was 8 years old and heard a moving sermon in church about a doctor: He went to medical school. He also pursued a love that began the summer before his junior year and married fellow Yalie Candy Rustin. Today they live outside Baltimore with Sonya and their three sons (Murray, 8, Ben Jr., 6, and Rhoeyce, 4). Carson tries to spend as much time at home as possible. "I don't want my kids to grow up with no father like I did," he says. "I came to the conclusion a while ago that you can work until midnight and not be finished or you can work until 6 or 7 and not be finished. I decided I'd rather work until 6 or 7."

Carson is raising his sons according to the laws of Sonya: two books a week, plus reports. He knows her scheme works, he says, "A lot of the kids I grew up with are dead from drugs and violence." And he is promoting his cause with a new book, *Think Big*, and lots of speeches. His mission in life, he believes, is to help others—particularly blacks. "It doesn't matter if you come from the inner city. People who fail in life are people who find lots of excuses," he says. "It's never too late for a person to recognize that they have potential in themselves." ■

DISCUSSING THE SELECTION

1. What were the three biggest obstacles to success in Ben Carson's life? Explain your choices by referring to specific parts of the article.

2. What turned his life around? What was the single biggest factor in his success today? Explain your answers by referring to specific parts of the article.

3. What incidents of racism did Carson experience? What enabled him to succeed even in such a racist situation?

4. In what two ways is Carson reaching out to help others? Which will reach more people? Which is more important? Explain your answers.

5. Reread the article about filmmaker John Singleton on page 107. How does writing figure in both these successful men's lives? What feeling do they have about the importance of having a father in the home?

THINKING CRITICALLY

1. Why do you think reading two books and writing two book reports a week made such a difference in Carson's school performance? What technique(s) have you used to become a better student?

2. Why do you think Carson wrote his two books? What influence do you think he would like them to have on young people in school today?

3. Why does the author include information about Carson's problems and weaknesses? She quotes Carson as saying he realized that if people could make him angry, they had control over him. What does this statement mean to you? How have you learned to control your anger?

4. In what way was playing basketball a problem for Carson? Could playing basketball or some other sport be seen as an asset for some young people? Explain your answer by describing your own experience or that of someone you know or have read about.

FOCUSING ON THE WRITING

Describing a Person

When you write about a person, keep these suggestions in mind

1. Think about the person(s) you want to describe. Write out your notes before you begin to write your essay or story. Write the person's name (and nickname if one exists). Describe the person physically and psychologically. Describe the person's typical dress, home, job, and ambitions. Write down the person's favorite colors, foods, and entertainment. (You may not use all this information in your essay, but it helps to think about the person before you begin to write.)

2. Write a story or an anecdote about the person or people you are going to describe. It may include a quote or several short quotes from a conversation. The quote(s) should make a point about who the person is and what makes the person special. In your essay or story, keep in mind that you are trying to create a complete picture of the person. Do not avoid conflicts and problems. They show the person as real and believable.

3. In your conclusion, explain why you wrote about this person. Why is this person important to you, and why should this person be important to others?

1. What specific details did Kramer include that show us the conflicts and difficulties in Carson's life?

2. Which anecdotes do you think contribute especially well to creating an interesting and full picture of Ben Carson?

3. What is the main idea of this article? Where is the thesis statement located? Explain your answer by referring to specific lines in the article.

4. Reread the concluding paragraph, and decide what its purpose is in this article. (See page 31 for more information about writing conclusions.)

5. What differences in writing would you expect if Ben Carson had written this article about himself? What do you think he would have added? What might he have deleted? Explain your answer.

CREATING YOUR TEXT

1. Reread the journal entry in which you wrote about a special technique or routine that has helped you succeed in school or in some other area of your life. Write an essay in which you explain your technique step by step (see page 149 for more information about writing a step-by-step process essay). Your essay should contain a description of the difficulty you faced, how you developed your technique or routine, a step-by-step description of it, and the results it has had in your life. In your conclusion, make suggestions about the ways other students could use your technique or routine to become more successful.

2. Carson's mother was the most positive influence in his life. Write an essay in which you describe the person who has been the most positive influence in your life up to the present. Describe the person in detail physically and psychologically. Include the specific incidents that demonstrate the influence this person has had on your life. What have you learned from knowing this person? What do you think this person has learned from you?

3. Carson mentions Sonya's laws; on page 48, Amy Tan presents her own mother's precepts. Write an essay in which you describe the laws or precepts you live by. How did you develop these laws or precepts? How have they influenced the person you are today and hope to be in the future? In your conclusion, explain what other people can learn from adapting your laws or precepts to fit their own needs.

REVISING YOUR TEXT

Reread your first draft with a classmate. Discuss the strong points and the weak areas. Review the essay together with the revision questions on page 11. In addition, discuss the following questions:

What makes the person(s) described in the draft stand out as unique individual(s)?

What specific quotation did you include that tells the writer about the way the person speaks?

What short, important detail(s) describe the person's appearance and make the person seem real?

What specific words and phrases in the draft make the reader think the person described is interesting enough to want to read about?

If the essay is a step-by-step process essay, are the steps in order? Do they start at the beginning and end in a logical place? Are they complete enough so that a reader could follow them?

Given your discussion, decide which parts of the draft need improvement. Make notes about these suggestions before you write your second draft. When you complete that draft, share it with your class.

ADDITIONAL PROJECT

Read one of Carson's books. As a class, decide what you have found out about Carson that you did not know or that could not be included in a short article. Decide on what basis Kramer made decisions about what to include and what to eliminate. Tell the class what you would include that Kramer did not, and explain why you think it is important.

> **EXPLORING YOUR IDEAS**
>
> Think about something you learned as a child that you had to unlearn or learn in a new way in school. For some people, this is language, or a behavior, or an attitude. Write about your experience and how it made you feel.

West Real

ALBERTO ALVARO RÍOS

Alberto Alvaro Ríos is an award-winning poet and a short story writer. He lives in Chandler, Arizona, and is a professor of English at Arizona State University. His books of poetry include *The Lime Orchard Woman* and *Teodoro Luna's Two Kisses*. He has won grants from the Guggenheim Foundation and from the National Endowment for the Arts. The selection that follows is from the Spring 1992 *Ploughshares*, a literary anthology edited by Ríos.

The West is a big place, but not my West. The West for me is where I lived—it is a house. And it's how I lived, and who I lived with. It's some people, and some streets, a border fence with Mexico in the distance, an arroyo* across the highway, a dry landscape, Coronado Elementary School, the Nogales Apaches High School fight song. My West is like that, a place to live. When I was old enough to think about the West, it was gone. It had moved into the realm of capital letters.

I learned the West best growing up in it, not talking about it. I was born in Nogales, Arizona, on the border of Mexico. My father is from Tapachula,

---

*arroyo: a hollow in the ground worn away by running water—depending on the season, the hollow may be wet or dry.

Chiapas, Mexico, and my mother from Warrington, Lancashire, England. I grew up around my father's family, but I look like my mother—which means I got to see two worlds from the beginning, and could even physically experience the difference growing up where I did: I could put, every day of my life, one foot in Mexico and one foot in the United States, at the same time.

For all practical purposes my first language was more or less Spanish, though the influences of my mother's British English clearly had its part. There was no problem with this, until first grade in the 1950s. That little kids can't make some very big decisions is not true. When we got to that first-grade classroom, my friends and I, we were told: You can't speak Spanish here.

That was crazy, of course, and we all raised our hands, saying, *Seguro que sí*—of course we can speak it! But no, they said, that's not what they meant. We were simply not to speak it, and some got swats,* even for speaking Spanish on the playground.

We knew one got swatted for something bad—our parents had taught us that. So if we got swatted for speaking Spanish, Spanish then must be bad.

There was a bargain in this, though: what we saw when we got to the first-grade classroom was clay, blackboards, cubbyholes, fingerpaints, kickballs that weren't flat. And when we got home that day, we looked around—and didn't see any of that stuff. We knew what we wanted. The decision was easy. And if learning English was going to get these things for us—well, we weren't dumb. We could play along.

But we kept learning. If speaking Spanish was bad, we then must be bad kids.

And our parents still spoke Spanish, so they had to be bad people. This was easy enough for children to grasp; so, though of course we loved them, we learned to be ashamed. One can imagine what PTA meetings were like—we didn't have any. None of us ever took the notes home.

By junior high school and the beginning of high school, I could no longer speak Spanish—which is to say, I didn't want to; I was embarrassed, and I didn't practice. Not until my later years of high school and college did I relearn Spanish, but that is what I had to do, relearn. And what I was relearning was not words, but my attitude toward those words. It was learning how to look at something in more than one way.

*swats: hits; slaps.

After all these years, however, this was the bonus. In having to pay double and triple attention to language—first to forget, and then to relearn—I began to see earnestly how everything, every object, every idea, had at *least* two names, and that the process, rather than my counting it as any kind of a detriment* in my life, worked instead, luckily, more like a pair of binoculars. It showed me how, by using *two* lenses, one might see something more closely, and thereby understand it better.

I was relearning how to look at something, period. A language implies, after all, a different set of ideas—different ways of looking at the world. My West is about edges, borders, about looking at something in more than one way, about all the things that make you do that. I can find no shame in this.

Still, there is sometimes a lingering confusion. The physical pain of being swatted, of thinking about being swatted—this doesn't go away so easily. It's hard to choose sides, to know which way to go. It's hard to think that you even have to choose sides.

I am reminded of the Fourth of July. As a writer, I lean toward thinking of such events as metaphor: a sky full of colors over Arizona, and how much noise that makes. There ought to be some kind of lesson in that: how we can be so scared by the noise and so dazzled by the sight, this confusion of perspectives. My Fourth of July is from childhood. The day is also the *día de los Refugios,* or the saint's day of people named Refugio. This was my great-grandmother and my grandmother's name, and coincidentally my mother-in-law's. Celebrating one's birthday as one's saint's day is common in Mexico.

We had a party every Fourth of July, and it was for the whole matriarchal† line, and for everything Mexican, which is what they were, from the whole other set of words to the green-tinted glasses. These women played such great roles in my life that birthday fireworks for them later in the evening always seemed right. But it was the noise of everything American.

Some things like this don't make any sense, but there they are together making perfect sense anyway. For me now, I still see one thing but hear another: I wonder, for example, how in Arizona we've come to find a rhyme between *no way* and *José,* or why anyone would buy patio stones with drawings of sombreroed and seraped peasants leaning their backs against

---

*detriment: harm or injury.
†matriarchal: related through the mother.

saguaros.* You'd think either the peasant or the homeowner or the artist should know better about leaning against a cactus. And these are stepping stones no less. I don't even want to guess at the metaphor there.

Several years ago I worked on what was then called the Papago Reservation near Sells. I took the third-graders on a field trip, and as we were walking back to the school they proposed playing a game. Sure, I agreed. What should we play? *Cowboys and Indians,* they said, and then began to run. They shouted at me to run as well, because, they said, *The Indians are going to get you, the Indians are going to get you.* When we returned to school and calmed down, I asked them if they were Indians. *No,* they said. *We're Papago.*

And of course. They knew what "Indians" were, and they weren't exactly that—they had seen the movies, with half-naked people shouting war whoops and shooting arrows. This isn't what they were. The people in their families wore boots, cowboy shirts, jeans; they drove pickup trucks; and they were good guys. They knew what they wanted. . . .

I am reminded of a small example used in every Spanish class about a central cultural difference between English speakers and Spanish speakers. In English, one says, *I dropped the glass,* should such a thing happen. It is an "I"-centered instance, rugged individualism in its smallest moment. In Spanish, one says, "*Se me calló el vaso,*" which means, "The glass, it fell from me." This is a different world view, a way of accommodating the world, of living with it instead of changing it. Which is the better view is not the point, but I do think that our notions of the West as representing rugged individualism may, in fact, be faulty. There's a messy middle, something in between. I think that's the language of this place. It's a rugged pluralism. ■

DISCUSSING THE SELECTION

1. In the first sentence, Ríos writes: "The West is a big place, but not my West." After reading the selection, what does this statement mean? Explain your answer by referring to specific lines from the selection.

*saguaros: cactus.

2. Why does Ríos feel split or divided into two worlds? How does this split affect the way he remembers school? How does it affect the way he remembers his childhood? Explain your answer by referring to specific lines from the selection.

3. What is the meaning of the incident Ríos describes when the children in his class play "Cowboys and Indians"?

4. In paragraph 6, Ríos writes about a "bargain" that the children learned was necessary to do well in school. What was the bargain? Compare the bargain Powell describes on page 210 with the bargain Ríos writes about in this essay.

5. In the last paragraph of the essay, Ríos refers to "rugged individualism" as part of an "I"-centered society. What does this mean? How does this relate to Quindlen's concept of "rugged individualism" on page 161? Ríos concludes that a better term is "rugged pluralism." What does this mean? Which term do you prefer and why?

THINKING CRITICALLY

1. Ríos describes ways in which children learn to speak and behave in school that are different from the ways they behave at home. How is this split true for you? Explain your reasons for the different behaviors. (Read the Tan essay on page 53 for her ideas on the different Englishes she learned to speak and understand.)

2. The headnote states that Ríos is a professor of English. In what ways do you think his early educational experiences affected the way he works with his students today?

3. Have any of your teachers told you about their early educational experiences? How has that influenced your relationship with those teachers?

4. What language(s) do you think Ríos's child speaks? What information in the selection did you use to arrive at your answer?

FOCUSING ON THE WRITING

Figures of Speech

Writers make their ideas clearer, richer, or more imaginative by using special literary devices or figures of speech. A commonly used device is the *simile,* in which comparisons are made using the words *like* or *as.* For example, a bare, wintery tree may be said to look *like* an old, wrinkled person.

Another is a *symbol,* through which an object is used to express an idea. For example, a red cape can be used to suggest anger and confrontation.

Metaphors are also often used by writers. In this device, a word, a phrase, or an idea that is usually used for one thing is applied to another without using the words *as* or *like.* For example, "All the world's a stage" or "Time is a river."

1. In paragraph 13, Ríos writes about the metaphor of the Fourth of July. Reread that paragraph, and decide what he means by this metaphor.

2. In paragraph 15, he refers to the metaphor of the stepping stones. Reread that paragraph, and decide what he means by this metaphor.

3. To support his view that there are cultural differences between English speakers and Spanish speakers, Ríos includes the following example in his essay:

In English, one says, *I dropped the glass,* should such a thing happen. It is an "I"-centered instance, rugged individualism in its smallest moment. In Spanish, one says, "*Se me calló el vaso,*" which means, "The glass, it fell from me." This is a different world view, a way of accommodating the world, of living with it instead of changing it.

Does this example effectively support his point of view? Would you have included other examples? If so, what other examples?

CREATING YOUR TEXT

1. Ríos felt alienated and angry because of his early experiences in school, yet he became a teacher. Write an essay in which you describe how feeling anger or alienation has forced you or someone you know to change. Explain the original situation, the reason for the anger, and the steps the person has taken to change.

2. At the top of a blank piece of paper, write on the left "rugged individualism" and on the right "rugged pluralism." For the next five minutes, write any words that you think of describing either of these concepts. Share these lists in class, and discuss what these terms mean to you. Write an essay in which you compare and contrast the concepts of rugged individualism and rugged pluralism. Reread the Ríos article and the Quindlen article on page 159. Look at your list, and think about the class discussion to help you develop your ideas. In your conclusion, explain whether you think the United States is an example of rugged individualism or pluralism, and why.

3. Look at your journal entry in which you wrote about something that you learned as a child that you had to unlearn or learn in a new way in school. Reread the Ríos article and the Tan article on page 53. Write an essay in which you describe what you learned, unlearned, and perhaps relearned at a later date. Describe your experience and how it has affected you as a learner today.

4. Should schools offer bilingual programs for all students? How would people in the United States be affected by knowing more than one language? Write an essay in which you discuss this idea. Support your point of view by explaining your own experiences learning in language(s) in school and the experiences of other people you know.

REVISING YOUR TEXT

Read your first draft with a classmate, looking at the revision questions on page 11. Decide together if your essay makes a clear point and develops it in a way that can be followed by your readers. In addition, discuss the following questions:

Are there any similes—comparisons using *like* or *as*? What is being compared? Do they make sense to the reader as well as to the writer?

Are any symbols used in the draft? What are they? Are they clear to the reader as well as to the writer?

Did you use any metaphors in your draft? What are they? Are they clear to the reader as well as to the writer?

If the essay involves comparisons and contrasts, what specific words are used to signal that to the reader? (See page 186 for more information about writing this type of essay.)

If the essay involves a step-by-step description, are all the steps stated? Is there a clear beginning and a logical ending? Can a reader follow the steps?

After discussing the draft and deciding how it can be improved, write a second draft and share it with the class.

> **EXPLORING YOUR IDEAS**
>
> Write in your journal about an experience you had in which reading (a letter, article, book, or any reading matter) made a difference to you. Describe the incident and what it meant to you.

Reading to Know

RICHARD RODRIGUEZ

Richard Rodriguez lives in California and is a writer and essayist. His book *Hunger of Memory* (1982), from which the following is excerpted, describes his transition from a home in which Spanish was spoken, to a school system in which English was taught. Ultimately, Rodriguez completed his doctorate in English literature and has taught English in college.

In our house each school year would begin with my mother's careful instruction: "Don't write in your books so we can sell them at the end of the year." The remark was echoed in public by my teachers, but only in part: "Boys and girls, don't write in your books. You must learn to treat them with great care and respect."

OPEN THE DOORS OF YOUR MIND WITH BOOKS, read the red and white poster over the nun's desk in early September. It soon was apparent to me that reading was the classroom's central activity. Each course had its own book. And the information gathered from a book was unquestioned. READ TO LEARN, the sign on the wall advised in December. I privately wondered: What was the connection between reading and learning? Did one learn something only by reading it? Was an idea only an idea if it could be written down? In June, CONSIDER BOOKS YOUR BEST FRIENDS. Friends? Reading was, at best, only a chore. I needed to look up whole paragraphs of words in a dictionary. Lines of type were dizzying, the eye having to move slowly across the page, then down, and across. . . . The sentences of the first books I read were coolly impersonal. Toned hard. What most bothered me, however, was the isolation reading required. To console myself for the loneliness I'd feel when I read, I tried reading in a very soft voice. Until: "Who is doing all that talking to his neighbor?" Shortly after, remedial reading classes were arranged for me with a very old nun.

At the end of each school day, for nearly six months, I would meet with her in the tiny room that served as the school's library but was actually only a storeroom for used textbooks and a vast collection of *National Geographic*s. Everything about our sessions pleased me: the smallness of the room; the noise of the janitor's broom hitting the edge of the long hallway outside the door; the green of the sun, lighting the wall; and the old woman's face blurred white with a beard. Most of the time we took turns. I began with my elementary text. Sentences of astonishing simplicity seemed to me lifeless and drab: "The boys ran from the rain . . . She wanted to sing . . . The kite rose in the blue." Then the old nun would read from her favorite books, usually biographies of early American presidents. Playfully she ran through complex sentences, calling the words alive with her voice, making it seem that the author somehow was speaking directly to me. I smiled just to listen to her. I sat there and sensed for the very first time some possibility of fellowship between a reader and a writer, a communication, never *intimate* like that I heard spoken words at home convey, but one nonetheless *personal.*

One day the nun concluded a session by asking me why I was so reluctant to read by myself. I tried to explain; said something about the way written words made me feel all alone—almost, I wanted to add but didn't, as when I spoke to myself in a room just emptied of furniture. She studied my face as I spoke; she seemed to be watching more than listening. In an uneventful voice she replied that I had nothing to fear. Didn't I realize that reading would open up whole new worlds? A book could open doors for me. It could introduce me to people and show me places I never imagined existed. She gestured toward the bookshelves. (Bare-breasted African women danced, and the shiny hubcaps of automobiles on the back covers of the *Geographic* gleamed in my mind.) I listened with respect. But her words were not very influential. I was thinking then of another consequence of literacy, one I was too shy to admit but nonetheless trusted. Books were going to make me "educated." *That* confidence enabled me, several months later, to overcome my fear of the silence.

In fourth grade I embarked upon a grandiose reading program. "Give me the names of important books," I would say to startled teachers. They soon found out that I had in mind "adult books." I ignored their suggestion of anything I suspected was written for children. (Not until I was in college, as a result, did I read *Huckleberry Finn* or *Alice's Adventures in Wonderland*.) Instead, I read *The Scarlet Letter* and Franklin's *Autobiography*. And whatever I read I read for extra credit. Each time I finished a book, I reported the achievement to a teacher and basked in the praise my effort earned. Despite my best efforts, however, there seemed to be more and more books I needed to read. At the library I would literally tremble as I came upon whole shelves of books I hadn't read. So I read and I read and I read: *Great Expectations*; all the short stories of Kipling; *The Babe Ruth Story*; the entire first volume of the *Encyclopaedia Britannica* (A–ANSTEY); the *Iliad*; *Moby Dick*; *Gone with the Wind*; *The Good Earth*; *Ramona*; *Forever Amber*; *The Lives of the Saints*; *Crime and Punishment*; *The Pearl*. . . . Librarians who initially frowned when I checked out the maximum ten books at a time started saving books they thought I might like. Teachers would say to the rest of the class, "I only wish the rest of you took reading as seriously as Richard obviously does."

But at home I would hear my mother wondering, "What do you see in your books?" (Was reading a hobby like her knitting? Was so much reading even healthy for a boy? Was it the sign of "brains"? Or was it just a convenient excuse for not helping around the house on Saturday mornings?) Always, "What do you see . . . ?"

What *did* I see in my books? I had the idea that they were crucial for my academic success, though I couldn't have said exactly how or why. In the sixth grade I simply concluded that what gave a book its value was some major idea or theme it contained. If that core essence could be mined and memorized, I would become learned like my teachers. I decided to record in a notebook the themes of the books that I read. After reading *Robinson Crusoe*, I wrote that its theme was "the value of learning to live by oneself." When I completed *Wuthering Heights*, I noted the danger of "letting emotions get out of control." Rereading these brief moralistic appraisals usually left me disheartened. I couldn't believe that they were really the source of reading's value. But for many more years, they constituted the only means I had of describing to myself the educational value of books.

In spite of my earnestness, I found reading a pleasurable activity. I came to enjoy the lonely good company of books. Early on weekday mornings, I'd read in my bed. I'd feel a mysterious comfort then, reading in the dawn quiet—the blue-gray silence interrupted by the occasional churning of the refrigerator motor a few rooms away or the more distant sounds of a city bus beginning its run. On weekends I'd go to the public library to read, surrounded by old men and women. Or, if the weather was fine, I would take my books to the park and read in the shade of a tree. A warm summer evening was my favorite reading time. Neighbors would leave for vacation and I would water their lawns. I would sit through the twilight on the front porches or in backyards, reading to the cool, whirling sounds of the sprinklers.

I also had favorite writers. But often those writers I enjoyed most I was least able to value. When I read William Saroyan's *The Human Comedy*, I was immediately pleased by the narrator's warmth and the charm of his story. But as quickly I became suspicious. A book so enjoyable to read couldn't be very "important." Another summer I determined to read all the novels of Dickens. Reading his fat novels, I loved the feeling I got—after the first hundred pages—of being at home in a fictional world where I knew the names of the characters and cared about what was going to happen to them. And it bothered me that I was forced away at the conclusion, when the fiction closed tight, like a fortune-teller's fist—the futures of all the major characters neatly resolved. I never knew how to take such feelings seriously, however. Nor did I suspect that these experiences could be part of a novel's meaning. Still, there were pleasures to sustain me after I'd finish my books. Carrying a volume back to the library, I would be pleased by its weight. I'd run my fingers along the edge of the pages and marvel at the breadth of my achievement. Around my room, growing stacks of paperback books reenforced my assurance.

I entered high school having read hundreds of books. My habit of reading made me a confident speaker and writer of English. Reading also enabled me to sense something of the shape, the major concerns, of Western thought. (I was able to say something about Dante and Descartes and Engels and James Baldwin in my high school term papers.) In these various ways, books brought me academic success as I hoped that they would. But I was not a good reader. Merely bookish, I lacked a point of view when I read. Rather, I read in order to acquire a point of view. I vacuumed books for epigrams, scraps of information, ideas, themes—anything to fill the hollow within me and make me feel educated. When one of my teachers suggested to his drowsy tenth-grade English class that a person could not have a "complicated idea" until he had read at least two thousand books, I heard the remark without detecting either its irony or its very complicated truth. I merely determined to compile a list of all the books I had ever read. Harsh with myself, I included only once a title I might have read several times. (How, after all, could one read a book more than once?) And I included only those books over a hundred pages in length. (Could anything shorter be a book?)

There was yet another high school list I compiled. One day I came across a newspaper article about the retirement of an English professor at a nearby state college. The article was accompanied by a list of the "hundred most important books of Western Civilization." "More than anything else in my life," the professor told the reporter with finality, "these books have made me all that I am." That was the kind of remark I couldn't ignore. I clipped out the list and kept it for the several months it took me to read all of the titles. Most books, of course, I barely understood. While reading Plato's *Republic*, for instance, I needed to keep looking at the book jacket comments to remind myself what the text was about. Nevertheless, with the special patience and superstition of a scholarship boy, I looked at every word of the text. And by the time I reached the last word, relieved, I convinced myself that I had read *The Republic*. In a ceremony of great pride, I solemnly crossed Plato off my list. ■

DISCUSSING THE SELECTION

1. What is Rodriguez's attitude toward books and reading? What evidence in the selection supports your answer?

2. What specific advice does the nun give Rodriguez that changes his attitude toward reading?

3. How does Rodriguez choose the books he reads?

4. What project does Rodriguez create for himself? What are the positive aspects of the project? What are the negative aspects of the project?

5. Rodriguez writes, "But I was not a good reader. Merely bookish, I lacked a point of view." What does this mean?

THINKING CRITICALLY

1. With other members of your class, decide what you think a "good reader" is. Make a list of the characteristics a good reader should have. How does a person who does not have those characteristics become a good reader?

2. Rodriguez describes his encounter with the nun who is helping him learn to read. What characteristics does this teacher have that help Rodriguez? What characteristics have teachers had who helped you become a better learner? If you were selecting teachers for your school, what characteristics would you look for? What kind of people do you think make good teachers?

3. On his own, Rodriguez reads much more than is expected in school. When you learn something new, do you usually learn it better in a classroom or by actually doing it? Explain, telling about your experience in learning something new.

4. Compare Rodriguez's experience with reading to Carson's as described on page 224. How does reading help these two young men become more successful in school?

5. In a later part of his book, Rodriguez writes,

[Other students] scorn his desire to succeed. They scorn him for constantly wanting the teacher's attention and praise. "Kiss ass," they call him when his hand swings up in response to every question he hears. Later, when he makes it to college, no one will mock him aloud. But he detects annoyance on the faces of some students and even some teachers who watch him. It puzzles him often.

Why do you think students often feel resentment for other students who seem to try too hard? In your experience, what happens to those students?

FOCUSING ON THE WRITING

1. List the names of the books and writers Rodriguez includes. If you are unfamiliar with some of the names, find out if classmates know them or if you can find information about them in your college library.

2. What in the tone of this selection suggests that Rodriguez is pleased with his program to become a better reader? Is he suggesting that something was missing? What specific evidence can you discover in the tone or feeling of the essay?

3. Reread the selection, copying down any questions Rodriguez asks. Which questions does he answer? Why do writers sometimes include questions they do not answer in their writing? How does this make you feel as a reader?

CREATING YOUR TEXT

1. Rodriguez asks the following questions: "What was the connection between reading and learning? Did one learn something only by reading it? Was an idea only an idea if it could be written down?" Write an essay in which you respond to these questions using your own experience, your observations of other learners, or your readings.

2. Rodriguez writes that in his school "the information gathered from a book was unquestioned." Many people feel that one of the most difficult concepts for students to understand is that books can and should be questioned. In addition to offering experiences and ideas, books may be one-sided, out-of-date, or simply incorrect. Write an essay in which you explain how you discovered that books present an author's point of view and should not be totally accepted without questions. Where and in what context did you learn this? How has it affected you as a reader today?

3. Write an essay in which you describe the ideal student. Describe in detail the characteristics of a person that make him or her a successful learner. As part of this essay, include an anecdote or story telling about a student or students (yourself or someone you have observed) who met your qualifications. In your conclusion, explain what you have learned about becoming a better student by thinking about the characteristics of the ideal student.

4. Write an essay in which you describe the ideal teacher. Describe in detail the type of personality, intelligence, and background that you think make someone capable to teach. As part of this essay, include an anecdote or story telling about a teacher you know who met these qualifications. In your conclusion, explain why the characteristics you have chosen are the most important ones.

REVISING YOUR TEXT

When you have finished your first draft of this essay, share it with a member of your class. Read the essay looking for its strong points and for the areas in which it needs improvement. Then review the revision questions on page 11 while reading the draft. In addition, discuss the following questions:

What specifically in the introduction makes one want to read the rest of the draft? If this needs improvement, what changes in the introduction would invite the reader to read on?

In what ways did the anecdotes or stories in the draft illustrate the main idea of the essay? What was the beginning, middle, and end of each of these anecdotes? How were they connected to the rest of the draft?

If people are described in the draft, what characteristics are provided that make these people unique and interesting to read about?

How does the draft end? What in the conclusion ties together the rest of the essay or adds an exciting or interesting idea to leave the reader thinking?

Keeping in mind the suggestions made during this process, write your second draft. Share this draft with your class.

ADDITIONAL PROJECT

"Reading to Know" is excerpted from Rodriguez's book *Hunger of Memory: The Education of Richard Rodriguez*. He has written a new book, *Days of Obligation: An Argument with My Mexican Father*, in which he continues to explore some of the themes of family, culture, education, and success. Some students should read *Hunger of Memory*, and others should read *Days of Obligation* (1992). Compare and contrast the ideas in these two books. How have Rodriguez's ideas about family, culture, education, and success changed over time? How do you explain these changes?

EXPLORING YOUR IDEAS

Look at the title of this article, and remember an experience in which you learned something for the first time and enjoyed it. Your experience could be in school, at home, with a friend, or on your own. Write about what you learned, how you learned it, and why you felt so good about this learning experience.

"It's Such a Pleasure to Learn"

WALLACE TERRY

Wallace Terry wrote this article for the March 18, 1990, issue of *Parade* magazine. In it, he tells about a remarkable 100-year-old man. A son of a former slave, John Morton-Finney earned eleven degrees and still practices law.

"*Arma virumque cano,*" I said, reciting in Latin the first words of Virgil's *Aeneid*. "*. . . Troiae qui primus ab oris,*" he continued, snatching the rest of the opening line out of my mouth.

I was surprised at my own memory. It had been three decades since I sat in my last Latin class. It had been even longer since he had taught one.

"*Italiam fato profugus Laviniaque venit litora,*" he continued, losing me in the rapturous recitation of his beloved ancient language. John Morton-Finney could not contain a soft chuckle. His eyes twinkled knowingly. He had beaten me. Not bad for a 100-year-old man.

John Morton-Finney is a very special old man. Born the son of a former slave, he served in World War I, became fluent in six foreign languages, earned 11 degrees, taught school until he was 81, and still practices law. His thirst for learning has never abated. In his 60's, he started college all over again, earning his fourth bachelor's degree at 75. Today he attends law-school seminars with the wide-eyed eagerness of a freshman.

I have interviewed many smart people in my career—Paul Tillich and Adam Clayton Powell, Jimmy Carter and Edward Teller. But John Morton-Finney has been smarter longer than anyone I ever knew.

So when I learned that he had turned 100, I traveled to his home in Indianapolis to learn the secrets of his love affair with knowledge, of his health, and of his unbowed faith in the American dream.

Morton-Finney peered through the door when I knocked at his home on the north side of the city. Then he motioned me into a living room filled with the Victorian furnishings he and his late wife had collected.

I looked at the mementos of his 100th birthday celebration. A proclamation from the Indiana Supreme Court citing him for being the oldest practicing lawyer in the state. A message from fellow Indiana University Law School graduate, [former] Vice President Dan Quayle. And another message signed by [former] President Bush.

A very private, humble man, he seemed genuinely puzzled that I wanted to know about his life. "There's nothing extraordinary about me," he scolded.

He is so shy, his daughter Gloria told me, he only danced at home. But talk history, and he explodes from his shell, racing over the centuries in lightning strokes, strewing the conversation with quotes from Pericles and Herodotus, Churchill and DuBois.

Morton-Finney reads three or four books at a time, making copious notes. Twenty books are stacked by his bed, next to five sharpened pencils and a TV set tuned to the news. More books paper the walls, climbing to the ceiling. Homer sits next to Cervantes. Cicero next to Shakespeare. Racine next to Chaucer.

Why does he keep reading so desperately? "I can get interested in so many things," he confided. "There is so much to know in this world. And it is such a pleasure for me to learn. Besides, a cultivated man would never say, 'I finished my education' because he graduated from college. There is no ending to learning."

In his childhood, Morton-Finney learned about his ancestors, who migrated from Ethiopia to what is now Nigeria. Enslaved in America, they were bought, sold, given away at the owner's whim. Morton-Finney's paternal grandfather was given by the owner to relatives as a wedding gift and taken to another part of Kentucky. The child who would become John's father was sold to another plantation. After President Lincoln issued the Emancipation Proclamation, John's grandmother, now free, went in search of her children.

"Grandmother told me she walked 12 miles barefoot, looking for my daddy," Morton-Finney recalled. "All she had was the dress she was wearing. When she found him, this white woman wouldn't let him go. 'He's mine!' she cried. But the owner's son, who had been fighting with the Rebels said, 'Mama, you have to give him up. It's the law.' Grandmother told me it was like glory. The owner had beaten this little boy to keep him under control. Now he was the happiest little soul she said she ever saw."

Ninety-five years after hearing that story at the knee of his grandmother, Morton-Finney's heart still swells. "Pioneer women showed no more bravery than the Negro woman did establishing her family after slavery. This is a stalwart character in American history."

The new family settled in Uniontown, Kentucky. Morton-Finney's father became a barber and married a woman from a family of free blacks. In 1889, their son was born. "I grew up in a Christian home," he told me. "That says it all."

Not quite. There was plenty of poetry reading and political debate. Morton-Finney grew curiouser and curiouser about the world. One day an older playmate read to him news reports from the Spanish-American War. "The illustrations fascinated me. It all made me want to read better." The next day, he bought his first book. It was Webster's *Common School Dictionary*. And it cost 35 cents, all the money he had.

When his mother died, she left his father with far too many children to manage, seven. So John was sent to live with his grandfather in Missouri.

The nearest school for blacks was six miles away. Each day Morton-Finney walked the journey, right past a school for whites that was only half as far.

He was segregated by custom. And by fear.

"Almost every day I would hear about a beating, burning, or hanging of a Negro," he recalled. "You have no idea how horrible it was. You learned to give up the road when white folks walked toward you. They could holler, and a gang would appear to beat you into the ground. I grew up afraid of white folks. I don't know that I ever stopped."

In 1911 Morton-Finney joined the Army and served a tour in the Philippines. Once out, he finished his first degree, at Lincoln College in Missouri and took a job teaching in a one-room schoolhouse. Then came the Great War, and he was back in uniform. "Oh, the destruction," he said. "I saw the survivors of mustard gas. Men spitting up parts of their lungs. I saw the graves of 30,000 Frenchmen."

How did he feel serving a nation in war that had enslaved his father and discriminated against him? "Although my country restrained me by law and by custom," he said, "it was still my country. There was no country in Africa that I belonged to. This is where I lived. I believed I should fight for this, my country. And I would do the same today."

After the war, Morton-Finney earned bachelor's degrees in mathematics, French, and history. He tried teaching languages at black colleges, but there was so little money that when he heard there were vacancies in the Indianapolis public schools, he moved there.

By then there was a Mrs. Morton-Finney. At Lincoln College, John had heard about a new French teacher, Pauline Ray from Geneva, New York, who had earned her B.A. at Cornell University. Morton-Finney signed into her class and won her heart. "We read poetry to each other," he recalled. "Talked history. We were very harmonious. I married a great lady. I married a mind. *Ma ange.*" His eyes moistened. "I called her that in French. My angel." She died in 1975.

In 1927, Indianapolis—under Ku Klux Klan influence—began segregating its public schools. Crispus Attucks High School was opened for blacks, and John Morton-Finney was the first teacher hired. It was, ironically, a showcase school, having more teachers with higher degrees than any other school in the state. Morton-Finney directed the foreign languages department, teaching Greek, Latin, German, Spanish, and French. Although he was proud of the high standards at Attucks, the segregation was a bitter pill.

Still, his love of learning held fast. Every semester, every summer, he would take a course. "I had set this ideal," he said. "No child could ask me a question that I couldn't answer or did not know how to find the answer." Soon he had earned master's degrees in education and French from Indiana University. In 1935 he finished his first law degree; there would be four more.

In 1957 he was asked to retire. He refused. The time to retire, Morton-Finney believes, comes when you decide and not someone else. "We waste a great treasure letting people retire too soon," he said. "It's called experience."

When I asked him to reveal the secrets of his long life, he said, "I take care of myself," as though that alone would silence me. "Moderation. Moderation in all matters is the key to a long life." And daily walks, fresh air, and wholesome meals, his daughter added. No snacks, no desserts, no caffeine, and no nicotine.

He has the same common-sense attitude toward race and race prejudice, enabling him to maintain his moorings in what America ought to be, rather than what it has so often been.

"We are making great progress," he said. "There is less prejudice today. Educated black people are getting along fairly well, although I worry about those with no skills. Jesse Jackson did something no one imagined when I was a boy—run for President. When Doug Wilder was elected governor of Virginia, it was the biggest surprise to me since a black man was elected mayor of Chicago. And you don't know how much the appointment of Colin Powell [see page 209], a black man, to be chairman of the Joint Chiefs of Staff means to me, an old soldier. It turned the world upside down."

And would he admonish black children who consider the pursuit of education "acting white"? His own lifelong pursuit? "When I was teaching high school," he said, "a bookseller came to me, seeking an order. He was white. Now, he apparently did not think highly of me teaching black children Latin and Greek, because he said, 'I don't believe in a black man getting a white man's education.' I asked, 'What is a white man's education?' I am still waiting for an answer. Education is education."

As I was about to leave, Morton-Finney beckoned Gloria, who is a former principal: "Please don't forget to pick up the new course announcements at Butler and the law school. I know there are going to be courses I'll want to take."

At that same moment, two miles away in a second-grade classroom at Mary E. Nicholson School, a 7-year-old boy stood up to read his composition. It was based on a news clipping his teacher, Betty Terry, had read to him about John Morton-Finney. "When I grow up, I want to be an 11-degree man," Ethan Daly read. "I might get 11 degrees teaching, being a lawyer, playing the piano. I wish the 11-degree man would come to our school and tell me how he did it." ■

DISCUSSING THE SELECTION

1. Why does the author include the Latin phrases in this article? What does he want his readers to think about Morton-Finney?

2. Before you discuss this selection in class, make a list of as many facts as you can remember about John Morton-Finney. Share and compare your list with a classmate. What facts did you both remember? Discuss why these were important to you.

3. Terry includes the names of many famous people in this article. List these people, and find out who they are and what they did. Write a short paragraph about each one so they will become names you know and can refer to in your writing and talking.

THINKING CRITICALLY

1. John Morton-Finney believes education can make a difference in a person's life. How do you define an "educated" person? How do you define an "intelligent" person? Explain the difference as you see it.

2. What in this article tells you about Morton-Finney's determination? Have you ever known anyone who succeeded in life because of his or her determination? Tell your class about the person.

3. Morton-Finney is described as having a commonsense attitude. What is a commonsense attitude? Describe an experience in your own life that shows you have or do not have such an attitude.

FOCUSING ON THE WRITING

Interviewing

Writers use interviews to learn about the subject. Here are some steps that can help you conduct an interview:

  Decide whom you want to interview. Write ten questions to ask the person.

  Make an appointment to meet with the person with whom you will conduct your interview. Bring your tape recorder, a fresh tape, your notebook with your questions written out, and a pen. Speak clearly, and ask questions if you do not understand someone's answers.

  After you leave, immediately make notes about your impression of the person. Describe the person's appearance, facial expression, body language, dress, and any other behavior that stands out in your mind. As soon as possible, transcribe your tape or write out your notes as completely as possible. You may show them to your interviewee, or you may need to make a follow-up call or interview to clarify some point.

1. What questions do you think the interviewer asked Morton-Finney? What did he find out by meeting with Morton-Finney that he might not have found out if he had interviewed him on the phone?

2. Compare the attitudes toward reading and writing described in the Kincaid story on page 216, the Kramer article on page 223, and the Rodriguez memoir on page 239 with those of Morton-Finney. As a reader, which selection did you prefer? Why? As a student, whose attitudes are closest to your own? Explain the reasons for your choice, referring to specific elements in the writing.

3. Writers make choices in every word they use as they write. Writing an interesting introduction is important to a writer because it makes a reader

want to read more. The first three paragraphs of "'It's Such a Pleasure to Learn'" contain some Latin phrases. Do these phrases make you want to read more about John Morton-Finney, or do they make you want to avoid reading this article? Would you keep the introduction as it is? If you would change it, what would you change and why?

4. Paragraph 4 begins with a topic sentence. Copy the topic sentence. List the specific details that Terry includes to support the topic sentence.

5. In paragraph 4, Terry summarizes the achievements of John Morton-Finney's life in one sentence. Copy that sentence in your notebook. What word is the subject of the sentence? What verbs are in the sentence? Why is one verb in a different tense from the rest?

CREATING YOUR TEXT

1. For this project, conduct an interview with someone. Try to find out specific details about the person's life and work. You can interview someone you know well, such as a family member, a neighbor, a store or restaurant owner, or teacher. Or you can interview someone you know only slightly, such as a neighborhood police officer, a doctor, a dentist, a social worker, or a neighborhood religious leader. The person need not be famous or glamorous. And he or she must be someone with whom you can talk and someone who is willing to talk with you. You may conduct one long interview or several short interviews. In your interview, focus on the person's attitudes toward education—toward reading and writing, specifically. How did these attitudes affect his or her decisions about higher education and job choices? What did you learn from interviewing this person?

2. Reread "'It's Such a Pleasure to Learn'" and "This Lady Came Down from the Mountains" on page 114 and write an essay in which you compare the lives and personalities of John Morton-Finney and Lou Crabtree. What about their early lives is similar? What about their professional lives is

similar? What differences have you discovered as you read about their personalities? In your conclusion, include what you imagine would be the perfect lines they would say to each other if they were to meet.

3. Choose one person you have read about so far in this book whose attitude toward life and/or education you admire. Write an essay in which you explain why you admire the person, what you have in common with the person, and what you learned about yourself from reading about him or her.

REVISING YOUR TEXT

When you finish your first draft, share it and your notes (the transcript, description, and so on) with a classmate or in a small group. Together, decide if you have included all the important information needed to create a clear portrait of the person and to emphasize that aspect of the person you think is important.

Then, in your journal, write about what you have learned about interviewing from this experience. What were your successes? What problems did you have? What would you do differently next time?

EXPANDING YOUR IDEAS

Collaborative Writing Projects

1. Think of a personal experience, involving school, about which you have not written for this class. Write about it for five minutes. Show your notes to a classmate. Together, write a draft based on one of your experiences, turning it into a story. As you work together, you may decide to add or delete some parts. You may decide to emphasize some aspects of the experience that at first you hadn't thought important. Rewrite the draft until you are ready to read it to your classmates.

2. Next, meet in a small group of three or four students. After reading all the drafts from step 1 carefully, choose one draft you especially like. As a group, read the revision questions for a story on page 13, and together revise the story until you feel ready to share it with the entire class.

3. After each group reads its draft to the whole class, the class can choose one story that everyone particularly enjoys. Together, on the computer (if you have a networking system) or on the chalkboard, all students can work together revising the draft to make a clearer, more interesting story. You may want to share the result with another class or submit it to a college magazine or newspaper as a class project.

4. Write a short paper about what it was like to write together as a group. What part was most difficult for you? What part was easiest? Why?

Each person can make a difference despite the fact that these are troubled and complicated times. By taking a stand and following through on it, a person makes a commitment to change and to the fulfillment of his or her potential.

Theme 5

Making a Social Commitment

Readings

"The Poor Man's Superman, Scourge of Landlords"
BY LARRY ROHTER

"El Patrón"
BY NASH CANDELARIA

"Aliza: Breaking Silence"
BY ALIZA MOLDOFSKY

"The Right Thing to Do at the Time"
BY GEORGE GARRETT

"Pan Asian Repertory Theatre's Tisa Chang"
BY FERN SIEGAL

"Meet Du Pont's 'In-House Conscience'"
BY JOSEPH WEBER

"The Voice of the Land Is in Our Language"

In "The Poor Man's Superman: Scourge of Landlords," Larry Rohter describes Super Barrio, a man committed to ensuring fair housing and human rights for poor people in Mexico City.

"El Patrón," by Nash Candelaria, is also about defying the system. In this story, a young man's moral beliefs lead him to stand up against his father and his country.

In "Aliza: Breaking Silence," Aliza Moldofsky writes about the abuse she was subjected to by her stepfather. She discovered that writing helped her not only to express her pain but also to get support from others.

Admiring the courage of his father, George Garrett wrote "The Right Thing to Do at the Time," a story about a lawyer who stood up against bigotry and the system in a small southern town.

In her article, "Pan Asian Repertory Theatre's Tisa Chang," Fern Siegal describes a different method of attacking bigotry. Tisa Chang created a theater that hires and produces work by Asian actors, who have often encountered prejudices in auditioning and hiring practices.

According to "Meet Du Pont's 'In-House Conscience,'" by Joseph Weber, Faith A. Wohl confronted and changed hiring and employment practices at a big corporation.

"The Voice of the Land Is in Our Language" describes Joseph Nicholas's decision to leave his job and return to his tribe to learn about its customs and language, and then to teach these to the children of the tribe.

Making Discoveries

In Your Journal

Write in your journal about a person you know, have seen on television or in the movies, or read about in a book who got involved in a movement or idea, or who took an action because of a cause in which he or she believed. What was the belief? What was the action? What was the outcome? What did you learn from this experience?

With a Classmate

Talk to your classmate about the person you described in your journal. Explain why you selected this person. What do the people you have each chosen have in common? What were the results of taking the action?

With Your Class

Discuss some of the people you have selected. What do they have in common? Discuss what makes people take an action. Discuss the results—positive or negative. Explain when you would take an action or join a cause, and why. Many people say that young people today are apathetic, meaning they don't get involved. Does this seem true of the people in your class? If it is, why do you think this is true?

EXPLORING YOUR IDEAS

Imagine that by putting on a mask or costume, you could do something for your community that you would be uncomfortable doing dressed normally. Write in your journal about the action you would take to improve some condition in your community. Explain why you would do this and what you think would be the result of your action.

The Poor Man's Superman, Scourge of Landlords

LARRY ROHTER

Larry Rohter's article, which appeared in *The New York Times* on August 15, 1988, is about a real-life superman and his defense of the poor and needy people in his community.

He is not faster than a speeding bullet, and he is definitely unable to leap tall buildings at a single bound. But wherever Government officials are indifferent to the needs of the poor, or landlords threaten tenants with eviction, Super Barrio is sure to be there.

Dressed in red tights, gold cape, face mask and a shirt emblazoned with the letters SB, Mexico's homegrown superhero leads the fight for fair housing, electricity, and sewers here. All it takes is a call to his telephone hotline, and Super Barrio will arrive at the scene of injustice in his Barriomobile, accompanied by lawyers, militants of the Assembly of Barrios, and often the press.

"I can't tell you how many evictions we have prevented," the masked man said in an interview at his Barrio Cave, an apartment in a public housing project here. "All I know is that having been thrown out on the street myself as a child, I wanted to do everything I can to defend the people's right to housing."

Recently, for example, a family with financial problems was summarily evicted from its rented quarters by the landlady, who then locked herself in the apartment. Summoned as a mediator, Super Barrio persuaded the landlady to allow the family to return to the apartment with a new lease with more liberal terms of payment.

Short, stocky, and bearer of a noticeable paunch, Super Barrio has also become a familiar sight at marches and political demonstrations around the capital. Wearing his mask and shiny but slightly worn costume, he has been admitted to meetings and public hearings at the Ministry of the Interior, the Ministry of Urban Development and even Los Pinos, the Mexican equivalent of the White House.

"Most of the time, Super Barrio is treated with respect," said Francisco Saucedo, a member of the board of directors of the Assembly of Barrios, a public interest group to which 50,000 poor and working-class families here belong. "Sometimes, though, we'll meet up with an official who is not sure how to treat him."

When Super Barrio was invited to testify at a hearing on housing at the Mexican Congress some months ago, his manner of dress became the center of controversy. When he appeared at the entrance of the chamber, legislators from the ruling Institutional Revolutionary Party, or PRI, took affront, accused him of being disrespectful, and instructed security guards to keep him out.

Ordered to remove his mask as a condition of being allowed into Congress, Super Barrio retorted he would do so only if the PRI legislators "take off their disguises too." But after opposition members threatened to walk out of the session in solidarity with Super Barrio, the ruling party relented and the masked man was allowed to testify in full regalia.

In an effort to capitalize on his successes, Super Barrio decided to become a candidate in the presidential election. Eventually he withdrew, throwing his support to Cuauhtémoc Cárdenas of the left-populist National Democratic Front, but 11 members of the Assembly of Barrios did run for Congress for Mr. Cárdenas's slate.

And when Mr. Cárdenas emerged from the voting booth on election day, he announced that he had cast his own presidential ballot for Super Barrio, which sent the masked man's stock rising even further. Super Barrio has since returned the favor by appearing at mass rallies in which Mr. Cárdenas presses his claim that widespread fraud in the elections deprived him of victory.

On one level, Super Barrio is an effort to blend comic book heroes such as Spiderman, Superman, and Zorro with a Mexican tradition of wrestlers who go into the ring disguised and are invincible so long as they are not unmasked. As Super Barrio himself explained his origin: "One day when I was in my room, I was enveloped in a brilliant red and yellow light, and when it dissipated, I was dressed this way. Then a voice said to me, 'You are Super Barrio, defender of tenants and scourge of greedy landlords.'"

But in a broader social context, both Super Barrio and the movement he has come to symbolize are really outgrowths of the earthquake that devastated Mexico City in September 1985. Many house and apartment buildings were destroyed, thousands of people were made homeless, and real estate speculation on a scale not seen before began.

In neighborhoods around the capital, families forced to live in the streets or with relatives banded together informally to press the Government for rapid reconstruction of new homes. In April 1987, after the bulk of the reconstruction was over, the groups united formally as the Assembly of Barrios to lobby for expansion of Government housing, utility, and sewer programs, and not long afterward Super Barrio made his first appearance.

"The reconstruction of the city is an achievement that has improved the lives of many people," Mr. Saucedo said. "Our reasoning was that if this much could be done, why not continue?"

As his fame has reached national proportions, Super Barrio has been invited to appear at events as diverse as university conferences in Puebla and antinuclear demonstrations in Vera Cruz. Locally, he is also broadening the scope of his activities to include issues such as police corruption, pollution, and transportation.

"Today my struggle is not only against landlords but against all those who commit injustices with the support of power or a Government post," Super Barrio said.

Like other superheroes, Super Barrio, who appears to be in his early 30's, makes a point of keeping his true identity a secret. But he did say that he lives in a rooming house in downtown Mexico City, has a wife and child, earns his living as a street vendor, and has in the past been a professional wrestler.

"We are all Super Barrio," he said when asked why he was so zealous about concealing his background. "If I take off my mask and disclose who I am, all of that changes and you lose the collective identity."

Because of his growing popularity, Super Barrio is being deluged with offers to appear in movies and comic books and even to return to the ring. But he says ideological scruples prevent him from accepting the deals.

"My struggle is a social struggle, not a commercial one," he said. "We are not confronting Martians, but landlords. Our enemies are not imaginary, but real." ■

DISCUSSING THE SELECTION

1. Why does Super Barrio dress in a costume while he performs serious and important acts? What specific events in the article indicate that people respect and treat him seriously even though he is dressed strangely?

2. Why do you think Super Barrio has created a myth to describe how he became the superhero he is today?

3. What specific incidents in the article support the idea that Super Barrio is trusted by the needy people of Mexico City? What incidents does Rohter include to support the idea that many of the people of Mexico City are poor and needy?

4. How did the events that followed the 1985 earthquake in Mexico City affect Super Barrio's life? Why did people begin to speculate in real estate? What did this speculation mean to the poor people of the area?

5. What is Super Barrio's attitude toward politicians? Explain this attitude, referring to specific incidents reported in the article.

THINKING CRITICALLY

1. Have you ever known anyone who defended the rights of the poor and needy? Tell the class about the person(s) you know and how this person's actions and/or life affected yours.

2. What does Super Barrio mean when he says, "If I take off my mask and disclose who I am, all of that changes and you lose the collective identity"? What is "the collective identity"?

3. Would you advise Super Barrio to take off his mask and costume and start to dress in a suit, shirt, and tie? Why or why not?

4. How does his statement "My struggle is a social struggle, not a commercial one" answer the people who make offers for him to appear in movies and comic books and even to wrestle again? Would you respond differently to this story if he accepted one of these offers? Why or why not?

5. What is the difference between a superhero and a hero? Name some men and women who fit each category, and explain the differences between them.

FOCUSING ON THE WRITING

1. In the first paragraph, Rohter makes an allusion to another superhero. Who? Why is this a good technique to get the reader's attention?

2. What other specific techniques does Rohter use to get his readers interested in reading this article? At what point in the article does he include

facts and more serious information? How does the change of tone affect your reading of the article?

3. What does the conclusion to this article tell the reader about Super Barrio? How does the style of the conclusion contrast with the style of the introduction? Why might the author have decided to write a serious conclusion?

CREATING YOUR TEXT

1. Write the word *hero* in the middle of your paper. Circle the word, and do a clustering activity with it by yourself or with a partner for five minutes (see page 5 for more information about clustering).

2. Look at the cluster you created, and reread the journal entry you wrote before you read this article. Write an essay describing a superhero. The person can be Super Barrio, someone you have read about, or someone you have imagined. Describe the actions this person would take and the causes in which he or she would get involved. What do you think ordinary people can learn from the actions of such an individual?

3. Write an essay in which you describe the heroes you had in your childhood and the heroes you have today. If these have changed, explain why.

4. Do people of today need heroes? In your essay, explain your answer including some examples of today's heroes. Explain why you think these people fit the category of hero. How have the lives of these people affected your life?

5. What effect do the movies, books, or television programs that depict superheroes have on our society? Write an essay in which you explain your point of view, describing your experiences or those of people you know or have read about. In your conclusion, explain why you feel as you do.

REVISING YOUR TEXT

Read your draft with a classmate, reviewing the revision questions on page 11. In addition, each classmate should answer the following questions about the other's draft:

What specifically, in the introduction, made you want to read more? If this needs improvement, make specific suggestions.

What details do you remember about the people described in this draft? What made them seem real or unique to you?

What one idea will you remember about this draft? How could the writer make this idea stand out even more?

Does the writer use any similes, symbols, or metaphors? (See page 236 for more information about these devices.) If so, do they make sense to you as a reader?

Using your answers to these questions, decide where your essay works and where it needs improvement. When you have decided how to improve your essay, write your second draft to share with the class.

> **EXPLORING YOUR IDEAS**
>
> Write about an event in which you or someone you know took a stand against someone in authority because of an injustice. As part of your writing, explain the context or background that led up to the event, the event and the action taken, and the outcome of the action. Include a description of the setting or place, the time of day, and any other details that bring the feeling of the event back to you.

El Patrón

NASH CANDELARIA

Nash Candelaria was born in Los Angeles and now lives in Palo Alto, California. His family is from Albuquerque, New Mexico. He has written many short stories, and a trilogy of novels about New Mexico: *Memories of Alhambra, Not by the Sword,* and *Inheritance of Strangers.*

My father-in-law's hierarchy is, in descending order: Dios, El Papá, y el patrón. It is to these that mere mortals bow, as in turn el patrón bows to El Papá, and El Papá bows to Dios.

God and the Pope are understandable enough. It's this el patrón, the boss, who causes most of our trouble. Whether it's the one who gives you work and for it pay, the lifeblood of hardworking little people—or others: our parents (fathers affectionately known as jefe, mothers known merely as mama, military commanders el capitán), or any of the big shots in the government (el alcalde, el gobernador, el presidente and never forget la policía).

It was about some such el patrón trouble that Señor Martínez boarded the bus in San Diego and headed north toward L.A.—and us.

Since I was lecturing to a mid-afternoon summer school class at Southwestern U., my wife, Lola, picked up her father at the station. When I arrived home, they were sitting politely in the living room talking banalities: "Yes, it does look like rain. But if it doesn't rain, it might be sunny. If only the clouds would blow away."

Lola had that dangerous look on her face that usually made me start talking too fast and too long in hope of shifting her focus. It never worked. She'd sit there with a face like a brown-skinned kewpie doll whose expression was slowly turning into that of an angry maniac. When she could no longer stand it, she'd give her father a blast: "You never talk to me about anything important, you macho, chauvinist jumping bean!" Then it would escalate to nastiness from there.

But tonight it didn't get that far. As I entered Señor Martínez rose, dressed neatly in his one suit as for a wedding or a funeral, and politely shook my hand. Without so much as a glance at Lola, he said, "Why don't you go to the kitchen with the other women."

"There are no other women," Lola said coldly. She stood and belligerently received my kiss on the cheek before leaving.

Señor Martínez was oblivious to her reaction, sensing only the absence of "woman," at which he visibly relaxed and sat down.

"Rosca," he said, referring to me as he always did by my last name. "Tito is in trouble with the law."

His face struggled between anger and sadness, tinged with a crosscurrent of confusion. Tito was his pride and joy. His only son after four daughters. A twilight gift born to his wife at a time when he despaired of ever having a son, when their youngest daughter, Lola, was already ten years old and their oldest daughter twenty.

"He just finished his examinations at the state university. He was working this summer to save money for his second year when this terrible thing happened."

I could not in my wildest fantasies imagine young Vicente getting into any kind of trouble. He had always impressed me as a bright, polite young man who would inspire pride in any father. Even when he and old Vicente had quarreled about Tito going to college instead of working full-time, the old man had grudgingly come around to seeing the wisdom of it. But now. The law! I was stunned.

"Where is he?" I asked, imagining the nineteen-year-old in some filthy cell in the San Diego jail.

"I don't know." Then he looked over his shoulder toward the kitchen, as if to be certain no one was eavesdropping. "I think he went underground."

Underground! I had visions of drug-crazed revolutionary zealots. Bombs exploding in federal buildings. God knows what kind of madness.

"They're probably after him," he went on. Then he paused and stared at me as if trying to understand. "Tito always looked up to you and Lola. Of all the family it would be you he would try to contact. I want you to help me." Not help *Tito*, I thought, but help *me*.

I went to the cabinet for the bottle that I kept there for emergencies. I took a swallow to give me enough courage to ask the question. "What . . . did . . . he do?"

Señor Martínez stared limply at the glass in his hand. "You know," he said, "my father fought with Pancho Villa."

Jesus! I thought. If everyone who told me his father had fought with Pancho Villa was telling the truth, that army would have been big enough to conquer the world. Besides—what did this have to do with Tito?

"When my turn came," he continued, "I enlisted in the Marines at Camp Pendleton. Fought los Japonés in the Pacific." Finally he took a swallow of his drink and sat up stiffly as if at attention. "The men in our family have never shirked their duty!" He barked like the Marine corporal he had once been.

It slowly dawned on me what this was all about. It had been *the* topic all during summer school at Southwestern U. Registration for the draft. "No blood for Mideast oil!" the picket signs around the campus post office had shouted. "Boycott the Exxon army!"

"I should never have let him go to college," Señor Martínez said. "That's where he gets such crazy radical ideas. From those rich college boys whose parents can buy them out of all kinds of trouble."

"So he didn't register," I said.

"The FBI is probably after him right now. It's a federal crime, you know. And the Canadians don't want draft dodgers either."

He took a deep swallow and polished off the rest of his drink in one gulp, putting the empty glass on the coffee table. There, his gesture seemed to say, now you know the worst.

Calmer now, he went on to tell me more. About the American Civil War; a greater percentage of Spanish-speaking men of New Mexico had joined the Union Army than the men from any other group in any other state in the Union. About the Rough Riders, including young Mexican-Americans, born on horseback; riding roughest of all over the Spanish in Cuba. About the War-to-End-All-Wars, where tough, skinny, brown-faced doughboys from farms in Texas, New Mexico, Arizona, Colorado, and California gave their all "Over There." About World War II, from the New Mexico National Guard captured at Bataan to the tough little Marines whom he was proud to fight alongside; man for man, there were more decorations for bravery among Mexican-Americans than among any other group in this war. Then Korea, where his younger brother toughed it out in the infantry. Finally Vietnam, where kids like his nephew, Pablo, got it in some silent, dark jungle trying to save a small country from the Communists.

By now he had lost his calm. There were tears in his eyes, partly from the pride he felt in this tradition of valor in war. But partly for something else, I thought. I could almost hear his son's reply to his impassioned call to duty: "Yes, Papá. So we could come back, if we survived, to our jobs as busboys and ditch diggers; *that's* why I have to go to college. I don't want to go to the Middle East and fight and die for some oil company when you can't even afford to own a car. If the Russians invaded our country, I would defend it. If a robber broke into our house, I would fight him. If someone attacked you, I would save you. But this? No, Papá."

But now Tito was gone. God knows where. None of his three sisters in San Diego had seen him. Nor any of his friends in the neighborhood or school or work.

I could hear preparations for dinner from the kitchen. Señor Martínez and I had another tragito while Lolita and Junior ate their dinner early, the sounds of their childish voices piercing through the banging of pots and pans.

When Lola called me Emiliano instead of by my nickname, Pata, I knew we were in for a lousy meal. Everything her father disliked must have been served. It had taken some kind of perverse gourmet expending a tremendous amount of energy to fix such rotten food. There was that nothing white bread that presses together into a doughy flat mass instead of the tortillas Papá thrived on. There was a funny little salad with chopped garbage in it covered by a blob of imitation goo. There was no meat. No meat! Just all those sliced vegetables in a big bowl. Not ordinary vegetables like beans and potatoes and carrots, but funny, wiggly long things like wild grass . . . or worms. And quivering cubes of what must have been whale blubber.

Halfway through the meal, as Señor Martínez shuffled the food around on his plate like one of our kids resisting what was good for them, the doorbell rang.

"You'd better get that, Emiliano," Lola said, daring me to refuse by her tone of voice and dagger-throwing glance.

Who needs a fight? In a sense I was the lucky one because I could leave the table and that pot of mess-age. When I opened the door, a scraggly young man beamed a weak smile at me. "I hitchhiked from San Diego," Tito said.

Before I could move onto the steps and close the door behind me, he stumbled past me into the house. Tired as he was, he reacted instantly to seeing his father at the table. "You!" he shouted, then turned and bolted out the door.

Even tired he could run faster than I, so I hopped into the car and drove after him while Lola and Señor Martínez stood on the steps shouting words at me that I couldn't hear.

Two blocks later Tito finally climbed into the car after I bribed him with a promise of dinner at McDonald's. While his mouth was full, I tried to talk some sense into him, but to no avail. He was just as stubborn as his father and sister. Finally, I drove him to the International House on campus where the housing manager, who owed me a favor, found him an empty bed.

"You should have *made* him come back with you," Lola nagged at me that night.

"He doesn't want to be under the same roof with his father." From her thoughtful silence I knew that she understood and probably felt the same way herself. When I explained to her what it was all about—her father had said nothing to her—it looked for a moment as if she would get out of bed, stomp to the guest room, and heave Señor Martínez out into the street.

The next day seemed like an endless two-way shuttle between our house and the I House. First me. Then Lola. If Señor Martínez had had a car and could drive, he would have followed each of us.

Our shuttle diplomacy finally wore them down. I could at last discern cracks in father's and son's immovable positions.

"Yes. Yes. I love my son."

"I love my father."

"I know. I know. Adults shoud be able to sit down and air their differences, no matter how wrong he is."

"Maybe tomorrow. Give me a break. But definitely not at mealtime. I can't eat while my stomach is churning."

The difficulty for me, as always, was in keeping my opinions to myself. Lola didn't have that problem. After all, they were her brother and father, so she felt free to say whatever she pleased.

"The plan is to get them to talk," I said to her. "If they can talk they can reach some kind of understanding."

"Papá has to be set straight," she said. "As usual, he's wrong, but he always insists it's someone else who messed things up."

"He doesn't want Tito to go to jail."

"That's Tito's choice!" Of course she was right; they were both right.

The summit meeting was set for the next afternoon. Since I had only one late morning lecture, I would pick up Tito, feed him a Big Mac or two, then bring him to the house. Lola would fix Señor Martínez some nice tortillas and chili, making up for that abominable dinner of the night before last. Well fed, with two chaperones mediating, we thought they could work something out.

When Tito and I walked into the house, my hope started to tremble and develop goose bumps. It was deathly silent and formal. Lola had that dangerous look on her face again. The macho, chauvinist jumping bean sat stiffly in his suit that looked like it had just been pressed—all shiny and sharply creased, unapproachable and potentially cutting, an inanimate warning of what lay behind Señor Martínez's stone face.

Tito and I sat across from the sofa and faced them. Or rather I faced them. Both Tito and Señor Martínez were looking off at an angle from each other, not daring to touch glances. I smiled, but no one acknowledged it so I gave it up. Then Lola broke the silence.

"What this needs is a woman's point-of-view," she began.

That's all Señor Martínez needed. The blast his eyes shot at her left her open-mouthed and silent as he interrupted. "I don't want you to go to jail!" He was looking at Lola, but he meant Tito.

Tito's response was barely audible, and I detected a trembling in his voice. "You'd rather I got killed on some Arabian desert," he said.

The stone face cracked. For a moment it looked as if Señor Martínez would burst into tears. He turned his puzzled face from Lola toward his son. "No," he said. "Is that what you think?" Then, when Tito did not answer, he said, "You're my only son, and damn it! Sons are supposed to obey their fathers!"

"El patrón, El Papá, and Dios," Tito said with a trace of bitterness.

But Lola could be denied no longer. "Papá, how old were you when you left Mexico for the U.S.?" She didn't expect an answer, so didn't give him time to reply. "Sixteen, wasn't it? And what did your father say?"

Thank God that smart-ass smile of hers was turned away from her father. She knew she had him, and he knew it too, but he didn't need her smirk to remind him of it.

He sighed. The look on his face showed that sometimes memories were best forgotten. When he shook his head but did not speak, Lola went on. She too had seen her father's reaction, and her voice lost its hard edge and became more sympathetic.

"He disowned you, didn't he? Grandpa disowned you. Called you a traitor to your own country. A deserter when things got tough."

"I did not intend to stay in Mexico and starve," he said. He looked around at us one by one as if he had to justify himself. "He eventually came to Los Estados Unidos himself. He and Mamá died in that house in San Diego."

"What did you think when Grandpa did that to you?"

No answer was necessary. "Can't you see, Papá?" Lola pleaded, meaning him and Tito. He could see.

Meanwhile Tito had been watching his father as if he had never seen him before. I guess only the older children had heard Papá's story of how he left Mexico.

"I don't intend to go to jail, Papá," Tito said, "I just have to take a stand along with thousands of others. In the past old men started wars in which young men died in order to preserve old men's comforts. It just has to stop. There's never been a war without a draft. Never a draft without registration. And this one is nothing but craziness by el patrón in Washington, D.C. If enough of us protest, maybe he'll get the message."

"They almost declared it unconstitutional," I said. "They may yet."

"Because they aren't signing women," Papá said in disgust. But from the look on Lola's face, I'd pick her over him in any war.

"If they come after me, I'll register," Tito said. "But in the meantime I have to take this stand."

There. It was out. They had had their talk in spite of their disagreements.

"He's nineteen," Lola said. "Old enough to run his own life."

Señor Martínez was all talked out. He slumped against the back of the sofa. Even the creases in his trousers seemed to have sagged. Tito looked at his sister, and his face brightened.

"Papá," Tito said. "I . . . I'd like to go home, if you want me to."

On Papá's puzzled face I imagined I could read the words: "My father fought with Pancho Villa." But it was no longer an accusation, only a simple statement of fact. Who knows what takes more courage—to fight or not to fight?

"There's a bus at four o'clock," Señor Martínez said.

Later I drove them in silence to the station. Though it felt awkward, it wasn't a bad silence. There are more important ways to speak than with words, and I could feel that sitting shoulder to shoulder beside me, father and son had reached some accord.

Papá still believed in el patrón, El Papá, and Dios. What I hoped they now saw was that Tito did too. Only in his case, conscience overrode el patrón, maybe even El Papá. In times past, popes too declared holy wars that violated conscience. For Tito, conscience was the same as Dios. And I saw in their uneasy truce that love overrode their differences.

I shook their hands as they boarded the bus, and watched the two similar faces, one old, one young, smile sadly at me through the window as the Greyhound pulled away.

When I got back home, Junior and Lolita were squabbling over what channel to watch on TV. I rolled my eyes in exasperation, ready to holler at them, but Lola spoke up first.

"I'm glad Papá got straightened out. The hardest thing for parents with their children is to let go."

Yeah, I started to say, but she stuck her head into the other room and told Junior and Lolita to stop quarreling or they were going to get it. ■

Candelaria *El Patrón*

DISCUSSING THE SELECTION

1. What does *el patrón* mean? What does this statement mean: "el patrón bows to El Papá, and El Papá bows to Dios"?

2. After reading this story, what do you know about "Señor Martínez"? From the information you can put together from the story, describe the man. What is his relationship to his son? What is his relationship to his daughter?

3. What do you know about Tito? Describe him. How does he feel about his father? Why does he refuse to register for the draft?

4. Why is the father so upset that his son has chosen not to sign up for the draft? What does signing up to fight for one's country mean to the father?

5. What in the story suggests that Tito wants to trust his father? What does Tito want to tell his father? What prevents this from happening? How does Lola's intervention inspire communication between the two men?

6. What in the story tells you that the father and son are more alike than different?

THINKING CRITICALLY

1. What is the order of power in your family? Reread the first paragraph of the story, focusing on the hierarchy of power in the Martínez family.

2. Why did Tito run away rather than directly confront his father? Have you ever run away from a problem and then found you had to confront it at a later time? Is there ever any time when it makes more sense to wait to

confront a problem rather than deal with it directly right away? Explain your answer using your own experience or your observations of others.

3. Explain what is meant in paragraph 74 by the question "Who knows what takes more courage—to fight or not to fight?"

4. What difference do you notice in the relationships between men and women in the two generations in this story—the father and his daughter, Lola and her husband, Tito and his sister?

5. What differences do you find between the way the family in this story resolves its problems and the way the family in "Three Thousand Dollars" on page 123 resolves its problems?

FOCUSING ON THE WRITING

Audience Awareness

When you write, you write to communicate your ideas to your readers, your audience. When you write, think about the person(s) who will be reading what you are trying to communicate.

Ask yourself the following questions about your audience:

Who are they? What do they do? What is their educational level?
What are their interests and concerns?
What do they know about my subject? What position do they already hold about my subject?
What are their political feelings or moral beliefs likely to be? What influence do they have on my topic?
How can I interest them in my topic?
What can I teach them or persuade them about my topic?
What do I want my audience to think about me and my ideas?

Candelaria *El Patrón*

1. For what audience do you think Candelaria is writing? What in the story supports your answer? What changes would you advise Candelaria to make if he were writing this story for a teen magazine? Explain the reasons for your advice.

2. The information in this story is revealed through the narrator. (Reread page 97 for more information on types of narration.) Decide what type of narrator Candelaria used. Use evidence from the story to support your answer.

3. What information does the narrator reveal about the following:

    What are the names of the characters in the story?
    What are their family relationships?
    Where does the story take place?
    How does the narrator of the story feel about the situation?
    Why does he feel this way?

4. What specific general ideas presented in "Only daughter," by Sandra Cisneros (see page 34), about her Mexican-American family are similar to the ones presented in "El Patrón" by Candelaria? What specific differences are there between the two styles of writing—one for an essay and one for a story?

CREATING YOUR TEXT

1. Spend five minutes freewriting on this story and on what it made you think about in your own life. To do this (see page 6), open to a blank page and start to write down any ideas that come into your mind. This activity may help you remember a story or an incident you will be able to use in your writing. The only requirement is that you write for the entire five minutes without stopping to reread, judge, or edit what you have written.

2. Read your freewriting, and reread the journal entry you wrote before you read "El Patrón." Write an essay that includes a story about someone who

took a stand against an injustice. In your conclusion, explain what you learned from this incident.

3. Many people feel that when they were young adults, they had difficulty communicating with their parents. They feel that the "generation gap" makes it hard for parents to understand their maturing children. Others feel that communication becomes easier as children become more mature. Discuss your feelings about this issue, and write an essay in which you use evidence from your own life, or from stories you have read, that explains why you feel as you do.

4. There has been an ongoing debate about whether women should be forced to register along with men for the armed services. Many people feel that fighting for one's country is a male duty. Take a position on this issue, and write an essay explaining why you feel as you do. Support it with your own experiences, observations, or readings about this issue.

5. Growing up often involves taking a position on an issue that differs from the position taken by one's family or peers. Write an essay in which you describe an incident in which you or someone you know took a position different from the family or peer position. Explain what the person learned about himself or herself through this experience.

REVISING YOUR TEXT

Review the first draft of your writing by reading the draft alone or with a classmate and then going over the revision questions on page 11 or 12.

In addition, think about the following questions as you prepare to write your second draft:

Is your position clearly stated?
What specific supporting details have you included that are personal?
What specific supporting details have you included that are general?
What audience did you have in mind when you wrote this? What changes did you make so your writing would be interesting to this group of readers?

EXPLORING YOUR IDEAS

In this story a fourteen-year-old girl reveals a terrible family experience. Today, people often reveal the details of their personal lives in magazine stories and on television talk programs. In your journal, write about a problem you learned about from one of these sources. Write about why you read these magazines or watch these kinds of television programs.

Aliza: Breaking Silence

ALIZA MOLDOFSKY

This story was written by fourteen-year-old Aliza Moldofsky after she came forward to reveal that her stepfather had been abusing her sexually for four years. As a result of her action, he was arrested, and she began to enjoy a new freedom in her life. Aliza has expressed her wish to have the piece published with her real name, saying that "If I printed it anonymously I would be a hypocrite to my message on honest communication, hiding behind a facade of non-existence."

She saw every room, every bed, every quilt in a different light. She no longer smelled him in the air nor did she hear the clinking of the ice cubes in his wine glass, coming to freeze her heart and mind. But, best of all, she would never have to endure his touch again, attempting to infuse carnal knowledge into a mind not so much pure as undesirous of such information. He was gone. She rejoiced.

It had lasted for three or four years, and now, in a few hours, it was finished—forever. Suddenly, she was so free that she didn't know what to do with herself: with that liberty. She felt reborn, and was lost in her "newness." Yet there she was also found—in herself, her life, and her world. She was healed of a sickness that was not even her own but had punished her since she was but a child. In reality, she was still a child, but she knew too much to ever reclaim that wide-eyed innocence that she wasn't altogether sure that she ever had in the first place. She had forgotten.

But she had finally taken the step that she had needed to take, and she was proud. She had spoken out of the depths of her silence and, surprising as it was to her, people listened. Surprising to her because she had been told again and again that they wouldn't hear or wouldn't care or wouldn't believe, but they did, and now, here she was, safe and strong and proud. The silence was over, and she could not turn off the flow of speech. They had listened, they had heard, and they had cared!

All she had had to do was ask for freedom, and it was. She felt godlike; she had asked for it, and it existed, and "it was good."

As she reflected, she recognized the link, the important step that she had overlooked for so many years—communication. In this modern world, people publicize telephones, television, magazines, books, and movies, but how many commercials are there for the spoken word? She hadn't printed her plea for help in Day-Glo letters across her forehead; she had just said, "Help me, please."

It all seemed so easy, looking back. One opened one's mouth and the words would be there, ready to burst forth upon others' unsuspecting ears, but, she reflected, sometimes the words weren't there; sometimes one had to search and fumble for the right phrase or vocabulary.

They don't teach you what to say; they just insist upon correct conjugation and usage. But she knew that, although she might still use the television or watch movies and such, she would always rely on language to be her salvation.

She prayed that others would speak, too, following her example. Now that she had found the truth of communication, she was impatient to share it with the rest of the world. Communicating bare human needs is far more important than using correct gerund phrases, she recognized with a sad smile.

Babies cry when they are in pain or want something, but once that child learns to speak, tears and screams are not enough—words are necessary to receive relief from distress. She now knew this and pitied the several friends she knew who were still suffering for not having the words or the strength or the will to tell their tales. But she knew in her heart that if and when they were ready, they, too, would speak the words that would bring them to the freedom she had already found.

"Learn to speak," she still begs, "learn to be able to ask for help and help yourselves. They can't help you until you tell them what's wrong, what's hurting you."

Then she falls silent, a rarity in her newfound expressive world—and she lets the weight of her message waft softly to the ears of the suffering around her.

> On July 31, 1990, Aliza's stepfather, Douglas Verity, pleaded no contest to the charges and received a 6- to 20-year sentence for molestation. He is to participate in a prison sex-offender program, and at the end of the 6-year sentence to be deported. ■

DISCUSSING THE SELECTION

1. How old was Aliza when she was first abused? Why did she wait so long to tell her secret? Why did she publish it with her name? What is the difference to a reader when a story includes the name of the author and when the author remains anonymous?

2. In paragraph 3, who told her there was no reason to reveal her secret because no one would listen?

3. What in the story suggests that Aliza felt anger at school and at her teachers because of the way she had been taught to communicate?

4. What does she hope will be the result of her coming forward with her story?

5. In the essay on page 159, Quindlen tells the results of a situation when a teenager was sexually abused but did not obtain help from the authorities. Compare the two situations, the one described by Quindlen and the one written about by Moldofsky. What does the reader learn from these two examples?

THINKING CRITICALLY

1. Do you think that Aliza should have written about what happened to her? Do you think that by doing this, she may be able to help other children?

2. Do you think that by telling her story, Aliza will help herself? In the past few years, people who have similar family secrets have been telling their stories on television shows. If you have ever watched such programs, discuss what you think is the result of appearing on such programs for the people involved.

3. Has anyone ever told you a serious family problem such as this? What type of help would you suggest the person try to get? What steps should a person in similar trouble take?

4. Given what you know from Aliza's story, do you think that her stepfather's sentence was fair?

FOCUSING ON THE WRITING

Specific to General—Induction

Writers sometimes begin with details about their subject and then lead to a general or main idea that is stated or implied in the conclusion of the paragraph or essay. This way of organizing ideas is called *inductive reasoning*. Some writers use this method for particular paragraphs, yet their overall essay may be organized deductively: a general statement is presented and then supported with specific details.

Some words used in the inductive method of organizing ideas are *therefore, consequently, as a result, in conclusion, to sum up,* and *thus*.

1. What details does Moldofsky begin with that lead her reader to conclude she has been sexually abused? What changes would she have had to make if she had begun with the general or main idea and then provided the specific details? Which method do you prefer for this essay?

2. Moldofsky wrote her story in third person, using *she* instead of *I*. Rewrite one paragraph changing *she* to *I*. How does this change the feeling or tone of the essay? Why do you think she wrote such a personal essay in the third person?

3. What words in this essay express emotion or feeling? What do you think Moldofsky wants her readers to think about the effect of her stepfather's abuse on her life?

4. For what audience do you think Moldofsky was writing? What in the essay supports your answer?

5. What is Moldofsky's thesis statement? Where does this statement occur in the essay? Is the statement general? Does it explain Moldofsky's attitude toward her subject? Try moving this statement to another place in the essay. How does this change its effect? Where would you have placed it in the essay and why?

CREATING YOUR TEXT

1. Some people believe that schools should provide counselors to help young people deal with serious family problems such as sexual, drug, alcohol, or physical abuse. Others believe these are private problems that should be taken care of in the family itself. Write an essay in which you take a position on this issue. (Read the Quindlen essay on page 159 and the Ames story on page 167 to get more information about some results of family problems on teenagers.) Support your ideas with your own experiences, those of people you know, or people you have read about.

2. Does publicizing the details of cases such as Moldofsky's situation make a difference in preventing this kind of crime from occurring? In your essay,

state your position on this issue and explain your point of view, referring to your observations of recent events in the newspapers and on television programs.

3. Although viewers seem to enjoy watching people reveal their problems and abuses on television, some people think these kinds of problems should not be handled on television. After rereading your journal entry, write an essay in which you explain how you feel about this subject. Tell about your own experience with these programs. In your conclusion, explain why such programs should or should not continue as they are.

4. A recent law allows some states to broadcast court trials on television. Many people believe this takes away privacy and does not permit a person to obtain a fair trial. They say that in the United States, a person is presumed innocent until proven guilty. Write an essay in which you discuss whether you think trials such as the one that took place with Aliza and her stepfather should be shown on television or whether they should be private. Think about the effects on the victim, on the person who may or may not have committed the crime, and on the viewers, both adults and children. In your conclusion, make sure your reader is clear on whether or not you support having such trials broadcast on television and why.

REVISING YOUR TEXT

When you complete your first draft, review the revision questions on page 11 with a classmate. Discuss where your draft succeeds in making its points and where it can be improved. Keep these suggestions in mind as you write your second draft. Share this draft with the class.

In addition, together, go through the following activities:

Locate the thesis statement.
Decide if it presents a general statement about the subject.

Decide if it presents the writer's attitude or position about the subject in a clear way.

If it does not, rewrite the thesis statement together.

Think about the audience that will read your paper. How can you make your ideas clearer to these readers?

> **EXPLORING YOUR IDEAS**
>
> Write in your journal about a time when you tried to do the right thing even though it was hard for you. Write down as many details as you remember from the incident. What led up to it? What action did you take? What was the result of that action? What did you learn from the experience?

The Right Thing to Do at the Time

GEORGE GARRETT

Born in Florida, George Garrett currently lives in Charlottesville, Virginia. He has written many works of fiction and won the T. S. Eliot Prize for Creative Fiction and the PEN Malamud Award for Excellence in the Art of the Short Story.

This is a true story about my father, a true story with the shape of a piece of fiction. Well, why not? Where do you suppose all the shapes and forms of fiction came from in the first place? And what's the purpose of fiction anyway, whether it's carved out of the knotty hardwood of personal experience or spun out of the slick thin air like soap bubbles? "What's the purpose of the bayonet?" they used to yell when I was a soldier years ago. The correct answer was: "To kill, *to kill*, TO KILL!"

The purpose of fiction is simply to tell the truth.

My father was a small-town southern lawyer, not a writer, but he was a truth-teller. And he would tell the truth, come what may, hell or high water. And since he loved the truth and would gladly risk his life (and ours, the whole family's) for the sake of it, he would fight without stint, withholding nothing, offering no pity or quarter against what he took to be wrong—that is, against the untruth. He would go to any length he had to. And that is what this story is all about—how far one man would go to fight for the truth and against what was and is wrong.

We were living in the cow town of Kissimmee, Florida, in the early years of the Great Depression. Disney World is near there now, and it looks pretty much like everyplace else. But it was a hard, tough place then, a place where life was hard for many decent people, black and white. And it was a place where some not-so-decent people had managed to seize power and to hold power and were extremely unlikely to be dislodged from power. Among the people in power in those days were the Ku Klux Klan, not a sad little bunch of ignorant racists in bedsheets but a real clan, a native-grown kind of organized crime family.

My father and his law partner were fighting against the Klan in court and in public with the promise that they would (as they, in fact, did) represent free of charge any person at all who chose to resist the Klan and wanted a lawyer.

This exposed position led to a whole lot of trouble, believe me. And in the end it led to the demise of the Klan as a power of any kind in central Florida. But the big trouble came later. This happened early on as the lines were being drawn and the fight was just getting under way.

Sometimes in the early evening we would go together, my mother and father and the other children, into town for an ice-cream cone: a great treat in those days. One evening we piled into our old car and drove into the center of town and parked in front of the drugstore. Went inside and sat on tall swivel chairs at the counter eating our ice-cream cones. We were all sitting there in a row when a young policeman walked in. Try as I will, I can't remember his name anymore. Just that he was very young and that my mother, who was a teacher then, had taught him in high school. He greeted her politely at first. He seemed a little awkward and embarrassed.

"Mr. Garrett," he said to my father, "I'm afraid I'm going to have to give you a red ticket."

"Oh really?" my father said, still licking his ice-cream cone. "What for?"

"Well, sir, your tail lights don't work."

"They did when I came down here."

"Well, sir, they sure don't now."

"Let's have a look."

So we all trooped outside and looked at the tail lights. They didn't work, all right, because they were broken and there was shattered red glass all over the street right behind the back bumper.

"I wonder who would do a thing like that," my father said, giving the young cop a hard look.

"Well, I wouldn't know, sir," he said. "I just work for the city and I do what I'm told. And I have to write you a ticket."

"Fine," my father said. "I understand that."

Then he surprised the cop and us too by asking if he could pay for the ticket right then and there. And the cop said yes, that was his legal right, and he said it would cost five dollars.

Now that was considerable money in those days when grown men with some skills were earning eight or ten dollars a week. Nobody had any money in those days, nobody we knew or knew of. Most of my father's clients, those who could pay at all, paid him in produce and fresh eggs, things like that.

My father peeled off five one-dollar bills. The cop wrote him a receipt. Then my father told my mother to drive us on home when we had finished our ice cream. He had to go somewhere right away.

He whistled loudly and waved his arm for a taxi. One came right over from the Atlantic Coastline depot directly across the way. He kissed my mother on the cheek and said he would be back just as soon as he could. Gave her the keys to our car and hopped into the cab.

None of us heard what he told the driver: "Let's go to Tallahassee."

Tallahassee was and is the state capital, a good three hundred or so miles away by bad, narrow roads in those days.

Much later we learned what happened. They arrived very late. Slept in the cab. First thing in the morning he got himself a shave in the barbershop. Then went to the legislature. Where, exercising a constitutional right to speak on this kind of matter, he quickly established that the town charter for Kissimmee, Florida, was completely illegal and unconstitutional. In a technical, legal sense that town did not exist and never had. It would require a special action of the state legislature to give the town a new charter and a legal existence. Having made his point, he thanked the legislators kindly and left the capitol. Woke the snoring taxi driver and said, "Let's go back home."

It probably cost him a hundred dollars for that ride. Maybe more. He never told us, and nobody, not even my mother, ever dared ask him.

By the time he arrived home there was a delegation waiting to see him at our house: the mayor, the chief of police, the judge, pretty much the whole gang. Legislators had been on the phone all day to them, and they were deeply worried. Because, you see, everything they had ever done, in the absence of a valid town charter, including collecting taxes, had been illegal. You can imagine what that could mean if people got it in mind to be litigious about things.

Everybody came into our living room. And the whole family, too, because, he said, we saw the beginning of it and deserved to see the end.

Before the mayor or any of them said a word, he explained to them exactly what he had done. And he told them that, under the state constitution, establishing a town was a very tricky legal business. He said the chances were a hundred to one that they would mess it up again. He wished them good luck, promising that if they ever bothered him or us anymore, he would go to Tallahassee again and close them down for keeps.

There was a lot of silence. Finally the mayor spoke.

"What do you want from us, Garrett?"

"Ah," said my father. "I knew it would come down to that. And I'm glad it did, because there is something I do want from you all."

They were all looking and waiting. I reckon they were ready to do or pay most anything. That's how things were handled.

"Damn it!" he said. "I want my five dollars back from that phony traffic ticket."

Long pause.

"That's all?"

"That's all. You give me my five dollars back and I'll give you back your receipt."

So they paid him the five dollars and he tore the receipt in two and they filed out of our house.

"You beat them, Daddy," I said. "You won!"

"That's right, boy," he told me. "And I taught them a very important lesson."

"What's that?" my mother asked, nervously.

"If they want to stop me now," he said, "they're going to have to kill me. And I don't think they've got the guts for it."

Then he laughed out loud. And so did I, not because it was funny, but because it seemed like the right thing to do at the time. ■

DISCUSSING THE SELECTION

1. What virtue did the father in this story hold above all others?

2. What had happened to the taillights? Why did this incident occur? What position had the father taken that made him vulnerable or likely to get into trouble?

3. Why does he pay the ticket and leave Kissimmee without an argument? What does he do when he is in Tallahassee?

4. Why does the mayor listen to him and then simply ask, "What do you want from us, Garrett?"

5. Why does he prefer to pay $100 to go to Tallahassee rather than have to pay $5 in Kissimmee?

6. In the end the father says, "If they want to stop me now, they're going to have to kill me." What does he think they want to stop him from doing? Do you think they will succeed?

THINKING CRITICALLY

1. Have you ever known anyone who valued one virtue above all others? Share your recollections about that person with the class. What did you learn from that person?

2. If this story had been in Theme 1 "Connecting with the Family" in this book, what would you expect to focus on? Why does this story belong in the section of the book that deals with taking a personal action?

3. Compare the father in Garrett's story with the father in the Lipsky story on page 123. Using the specific incidents and descriptive details presented in the two stories as evidence, explain what virtue each man valued most. What lesson did each man want to teach his son? How did each man feel about standing up to someone to do the right thing? Which man's values do you admire more? Why?

FOCUSING ON THE WRITING

Tone

A writer's choice of words and way of presenting ideas suggest her or his attitude toward the subject. The three main types of tone are *informal*, *straightforward*, and *formal* or academic.

Most textbooks and some essays are academic or formal. The writer may seem detached from the information. Today, many essays and stories are written in either an informal or a straightforward tone. Within these main categories, writers also may adopt a humorous, ironic, sarcastic, light, or serious tone depending on their attitude toward the subject.

Writers can change their tone by their choice of words, the length and style of their sentences, and even the very ideas and order in which they present them.

1. Which of the preceding types of tone best describe the tone of the Garrett story? What in the story supports your choice?

2. What is the tone of the Moldofsky essay on page 281? of the Rohter article on page 262? What in these selections suggests a different tone and attitude on the part of each writer?

3. What is the thesis statement (see page 60 for more information) in this story? Where is it stated? What convinces you that this statement reveals Garrett's general attitude?

4. Garrett begins by explaining that the purpose of fiction is simply to tell the truth. In your experience as a writer, do you write about incidents that tell, as Garrett describes it, "a true story with the shape of a piece of fiction"? What does this description mean to you?

5. Do you think Garrett has any purpose for telling this story beyond telling the truth? What do you think he wants his readers to get from reading this story?

6. When you write a story, how do you decide where to fictionalize what really happened? Reread some of the stories you have written earlier this semester. What parts of the characters are real and what parts fiction? Are there any characters in your stories that are composites or combinations of several people you know described as one person? Explain how you did this when you wrote. How do you write the dialogue that people say? Do you ever remember the exact words, or do you try to get a feeling more than accuracy? Discuss these ideas with your classmates. Write about them in your journal so you will have a better understanding of your own writing process.

CREATING YOUR TEXT

1. Write the story of a person who did the right thing. In your essay, begin by explaining the background for the incident, the place, time period, people involved, and the incident itself. Then explain what the person did, including as many details as necessary to describe this incident clearly.

In your conclusion, focus on the meaning of the incident and what you learned from it.

2. "And that is what this story is all about—how far one man would go to fight for the truth and against what was and is wrong." Write an essay in which you describe an incident in which someone had to decide whether or not to tell the truth. Explain to your readers how the person decided and the action the person took. In your conclusion, focus on the factors a person should keep in mind when deciding whether to tell the truth or not.

3. Is it better to confront a bully? Or is it better to avoid the confrontation and not encourage the anger of the bully? Explain your point of view, answering these questions. Support it by describing an action you or someone you know took and the outcome of the action. What did you learn from this experience?

REVISING YOUR TEXT

Reread your first draft and focus on what you have written. Decide whether you need to add more details or delete some details that confuse the point of the story. Ask the following questions:

What do you want your reader to come away thinking about this subject?
What is your tone? How is your attitude reflected in the tone you chose for this piece of writing?

Write your second draft, keeping the preceding ideas in mind.

Share your second draft with a classmate. After your classmate has read what you have written, ask him or her to tell you the incident again and explain why the incident was important to you. Listen to the retelling of your story. If important details have been left out, you may need to re-emphasize them when you rewrite the next time. If there is confusion, clarify that part of your story. Discuss the changes you should make. Rewrite your next draft to share with the class.

ADDITIONAL PROJECT

As part of gaining a broader picture of the context in which the Garrett story was written, students can read and discuss *To Kill a Mockingbird*, by Harper Lee. The class can also view the film based on the Lee book, *The Autobiography of Miss Jane Pittman*, or view episodes of the television program "I'll Fly Away." With these experiences in mind, discuss race relations in the United States in the past and today. Discuss ways in which the class can act to improve their understanding of each other.

EXPLORING YOUR IDEAS

At the age of nine, Tisa Chang told her father that she wanted to be a Chinese "Joan of Arc" and save her people. If you could create one project that would help the people in your family, your community, or your ethnic, racial, gender, or religious group, what would it be? Write about it in your journal, and explain why you would take that particular action.

Pan Asian Repertory Theatre's Tisa Chang

FERN SIEGAL

Fern Siegal wrote this article for the March–April 1992 issue of *Ms.* magazine. Siegal describes a woman who fulfilled her dream to establish a theater that employs Asian-American actors and to produce plays that present Asian-American themes.

"When I was nine, I told my father I wanted to be the Chinese 'Joan of Arc' and save my people," remembers Tisa Chang. True to her word, she has fostered a rebellion, but her battles are fought onstage. Her weapons—commitment and integrity—are the hallmark of Pan Asian Repertory Theatre, the Manhattan company Chang founded in 1977. [1]

"I was so tired of Westerners using Asian-ness as an exotic characteristic, seeing an Asian woman either as a courtesan* or a cute little thing who puts up with a big male," Chang sighs. "I don't like stereotypes. I don't like injustice. These were seeds that shaped my resolve to direct. Whatever elements you use in theater have to coalesce into a totality." [2]

*courtesan: a prostitute.

Call it destiny. Tisa Chang, who claims to be the only female Chinese theater director in the United States, has created the most successful Asian American resident ensemble in the country. Chang founded the group 15 years ago with money she earned as an actress, parlaying* blood, sweat, and tears into a company that's showcased more than 100 playwrights, actors, directors, and designers. Her first-year budget of $8,500 has grown into an impressive $500,000.

What sustains Pan Asian? A clear goal: to present professional productions of plays that employ Asian American theater artists, and to encourage the production of new plays with contemporary Asian American themes. To date, the theater company has mounted more than 50 full productions and 18 world premieres, and toured nationally and internationally. And acclaim† has followed.

Pan Asian won a Special Theatre World Award in 1988, and one of its performers, Ernest Abuba, won the coveted‡ Obie** Award. Chang herself earned the 1991 Barnard Medal of Distinction and was presented with a Certificate of Tribute from Los Angeles for Leadership and Advocacy.

Theater, she resolutely*** believes, demands "total commitment. You give up everything. I consider myself an iconoclast.**** Pan Asian's dare was 'Look at us as we want to be seen, not as society wants to slot us.' What we didn't have in dollars we made up for in inspiration." Indeed, from its inception, Pan Asian defied convention.

"Pan Asia" encompasses the Pacific Rim, India, and the Central Asian republics. Chang's innovative theater troupe was the first to commission translation of Chinese classics, to present plays that addressed the United States internment of Japanese Americans during World War II and such intercultural projects as a bilingual version of Shakespeare's *A Midsummer Night's Dream*. Their audience is equally cross-cultural: only 50 percent Asian.

Chang takes personal pride in *Teahouse*, a 60-character play spanning 50 tumultuous years (1898–1948) of modern Chinese history. "My family was part of that history," explains Chang, the daughter of a career diplomat. "I am

---

*parlaying: betting on another race or contest with money earned from a gamble.
†acclaim: loud applause, approval.
‡coveted: envied, longed for.
**Obie Award: off-Broadway theater award.
***resolutely: determinedly.
****iconoclast: a person who goes against the traditional or respected institutions.

extremely aware of my early influences and feel a strong obligation to them. The more successful plays deal with mythic forces that duel with reality and identity. It's like having an old soul that goes back several centuries," she smiles. "I have an old soul."

And her "old soul" is incensed* by the modern subjugation of women. "There are still Chinese mail-order brides and Bangkok brothels. Isn't theater's function to inform, educate, improve?

"For example, in our staging of *Sunrise* the prostitutes aren't colorful playthings. We delve into real characters, question why a society has women in these positions. *The Dressing Room*, a surreal Japanese comedy, is a play-within-a-play—the characters are four actresses who vie for the role of Nina in *The Seagull*. Author Kunio Shimizu discusses identity and assimilation; the women are fully dimensional characters. *Cambodia Agonistes* profiles a dancer whose psychosomatic blindness results from witnessing the Pol Pot horrors."

Chang's dream flourished by combining artistic vision with sound fiscal policy. Her budget is derived from box-office earnings, government grants, and corporate gifts. Initially, every cent was plowed back into the theater company; now salaries are a top priority. Her offices are donated by the experimental theater group LaMama, and she's secured a reasonable lease from Playhouse 46, the off-Broadway venue where Pan Asian performs.

"I see myself as a crusader," says Chang. "I lead ideas into theatrical battle. My mission is to create great theater and advance the artistic maturation of my people. Sun Tzu wrote, 'To win without fighting is best.'" ∎

DISCUSSING THE SELECTION

1. What are stereotypes? What stereotypes does Chang observe in the ways that Western people view Asians, particularly in theater?

2. Chang considers herself to be an "iconoclast." What specific examples in the article support her view of herself?

*incensed: angered.

3. According to Chang, what is theater's function? Referring to the article, explain how her theater fulfills this function.

4. What was Tisa Chang's personal dream? How does her dream indicate her commitment to her people? What steps did she take to fulfill this dream? What indications do you have that she is still working to fulfill her dream?

THINKING CRITICALLY

1. Think about plays, movies, television programs, or commercials in which actors were stereotyped by their race, age, gender, or religion. What characters did they play? How were they stereotyped?

2. Tell the class about any person you know who fits the description *iconoclast*. Why does this term describe the person well? Are you an iconoclast in any way? Explain your answer.

3. Should race, gender, ethnic group, and age play a part in casting actors in plays, movies, or television programs? How can this lead to stereotyping of actors and actresses? How can it lead to racial, gender, ethnic, and age stereotypes, too? What can be done to prevent this stereotyping?

FOCUSING ON THE WRITING

1. Read the introductory paragraph to this article. Read the conclusion. How do these connect or tie together the article? What do they share in relation to the theme?

2. Why does Siegal include the quotation from Sun Tzu? What does it mean in relation to this article and to Chang's goal?

3. In paragraphs 8 and 10, Chang describes some of the original plays her theater has staged. Reread the descriptions, noticing how she presents a brief but thorough explanation so that readers who are not familiar with the plays know what they are about. What individual elements are included in the description of each play? How do these descriptions of the plays support the main idea of the Pan Asian Theatre?

CREATING YOUR TEXT

1. Reread the journal entry you wrote before reading this article. Write an essay in which you describe in detail one project you would create, based on your abilities, skills, and desires, that would help the people in your family, your community, or your ethnic, racial, gender, or religious group. In your essay, explain how you made your choice, and the steps you would have to take to fulfill your goal. In your conclusion, explain what you believe the effect of your project would be.

2. Write an essay in which you define *stereotype* (see page 163 for information on writing a definition essay). Tell a story in which stereotyping an individual led to an inaccurate understanding of the person. Explain how the situation was resolved. Tell your reader what you learned from this experience.

3. Before you write this essay, watch television during prime time for one or two nights. Make notes about the roles in which Asian-American, African-American, Latino, older, younger, physically disabled, or women actors are cast. (Focus on any one of these groups.) Write an essay in which you carefully describe what you have observed, thinking about the questions that follow and any others that occur to you as you do this project.

In what roles are the people you have chosen to focus on, cast?
Do they have power, or are they victims in the situation in which they are involved?
Are they portrayed as intelligent?

Are they portrayed as kind and loving?
Are they portrayed as violent?
Are they portrayed as serious?
Are they portrayed as fools?
Are they rich, middle income, or poor?
Are they employees or employers?

Describe in essay form what you have observed, and explain what your observation tells you about stereotyping and television. In your conclusion, take a position on whether or not you think any changes should be made in television programming in relation to stereotyping, and explain why or why not.

REVISING YOUR TEXT

Reread your draft, focusing on the revision questions on page 12. Think about whether you have provided enough examples for your reader to understand your point of view. Reread your draft thinking about the following:

What examples have you included to illustrate your point of view? Do you have enough examples? too many? If you have too many, list them in order of importance. Which one most illustrates your point of view? which one least? Looking at this list, decide which to keep and which to discard.

Have you provided enough background to convince your readers that your examples are significant?

What have you included to make your essay interesting and informative to read? What have you included in the essay to move the reader from one idea to the next?

How can your conclusion better express your main idea in an interesting and new way?

EXPLORING YOUR IDEAS

Imagine that you have the opportunity to become the "in-house conscience" or the person who makes decisions about ways for your school to become more sensitive to the needs of students. Write about the changes you would make.

Meet Du Pont's 'In-House Conscience'

JOSEPH WEBER

Joseph Weber wrote this article for *Business Week*. It is about a corporate executive who is taking a personal action to ensure better working conditions for employees and their families.

Faith A. Wohl doesn't come across as an agitator. The gracious, gray-haired Du Pont Co. executive is a 55-year-old grandmother of six (soon to be seven) whose idea of relaxation is grocery shopping and visits to the library on weekends. Wohl is also a passionate advocate of pro-family policies—and Du Pont's "in-house conscience," says Nicholas Pappas, a recently retired executive vice-president. Under her prodding, once-staid Du Pont is turning into a corporate ground-breaker that helps its employees balance family life and careers. [1]

In the past three years, the company has paid out $1.5 million to build and renovate child-care centers near its major work sites around the country. In its home base in Wilmington, Delaware, it spent $250,000 and enlisted top executives to set up Child Care Connection, a state-wide day-care referral [2] service that's used by 75 companies. Du Pont now offers a generous and pacesetting leave policy for birth, adoption, or a relative's illness—six months of unpaid time off, with full benefits, on top of six weeks' paid time off. That's twice the unpaid leave recommended by the current family-leave bills pending in Congress. In such family-friendly policies, Du Pont is clearly "one of the leaders," says Arlene A. Johnson, program director for work-force research at the Conference Board.

3   Give some of the credit to Wohl, who operates under the clunky title of "director of work force partnering." She represents one of a new breed of specialists—also known as work-family coordinators—cropping up at corporations around the country. Their job is to champion programs that address employees' personal and social concerns—issues that, if not strictly job-related, can nevertheless pose workplace problems. At Du Pont, Wohl's 19-person staff runs rape-prevention and sexual harassment programs. It also sponsors three-day workshops that teach employees how to confront their biases about race and gender.

4   Closest to Wohl's heart, however, are the company's family-oriented activities, such as job-sharing for working mothers or the new Flying Colors program. Flying Colors offers grants to day-care providers that upgrade their services beyond those that meet the minimum legal requirements.

5   Wohl herself could have benefited from some corporate-sponsored day care when she began her career with Du Pont 18 years ago. Accepting that position in public relations meant moving her family to Wilmington from Long Island, N.Y.—with no opening for Wohl's husband, Howard. He is 17 years older than Faith, and—after assessing their options—decided to be a stay-at-home dad for their three children, coolly figuring that her career had more mileage than his. It was a move that made him one of the early Daddy Trackers.

6   Wohl zipped through top assignments in public relations, including preparing the $40 billion company's annual report and working as the staff executive on Du Pont's high-profile affirmative-action committee. It was in 1989 that she was recruited to the mostly male human-resources department.

7   Although she has only been on the job three years, her programs already impress the rank and file. "I'm seeing more change every day—I think the whole mindset is different," says secretary Dorothy A. Morley. Morley should know. She worked at Du Pont from 1962 to 1973, rejoining the company in

January after hearing Wohl discuss programs for elderly care and "the new Du Pont" at a conference.

Wohl's style is to persuade rather than confront. Her feelings may be passionate, but her presentations are clinical, filled with statistics so dear to Du Pont management. At the heart of Wohl's research: surveys of company employees around the U.S. One recent scan of 8,500 Du Ponters found that 56% of the company's male employees favor flexible work hours, up from 37% five years ago (and compared with 76% of women favoring the option). Another surprising finding: 40% of Du Pont men had considered moving to another employer in order to get more job-scheduled flexibility, up from 25% three years earlier. In response, Wohl's team is already meeting with managers to design part-time and flextime schedules.

But Wohl does more than trot out survey results. To put the squeeze on middle managers who may think a suggested innovation is fine for others but not for their departments, Wohl seeks help from above and below. She musters support from Chief Executive Edgar S. Woolard Jr.—who regularly proclaims his commitment in internal newsletters and memos—and his operating-committee colleagues, partly by trumpeting Du Pont's progressive policies on network TV and in magazines. Then she regularly meets with lower-level staffers in sessions that create enormous in-house publicity for the programs.

Wohl and her staff have also set up some 50 "work-life" committees at work sites around the country, where employees can offer new programs and suggest changes to existing ones. And if midlevel managers still resist, they're very likely to get visits from her staff—or from Wohl herself. "She doesn't roll over and play dead," says Michael B. Emery, a senior vice-president who co-chairs the company's domestic Valuing People (formerly Affirmative Action) committee.

Not that Wohl's track record is perfect. She describes a heavily subsidized day-care center near one of the big Du Pont office work sites outside Wilmington that was a big bust, with parents complaining about the poor care their children got. (Du Pont has since replaced the center's staff.) And for all the company talk about equal opportunity and progressive hiring, Du Pont has only one woman vice-president, out of about 70, and eight female business directors (including Wohl) out of some 200. Among minorities, the company's record is a little better—six black vice-presidents.

But Wohl keeps the faith, constantly planning new projects—from the practical, such as buses to take employees' children from offices to summer camps, to the visionary, such as month-long summer vacations similar to those offered by French corporations. Then, there's her ultimate goal: "To someday make my own job obsolete." ■

12

DISCUSSING THE SELECTION

1. What personal information do we know about Wohl? What aspects of her background might contribute to making her more sensitive to the needs of the employees of Du Pont?

2. What specific changes has Wohl made in Du Pont Co.?

3. What is the role of the work-family coordinator in a corporation? What educational or personal background does Wohl have that makes her qualified for this job?

4. What is a "Daddy Tracker"?

5. In paragraph 11, Weber suggests that Du Pont does not perfectly meet the criteria for an equal opportunity company. What problems does he point out?

THINKING CRITICALLY

1. What is your opinion about men who stay home to take care of their families while their wives go out to work? Tell the class about a family you know or know about that lives this way. What has the effect been on the family members?

2. Should corporations offer day care to their employees even if it means a cut in other benefits or salaries for their employees?

3. Should colleges offer day care services for the children of their students? How should it be paid for?

4. Compare the way Faith Wohl agitates for change with the way Super Barrio (see page 262) agitates for change.

5. When you look for a job, do you look at the company's record on equal pay and opportunity? If you are interested in getting this information, what should you do to find it?

FOCUSING ON THE WRITING

Order of Importance

As you begin to write, you decide how to organize your ideas. One method of organization involves beginning with the most important point and ending with the least important. In this way, you get your readers' interest at the beginning. However, unless you include interesting material throughout, you can lose your readers along the way.

Another method involves beginning with the least important point and ending with the most important. Readers' interests are maintained to the end if you make an effort to add new information to connect your ideas throughout the piece of writing.

Some words used in this type of writing include *most important, equally important, least, for example, first, second, third, next, prior to, before, after, when, then, later,* and *as soon as.*

1. Does Weber begin with the most important point or the least important point? Support your answer by mentioning specific evidence from the article.

2. Compare the way Weber orders his ideas in this selection with the way Rohter (see page 262) orders his ideas in "The Poor Man's Superman: Scourge of Landlords." Support your answer by mentioning specific evidence from each article.

3. Why does Weber explain in the first sentence that Wohl "doesn't come across as an agitator"? What is he trying to establish about her personality? For what audience might Weber try to prove that Wohl is an agitator? How could he do this?

4. Weber is writing this article for *Business Week*. What does his article tell you about his audience? If you were writing this article for your college newspaper, what changes would you make? Explain your response.

5. Weber begins many paragraphs with a topic sentence and then presents supporting details to prove his point. Analyze one of the paragraphs in the essay by answering the following questions:

What is the topic sentence?
What are each of the supporting details?

CREATING YOUR TEXT

1. Wohl makes changes from inside the system, while Super Barrio makes changes from outside the system. Write an essay in which you compare these methods and decide in which situations one is more effective than the other. (See page 186 for more information about writing a comparison-and-contrast essay.)

2. Many people cannot attend college because they do not have child care for their small children. Write an essay in which you take a position as to whether colleges should or should not provide free day care services to their students. What if this means a raise in tuition for all students?

3. Write an essay in which you explain why you think that women should or should not be given paid leave to stay home with their new babies. If so, how much and why? Explain whether men should or should not be given the same benefit. Use your own experience or observations of others to explain your position.

4. "As women move into higher positions, in some cases it may make sense for women to work while their husbands stay home and take care of the children." Do you agree or disagree with this statement? Write an essay in which you take a position on this issue, referring to the article you have just read and to your own experiences or observations.

REVISING YOUR TEXT

When you have finished your first draft, share it with a classmate. Review the revision questions on page 11. Together, decide on the strong points in your essay and the places in which it needs improvement.

With your partner, discuss your method for organizing your essay:

Did you use chronological or time order?
Did you order your information from most important to least? from least important to most? from general to specific? from specific to general?
How did the information in your essay help you determine the way you were going to organize it?
What audience did you have in mind when you wrote this?
What information did you include specifically for your audience? How did this affect your choice of words?

After discussing all these questions, write your second draft. Share it with your class.

EXPLORING YOUR IDEAS

Think about your family, your culture, and your traditions. Imagine that you are going to take an action to ensure the continuing of one aspect of your culture or traditions to pass on to future generations. Write about what you would save and why. Write about what you would do to make sure the next generation learns what you already know and think is important for your people.

The Voice of the Land Is in Our Language

This selection appeared in a series of articles that described ordinary people who made a difference. As you read it, think about Joseph Nicholas and why his story was chosen for this series and for this book.

1   In 1965, Joseph Nicholas was earning a decent living in Bangor, Maine, as a barber, a trade he learned in the Navy. But something was missing and he knew it.

2   He was haunted by memories of his grandparents and their pride in being People of the Early Dawn, The Passamaquoddy Indians, who had lived in what is now Maine ("the land where the sun rises first") for at least 3,000 years.

3   Nicholas quit his job and returned to his roots on the Passamaquoddy Indian reservation at Pleasant Point in northern Maine. His mission was two-fold. First, he wanted to do everything he could to ensure that New England's last living Indian language survived. Then he wanted to help instill in the tribe's younger generation the cultural pride his grandparents had given him.

In the late 1960's, some might have questioned the wisdom of leaving a stable job to head back to the reservation. At that time, over 80 percent of the Passamaquoddies were unemployed and living in shacks with dirt floors and no plumbing. The average life expectancy was 47 years. Morale was low.

Although the Passamaquoddies fought bravely in every U.S. war since the Revolutionary War, Maine did not allow them the right to vote until 1954. English had long ago replaced the Passamaquoddy language in the reservation schools, and TV was making English the language of choice at home.

The first thing Nicholas—an unflinching optimist—did was to get the children dancing again. For the first time in 35 years, ritual dances were performed, as Nicholas taught the children the way his grandparents had taught him when he was 12.

"Since they had never thought of Indians as winners—they'd seen too many John Wayne movies—many of the children were reluctant to wear costumes," he recalls. But he encouraged them by narrating the dances in a positive manner, and they soon danced with pleasure and with pride. That was the beginning.

Now 62, Nicholas, a former tribal councilor and state representative, is more involved than ever. He and David Francis, Sr., a former blueberry picker and self-made linguist, are fighting to keep the Passamaquoddy language from slipping into extinction.

If the trend of not speaking the language continues among the young, they see it disappearing by 2035. "The voice of the land is in our language; it has to survive," Nicholas says.

To ensure that survival, Francis worked with linguists at M.I.T. [Massachusetts Institute of Technology] so that now, for the first time in history, the Passamaquoddy language can be written. The verb-based language, with no adjectives and no sexism—no differentiation is made between men and women—now has an alphabet of 27 letters. A federally funded program assures that each family gets a copy of the first Passamaquoddy dictionary.

In addition, the two tribal elders have seen to it that the reservation schools are now bilingual. Booklets and videotapes, another first, tell the story of the Passamaquoddy culture. A year ago, Nicholas founded the tribe's first museum.

Thanks to the efforts of Joseph Nicholas and David Francis, the children of the People of the Early Dawn can now write as well as say, "Nkihcitomitahatomon wetapeksi." (I am proud of my roots.) ■

DISCUSSING THE SELECTION

1. What changes did Joseph Nicholas make in his life?

2. What specific elements of his culture has Joseph Nicholas tried to save for future generations?

3. Make a list of the steps Nicholas took to fulfill his goal. Which steps are similar to those you have read about in any other selections you have read in this book so far?

4. In the selection, it is written that Nicholas's mission or goal is twofold. What are the two goals? What is the main difference between them?

THINKING CRITICALLY

1. Nicholas is described as "an unflinching optimist." In general, are you an optimist or a pessimist? What is an example of something that happened in your life that shows you are an optimist or a pessimist?

2. Nicholas has a strong purpose in his life. What mission or purpose do you have in your life today? Tell the class about a person you know who has a strong purpose in life. What is the person doing to accomplish that purpose?

3. Nicholas took an action that changed his entire life's direction. What one step have you taken that has changed your life the most? Explain your answer.

4. Reread the Ríos essay on page 231 focusing on the way the children in his essay feel about being Native American. How do you think Nicholas would feel about their attitude? How do you think he would try to change it?

FOCUSING ON THE WRITING

Analyzing

Writing is a useful way to analyze or deeply understand a process, an object, a person, or an event. To analyze, writers break their subject down into its parts and subparts and determine the essential features. The analysis includes a critical discussion of what these parts mean, how they compare to others, and how and why they relate. In addition to examining the essential parts, in some cases, writers also examine the way in which their subject fits into the larger picture.

Some words used for analyzing are *to clarify, in other words, for instance, similarly,* and *as a result.*

1. Nicholas analyzes the Passamaquoddy language. What essential parts or features are mentioned in the article? Knowing about the structure of a language can sometimes tell you about its people. What does the information about the language tell you about the Passamaquoddy people?

2. In the selection, a few words from Native American or Indian languages are defined. Which words are these and what are the definitions? Why do you think these Native American words were included in this article? In the Cisneros essay (see page 34) and in the Ríos essay (see page 231), the authors also used non-English words. Are there any other selections in this book in which this occurred? Why did the authors of those articles include these words and phrases? How did the writers help their reader understand their meaning?

3. Writers make careful choices when they write, especially if they want to influence their reader's point of view. In this selection, the author includes some history of the Passamaquoddy people. Reread the selection, and write down any historical facts you discover about them. What is the purpose for including the historical information about the Passamaquoddy people? What do you think the author wanted the reader to think about these people after reading this selection?

4. When we write, we use different tenses (past, present, and future) to express changes in time. Notice the different tenses in this selection. Find the places in this article in which the tense changes. Where do these changes occur? Why does the tense change in these places?

5. Paragraph 4 ends: "Morale was low." Make a list of the supporting details in this paragraph that lead to this conclusion.

6. The events in this article are arranged in time or chronological order (see page 206 for more information on chronological order). List all the words and phrases in this selection that indicate time and order. Where are these located, and what ideas do they connect in the selection?

CREATING YOUR TEXT

1. Write an essay in which you describe either "an unflinching optimist" or "a downhearted pessimist." Think about the way in which the person moves, talks, and acts. In your conclusion, analyze the characteristics of either of these types of people.

2. Nicholas is trying to save the dances of his people. Write an essay in which you describe one group activity—such as the singing in your religion, dance styles, special foods, or holiday celebrations. Explain why you think this activity tells something about your culture or group that is important for the next generation to know about.

3. Most linguists, people who study language, notice a difference between informal and formal language. They observe that the way people speak with their friends and family on the streets or at home differs from the way they speak at school or at their jobs. (Look at the Tan essay on page 53 for her views on formal and informal language.) Write an essay in which you compare the two types of language, focusing on what you have observed as you have watched and listened to people talking. Be specific and focus on two or three examples of each at most, so you will have time to explain the differences in the way people express the same ideas in formal and in informal language. Analyze why these differences exist and why people communicate differently in different circumstances.

4. Imagine that you receive a grant to open a museum in your neighborhood. In detail, describe the museum you would create. Tell your reader about the building you would choose, how you would fix it up, what you would see when you opened the front door, and what would be in each room. What type of special programs would you design for your neighbors? (This essay can be broken into a group of essays, with individual students describing particular rooms or special programs in the museum, for example. The students doing this should present their essays as a group project to the entire class.)

REVISING YOUR TEXT

When you finish your first draft, read the revision questions on page 12, going over your paper on your own. Once you have done so, discuss your essay with a classmate focusing on the following questions:

In what order are the ideas presented? Why are they ordered in a particular way?

What particular words and phrases connect the ideas from paragraph to paragraph? Is there any place in the draft in which the ideas do not connect?

If the writer analyzes a process, idea, or situation, where in the draft is the idea being analyzed (broken down into smaller parts)? What are the essential features, according to the writer? How do these relate to each other? What words signal that comparisons and/or contrasts are being made?

Do you have a better understanding of a process, idea, or situation after reading this essay? If you are unsure about this, what would improve the essay?

As part of deciding on which changes you should make to improve your second draft, think about the audience or readers for whom you wrote this essay. What words did you use, and in what order did you present your ideas?

Write your second draft to share with your whole class.

Expanding Your Ideas

EXPANDING YOUR IDEAS

Collaborative Writing Project

1. In small groups of four or five students, decide on a problem you would like to understand better. For example, why does it take so long to register at this college? Why is there so much crime in this neighborhood? Why is it hard to get food after midnight near the college? Why is there no child care for students' children on campus? Why do certain majors make it difficult for college graduates to obtain a job after graduation? Why do so few men major in nursing? Why do so few women take advanced math courses? These are only suggestions. Use your own situation to come up with problems that are relevant for you. You can choose a large problem or one that has a narrow focus that affects only you or the students in your class or college. Together, write a statement defining your problem.

2. Decide on roles for your group members that match up with their particular expertise. Someone may be good at using the library and finding out which are the best sources of information. Certain students may enjoy doing research. Others may enjoy summarizing large documents into smaller, more accessible pieces of writing. Someone else may be good at making phone calls. Other students may be good interviewers. Some students may be proficient with computer word processing. Talk with the members of the group to find out what roles people feel most comfortable handling on this project. Everyone must do something, and everyone must cooperate in order to complete the project.

3. The first step in the project involves gathering data about your problem. This may entail trips to the library, the college administration offices, local municipal offices, and so on. It may involve contacting people and conducting interviews over the phone or in person. The second step is to integrate the data into a form that can be shared among all group members. The next step is to order the information from most to least important. The final step is to decide on solutions to your problem that can be presented to the class as a whole.

4. Finally, each group presents the results to the class, with different people taking responsibility for presenting various parts of the project. The presentations should include a statement of the problem, the steps the group took to gather information, the relevant information found by the group, an analysis of the reasons for the problem, and a group suggestion for improving the situation described.

Becoming part of a group is a way of working with others to make change. Together, individuals affect society and find purpose in their own lives as well.

Theme **6**

Reaching out to the Community

Readings

"Coat for the Homeless Is Shelter, Too"
BY MICHAEL DECOURCY HINDS

"Two Institutions Solve Common Problem"
A description of a collaborative project

"Cinderellas in Toe Shoes"
BY DAVID GROGAN AND JANE SUGDEN

"Learning the Art of Bringing Up Baby"
BY SALLY JOHNSON

"The Value of Volunteering"
BY CHARLES A. LARSON

"Merit Gets Them Nowhere"
BY ALBERT SHANKER

"The Hiroshima Maiden"
BY MARILYN KRYSL

In "Coat for the Homeless Is Shelter, Too," Michael deCourcy Hinds describes what develops when a class of students and their teacher try to make a small but potentially lifesaving change in the lives of homeless people.

"Two Institutions Solve Common Problem" describes the way a nursing home and an animal shelter created a program that improves the lives of all concerned.

David Grogan and Jane Sugden collaborated on an article, "Cinderellas in Toe Shoes," which tells about a grant-funded program that provides free ballet lessons to children living in homeless shelters.

Helping children is also the goal of the program described by Sally Johnson in "Learning the Art of Bringing Up Baby." This parent-child program works to break the cycle of abuse.

Charles A. Larson, in his essay "The Value of Volunteering," describes his experience as a Peace Corps worker and advocates volunteering as a way to grow as a person and at the same time to connect with others.

In "Merit Gets Them Nowhere," Albert Shanker—the head of the huge American Federation of Teachers—describes his concern about the lack of equality for women in the workplace.

"The Hiroshima Maiden," by Marilyn Krysl, is a story about the effect of war on one Japanese girl who seeks medical assistance in the United States, the country that caused her injury.

Making Discoveries

In Your Journal

Write in your journal about a situation in which you did something through your school, religious group, club, or other organization to help a needy person or group. Describe what this experience was like for you. Think about whether you prefer to act alone or in a group, and why.

With a Classmate

Talk to your classmate about the experience you have written about in your journal. Explain why you chose this experience. Discuss what your individual experiences have in common. Discuss whether you prefer to act alone or in a group, and why.

With Your Class

Discuss some of the experiences you have selected. What do the experiences have in common? Discuss how people felt during these experiences. Why do some people in your class prefer to act alone, and others as part of a group or organization?

EXPLORING YOUR IDEAS

This article tells about a class project in which students select a group of people with special needs and design a piece of clothing or other object that will be useful for them. The school then gets the item manufactured. Write in your journal about the group of people with special needs that you would like to help. Explain what piece of clothing or other item you would like to design to make their lives easier. What ability do you have that would make you an asset on this project?

Coat for the Homeless Is Shelter, Too

MICHAEL DECOURCY HINDS

Michael deCourcy Hinds, who was born in Boston, Massachusetts, and now lives in Brooklyn, New York, is a staff writer for *The New York Times*. With his wife, Susan Lapinski, he wrote *In a Family*, a joint diary of pregnancy and the birth of their first child. His article dealing with a unique approach to helping the homeless appeared in the "Philadelphia Journal" of *The New York Times* on March 2, 1992.

An apparel professor whose students have produced stuffed caterpillars for children with cerebral palsy and cloth blocks with Braille characters for blind toddlers has come up with an elegant robe that would move well on a runway with pieces designed by Giorgio Armani or Issey Miyake. But the latest project was designed for the homeless and can double as a sleeping bag.

In this project, form is secondary to function, said the professor, David L. Wilson, who is director of fashion and apparel programs at the Philadelphia

College of Textiles and Science, a four-year independent college. "We wanted to provide moveable shelters for the hard-core homeless who don't have a place to go in severe weather," he said.

Interest in the effort to cloak the thousands of people who sleep on Philadelphia's streets has spread. Scores of volunteers have joined the manufacturing effort, textile companies donate fabric, and the college has fielded dozens of inquiries from groups as far away as Alaska about producing the coats, known as Shelter-Paks.

"It makes you feel good," said Mitzi Miraflor, one of the students. Matthew Mehrman, an assistant professor of textiles who is coordinating the project, vows, "We are going to keep making Shelter-Paks until the problem of the homeless is resolved."

Shelter-Pak is, as Professor Mehrman says, an "engineered garment" for people with very special needs. The coat was designed to have simple lines and somber colors to serve as a kind of urban camouflage for the homeless, who often say they avoid harassment by being inconspicuous.

The hooded, full-length coat is designed to be as warm as a sleeping bag, but unlike a sleeping bag it has no zippers or Velcro snaps that would restrain a person under attack. It has no buttons to pop, only a belt to tie. The pockets are deep, one as deep as a duffel bag.

In warm weather, the coat can be folded inside the large pocket, carried as a backpack or used as a pillow. It weighs slightly more than five pounds and is reversible, with one side made of wool and the other of a waterproof nylon. It comes in two sizes, several colors, including black, purple, blue, and tan, and is unisex. It is made of about $50 worth of material.

Each semester, Professor Wilson's students select a group of people with special needs, do research on the kind of clothing they require, meet with some of the people they are trying to help to discuss the project, design a prototype and manufacture it.

Over the last three years, in addition to the stuffed animals and Braille blocks, the class has produced loose-fitting overalls for burn victims, smock-style dresses for battered women, and uniforms for an inner-city baseball team and its cheerleaders.

The projects began in the fall of 1990 as a student design competition to mix design with social awareness.

Shelter-Pak quickly grew beyond a competition, as the best ideas of the entries from about 60 students were combined. There have been so many refinements in design and manufacturing that only Professor Mehrman knows how to cut out the complicated patterns. So far, only 80 Shelter-Paks have been distributed. The pace of production is expected to pick up this summer, when he completes sewing instructions and develops a computer program to generate paper patterns.

The demand for Shelter-Paks on the street is overwhelming, said Brother Bill McDonald, who has distributed most of the coats. He is a member of The Servants of the Poor, a Roman Catholic order that ministers to the homeless and operates a shelter that houses 13 men. "Everyone wants the coat," he said. "I can use it to barter for good behavior because people will do anything for it."

Jesse D. Evans, a resident of the shelter, was wearing his Shelter-Pak when he accompanied Brother Bill on a recent visit to the College of Textiles. He is 30 years old and said he became homeless early last year when as a result of being shot he developed problems with his health and with drugs and alcohol.

Mr. Evans said he lived in his Shelter-Pak on City Hall Plaza over the winter. "It saved my life," he said. "And it kept me above water, as far as fashion goes."

Professor Mehrman said that when the patterns and instruction kits were completed, he would provide them free to anyone who sends a written request to Shelter-Pak, c/o Philadelphia College of Textiles and Science, 42101 Henry Avenue, Philadelphia, PA 19144. ∎

DISCUSSING THE SELECTION

1. What are some of the functions of the Shelter-Pak?
2. In paragraph 2, the professor says that in this project "form is secondary to function." What does this mean? In most clothing design, which is more important, form or function? Explain your answer. Give an example of an

item of clothing in which form is more important and one in which function is more important.

3. List the problems of the homeless that the designers took into account as they designed the Shelter-Pak. What did they include in their design to deal with these problems?

4. What does the term "urban camouflage" mean? How can a piece of clothing meet this requirement?

THINKING CRITICALLY

1. What experience do you have with the homeless in your community? What do you do when you see a homeless person in need? Why are the homeless subject to harassment in our society?

2. What other problems should the designers on this project have dealt with or thought about as they worked on the Shelter-Pak? What adjustments should they make in the design to respond to the problems you have uncovered?

3. Why do you think so many outside volunteers have gotten involved in this project?

4. Reread the descriptions of other projects designed by the students in this college. Given social needs you have observed, what other projects should the students work on?

5. Do you think that political groups who are fighting for rights for the homeless would support this project or oppose it? Explain your answer.

6. Would you take a course in your college that involved work on a project that would benefit some group? Does your school offer such a course? What could you do to create such a course?

FOCUSING ON THE WRITING

Describing an Object

When you write about an object, think about the following questions:

What does it look like? What shape is it? What size is it? What color is it? What does it feel like to the touch? Does it resemble any other common object? Make sure to include enough details so the reader(s) can almost see it.

Why should your readers know about this object? Why is it important to you?

1. What details did Hinds include to describe the Shelter-Pak? Are there any other details you would have liked him to include?

2. Reread the Hinds article, focusing on his method of organization. List the ideas that are presented in this article. Decide if the most important ideas come first or last. (See page 307 for more information about this.)

3. What ideas not included in this article would you like to know more about?

4. Reread the quotations in the article, thinking about why the author included them. Explain the purpose of those quotations.

CREATING YOUR TEXT

1. Reread the journal entry you wrote before reading this article, and then reread the article itself. Think about your class discussions. Imagine you

have entered a competition, such as described in the article, that involves your designing an item to help a needy group. Write an essay in which you describe in detail the type of object you would like to design. What problems must you stay aware of as you create your design? Describe your design and the materials that you would need to develop a sample or prototype. What do you think would be the result of your project? The goal of your essay is to convince a reader that your project is a valuable one.

2. What steps should our society take to help the homeless? Write an essay in which you describe a plan to make changes that would help the homeless lead more productive and safer lives.

3. Write an essay in which you choose the *five* most important inventions of the past fifty years. Describe the inventions you chose, and explain why these have made a difference in your life and/or our society today.

4. In our lives, we all have seen homeless or needy people. Each time, we have to decide whether or not to help them. Write an essay in which you explain how you decide whom to help and whom to ignore. Include a story describing an experience that you or someone you know had with a homeless or needy person. What did you learn from this experience?

REVISING YOUR TEXT

Discuss your first draft with a classmate, reviewing the revision questions on pages 11 and 13. In addition, talk about the following questions:

Why did you choose to write about this subject? How does your feeling come across to your reader(s)?

What specific details does the reader remember from this essay? Why did these remain with the reader? What did the writer do that made them stand out for the reader?

From the beginning of the essay, is it clear to the reader what the essay is about and what the writer's feelings about the subject are? If not, how could these aspects be made clearer?

Is the conclusion powerful and to the point? If not, how could it be improved?

Together, decide which parts of the draft are the strongest and which need to be improved. Think about the method you have used to organize your essay. Think about the tone you have taken to present your ideas. Write your second draft, keeping your discussion and the suggestions made in mind. Share this draft with your class.

EXPLORING YOUR IDEAS

This article involves a nursing home and an animal shelter. In your journal, write your reflections or thoughts on either a nursing home or an animal shelter. What do you know about these institutions and the role they play in our society?

Two Institutions Solve Common Problem

This article appeared in *The New York Times* on February 11, 1992. It deals with a unique solution to the loneliness felt by people living in a nursing home and that felt by animals living in a shelter.

Agnes is 96 years old. She lives in Room 109 of a Westchester County nursing home. Most days Agnes sits quietly in her wheelchair. She reads. She snoozes. She stares. She walks.

Then comes Tuesday. Agnes is up. She dresses. She eats. She's alert. She's ready.

"Oh, my," she says right after lunch, "here comes Mattie! Here she is. Hello, Mattie. Hi, Mattie. You came. How are you today?"

Mattie is a dog, another institutional lost soul of sorts. She's a stray, collected in Ossining by Westchester's Society for the Prevention of Cruelty to Animals four years ago. For years Mattie waited in her quarters for someone to take her home, or at least to visit. No one did.

Then, in 1990, the society started a special program. It's called Animal Therapy. Every week four dozen volunteers take dogs into 32 county nursing homes. Mattie goes every day. The shelter believes that humans' mental and physical health often improves when they interact with animals.

Americans know this intuitively. Today their households contain millions more pets than children. Now the anecdotal and scientific evidence mounts, showing that association with animals offers benefits from reduced hypertension and loneliness to increased optimism and survival rates from heart disease.

Like a growing number of the country's animal shelters and nursing homes, Westchester's saw the benefits. The visits give patients an eagerly anticipated living link to the outside world. The pets make great conversation catalysts, providing furry, panting reasons to reminisce about pets or family. Nursing home staffs report increased chatter and liveliness among patients long after the visits.

Agnes and other residents track the days by Mattie's visits. Some intimate links also develop between volunteers and patients. Not counting a healthy dose of treats, the animal also benefits from the friendships, the touching and the change of pace from its institutional life. The dog becomes more sociable and thus easier to place permanently, especially during these winter months when adoptions are fewest.

"We can't find anything wrong with animal visits," says Mimi Einstein, society president and a regular volunteer. "Except maybe we'll soon lose Mattie to a permanent home."

Now, of course, everyone knows that pets don't think like people. It's sentimental hogwash to attribute human characteristics to coincidental animal behavior. How could a stupid dog know what a bunch of humans in long rows of wheelchairs are saying as she trots regally down the nursing home hallways?

"Oh, look, everyone. Here comes Mattie! Hi, Mattie."

"Hi, Mattie."

"Hi, Mattie."

"C'mere, Mattie."

Mattie got her name from the condition of her all-black coat when found. She is always shiny-clean and soft now, thanks to Lori Lewis, a dog groomer who donates her time and hair dryer. Mattie seems to nod right and left as her subjects offer greetings. Any outstretched hand draws a pause, often a lick, in exchange for pats. "Aren't you a good girl? Yes, you are. Oh, thank you. I love you, too."

It's probably just coincidence that Mattie makes a right turn, two lefts, and another right to position herself by Agnes's drawer, which happens to contain cookies saved from recent dinners. Agnes thinks Mattie remembers. Mattie puts her head on Agnes's thigh. Her golden eyes seem to plead. She nudges Agnes's hand. The woman interprets this as a request to resume patting. "We used to have a dog," Agnes says. "A house isn't a home without a dog." And she starts reminiscing. Mattie and Ms. Einstein listen intently.

Everywhere, Mattie's presence sparks conversations. Later in her round, Mattie trots into Room 321. "Oh, you're late," says Marian. "I have a surprise for you." She opens a tin box. Out come chocolate-chip cookies, Mattie's favorite, as it happens. Mattie, who does not seem at all surprised, crunches them gently while Ms. Einstein and Marian chat.

When Marian is a little slow handing out cookie No. 3, Mattie places a paw on the woman's knee. Marian laughs for the first time all week. When Mattie leaves, Marian watches all the way down the hall.

Then comes Mattie's last stop before returning to her cage at the shelter. It's Pearl's room. But Pearl is not well. Her tearful daughter says the 92-year-old woman stopped eating more than a week ago when her son died. Pearl lies there, eyes open, but never moving. "She just wants to go," her daughter says.

Mattie places her chin on the sheet. No response. She puts her front paws on the bedrail. She stands up and leans over the mattress. Slowly, Pearl's head turns. A spotted hand moves. She caresses the dog's floppy ears. Mattie licks the bony fingers. Pearl smiles.

Probably just a coincidence. ■

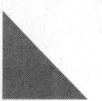

DISCUSSING THE SELECTION

1. What evidence is presented in the article that a relationship develops between the residents of the nursing home and the animals that come to visit them?

2. In paragraph 6, a difference is made between "anecdotal and scientific evidence." Decide which of the following is anecdotal or opinion and

which is scientific or factual (see the Klass article on page 174 for more information about these categories):

   a. Agnes smiles when Mattie comes into her room. She is alert and eats better at lunch time. The dog's visit makes a difference to her.
   b. Agnes's blood pressure goes from 180/90 to 140/75 after the visit from Mattie. The dog's visit seems to make a difference to her.
   c. People who receive visits from the dogs live an average of three years longer than people who do not visit with the dogs. The dogs' visits seem to make a difference.

   Based on your choices, what is the difference between scientific and anecdotal evidence?

3. What role do volunteers play in the Animal Therapy program?

4. How does Pearl's response to the dog support the idea that having dogs in the nursing home is good for the residents?

THINKING CRITICALLY

1. If you have ever had a special relationship with a dog or other animal, describe to the class the animal and your relationship.

2. Why do you think some of the people described in this article relate better to animals than to people?

3. Do you think that young people can learn something by visiting a nursing home? Discuss what patients and visitors can gain from this experience.

4. Do you approve of the way older people are treated in the United States? If you could improve any aspect of the lives of older people in this country, what would you change? Why? How would you go about making this change?

5. Why are there so many stray animals in the United States? Why are there

so many animal shelters in this country as well? What could people do to make sure that animals are better treated in our society?

FOCUSING ON THE WRITING

Sentence Variety

It is important to vary the length and design of your sentences. If a writer uses all short, choppy sentences or all long, complex sentences, the writing can become boring and predictable. Good writers use a combination of short, medium, and long sentences.

Some sentences may be simple. Some may be compound, using such words as *and, or, for, but, so, nor,* or *yet.* Others may be complex, using such words as *although, even though, because, since, if, when, after,* or *before.*

Try to vary your sentences to make your writing interesting and unpredictable.

1. Notice the number of short sentences in the beginning of this selection. What other types of sentences do you find? Is there enough variety in this article for you as a reader?

2. Review another article you have read in this book, and notice the types of sentences used in that selection. Review one of your own essays, noticing the variety in your own sentence structure.

3. What difference do you find in the writing in paragraphs 1 to 3 and in the rest of the article? What seems to be the purpose of the introductory paragraphs?

4. In paragraph 10, the terms "sentimental hogwash" and "stupid" are used.

What is sarcasm? How is it used in this paragraph? What is the purpose? Is it used in any other part of the article?

5. In the article, the speakers of the dialogue are not identified. How do you as a reader know who is speaking? What indicates this to you?

CREATING YOUR TEXT

1. Write an essay describing a relationship you have or had with a dog or other animal that made a difference in your life. Describe the animal in your essay. Include an anecdote or story that illustrates your relationship. In the conclusion, explain what you gained from this relationship.

2. Write an essay in which you describe a person who relates better to animals than to people. Describe the person, and explain the circumstances of the person's life that explain his or her feelings. What is your relationship to the person? What have you learned from observing the person's relationship with animals?

3. Write an essay in which you describe a nursing home or an animal shelter. Explain your reason for being there and the way you feel about it looking back in retrospect. What did you learn from your experience in either of these institutions? What would you change about them to make them more humane and caring?

4. Imagine that you are writing a brochure describing the qualities needed for a volunteer in either a nursing home or an animal shelter. Choose one of these institutions, and write an essay describing the kind of person who would fit in well and be an effective volunteer. What characteristics are important? What knowledge should the person have? What experience would you prefer? What training would you offer? In your conclusion, emphasize the one characteristic you think is more important than any other for the person to become a successful volunteer.

REVISING YOUR TEXT

Read your first draft with your classmate, discussing the strengths of the writing. Turn to the revision questions on pages 11 and 13, and reread the essay, looking for ways to make your writing clearer and better able to communicate your ideas.

Notice the types of sentences you used in your writing. Was there enough variety? How did you order your ideas? For what audience did you direct your writing? What changes can you make in any of these aspects to make your writing more effective?

After thinking about these questions, write your second draft and share it with your class.

EXPLORING YOUR IDEAS

Dance and music are powerful means of expression for most people. Think about what dance means to you in your life. Write in your journal about your experiences dancing at home, by yourself, with another, with a group, or in front of others. You may even write about how you feel when you watch other people dance.

Cinderellas in Toe Shoes

DAVID GROGAN AND JANE SUGDEN

David Grogan and Jane Sugden's article, which appeared in the July 15, 1991, issue of *People* magazine, concerns a special project begun by ballet dancer Diana Byer to help children learn to dance.

Gunshots often ring outside the Convent Avenue Family Living Center, a homeless shelter in New York City's Harlem where Shara Overton, 8, lives with her mom and four of her five siblings. A ruffled pink tutu hangs from Shara's bunk bed, and a *Nutcracker* ballet poster hangs on the wall. "I want to be a dancer so I can help my family out," says Shara, lying on the bed and drawing in a ballet coloring book. "I want to be just like Diana when I grow up."

Shara is not talking about the Princess of Wales. Nor is she just daydreaming. She is talking about her teacher, Diana Byer, who is giving Shara and four other children she found at the shelter free ballet lessons. As artistic director of the New York Theatre Ballet, a well-regarded, 10-member troupe that tours such towns as Durango, Colo., and Harrisburg, Pa., to "bring ballet to people who would not ordinarily have a chance to see it," Byer, 44, has a full-time job just keeping her company afloat. She acts as her own fund-raiser, secretary, and janitor, and she even operates the elevator to her fifth-floor studio in mid-Manhattan. But Byer felt something was missing. "In the back of my mind, I kept thinking, I need to do something in society," Byer says. "Here I am in this ballet studio morning, noon and night. How could I do something that might affect somebody in a positive way?"

When a colleague told her about city programs for homeless children, inspiration struck. In December 1989 Byer gave five days of dance instruction to children from a homeless shelter in Chinatown. Last year, bolstered by $14,000 in city and corporate aid, she offered a 10-week course to 30 kids, ages 7 to 11, from Shara Overton's Harlem shelter. When the money ran out, Byer couldn't bear to bow out. "It was breaking my heart," she says. So she has continued to give free lessons to five of the most promising children—Shara, plus three other girls and a boy. Often she has dipped into her own pocket for subway fare and leotards. "These kids really touch you," she says. "I want to fix everything in their lives, but I can't. What I can do is let them know that someone cares about them."

The message sinks in slowly. "Most of these children are afraid," says Byer. "But the first day they came through the door, I hugged each individual child. When I talk to them, I get down to their level. I hold their faces in my hands and speak very gently." She doesn't coddle them, however. The shelter students are held to the same standards as Byer's 60 paying pupils. "You are good dancers, but you make bad circles," she told her charges as she organized them for an arm exercise during a recent class. "I show them respect and they show me respect, or they are out of the class," she says. "We're not twinkle toes. I hope some of the children will go on to be professional dancers. But what matters is that they give their all."

Byer certainly does: 90-hour weeks, no vacations, a no-frills life. She grew up in Trenton, the daughter of a salesman and a homemaker. "When I was a kid, there was a lady who was drunk and fell in the snow," she recalls. "I brought her home to my mother because I felt badly for her. I've always done what I felt." Dance was her first love. "I can't remember ever wanting to do anything else with my life," she says. After launching her professional career in 1964, at age 18, following a year at Juilliard, she lived for years like a gypsy, performing with various dance companies. Then in 1977 she founded the New York Theatre Ballet and its accompanying school. Like many dancers, Byer has pursued her muse at the expense of a family life. Her marriage to Ken Ferris, a movie cameraman, ended after seven years, in the mid '80s. "It was very difficult with his job and my job," she says. She has no children, but she has been like a second mother to many of her homeless students. On three occasions she has taken them to see major ballet companies at Lincoln Center. Recently she bought Shara the book *Black Dance in America*. "I like to read a lot more since I came to Diana's classes," Shara says.

Byers considers Shara and Courtney Williams, 9, another girl she found at the shelter, two of her most promising pupils. "Shara has a wonderful body for dance and powers of concentration that are rare in a child her age," Byer says. "And Courtney is a beautiful jumper who can hover in the air a moment."

The girls appeared in her company's rendition of *The Nutcracker* in December 1990 in New York City, but if either of them forges a career in ballet, Byer says, "it would be a miracle. Dancing is a hard profession, and they have so many strikes against them. But I hope this will make a difference in their lives. It's gaining self-esteem," she says. "That's what's important." ■

DISCUSSING THE SELECTION

1. How does Shara's explanation of why she wants to dance show her feeling of responsibility? What do we learn about this child from reading this article that explains why she might feel such a responsibility at such a young age?

2. In paragraph 4, Byer states that "most of these children are afraid." What in the article supports the fact that the children have reason to be afraid at first?

3. How did Byer become involved in teaching homeless children to dance? What do you think she has gained from this experience?

4. What specific information is provided in the article that tells the reader that Byer is responsible and hard-working?

5. What characterizes her relationship with the children in this project? What details in the article helped you answer this question?

THINKING CRITICALLY

1. What difference do you think the dance lessons will make in the lives of the children involved? Will there be a long-term difference? What do people gain from being involved in projects such as this? Explain your answer, describing your own experience or that of people you know.

2. What ability do you have that you could teach to others? Have you ever taught anyone what you know? How do you think you would feel as a teacher?

3. Do you know anyone who has a career in the arts—dance, music, writing, painting, and so on? What specific steps did that person take to become a professional in his or her field?

FOCUSING ON THE WRITING

Describing an Event

When you describe an event in your writing, think about the following questions before you begin:

Where did it take place? Describe the place in detail.
What was your role in the event? Why were you there? Where were you sitting? Whom were you with?
What happened? Focus on one of the following types of ordering of your ideas—chronological order or telling the event in time order, moving from the most important action to the least important action, or moving from the least important action to the most important one.

> Try rewriting and organizing the event in different ways until you decide on the one that tells your story the best.
>
> What one moment stands out in your mind? Make sure your readers know about this moment and why it was important to you.

1. What event from this article stands out in your mind? How did the writers organize the telling of the event? What would you like to know about it that is not contained in this article?

2. To whom and to what does the title of the article refer? Reread the article, and decide on whom the article actually focuses. What specific information in the article helped you make your decision? Given your answer, is the title misleading or appropriate?

3. This article first appeared in *People* magazine. If you have ever read this magazine, who do you think the reading audience is? What about this article supports your answer?

4. Is there anything about Byers, her project, or the children that you wanted to know more about but was not included in the article? Why do you think the authors did not include this information? How could they have obtained this information?

CREATING YOUR TEXT

1. For five minutes, write about your experiences with any of the following art forms—dance, music, writing, acting, painting, sculpting, or photography. Focus on one of these that is meaningful to you.

2. Reread your journal entry about dance and the writing you did earlier in class about the arts. Write an essay in which you describe the importance of art in your life. Focus on one art form (music, dance, painting, sculpting,

acting, and so on). In your essay, tell about one incident or event that illustrates your feelings about this art form. Give enough details so your readers can understand why this art form is meaningful to you. What have you learned about yourself through art?

3. Write an essay in which you describe an experience of watching live performers dance, sing, act, or play music. The event may have taken place in a theater, in a church, at a party, or on the street. Describe the people and the art form in which they were involved. Compare the differences in observing a live performance and in watching people perform on television or in the movies. Which do you prefer and why?

4. Write an essay about a performer whose work you admire. You may write about an actor or actress, a singer, a dancer, or a circus performer. Describe the performer and the work he or she does, and explain why you admire the person and the work.

REVISING YOUR TEXT

Share your draft with another student in the class. Read the essay, making sure that your reader understands why you have chosen this art form and what it means to you. Review the revision questions on page 11 to help you identify your strong points and the places where you need to improve in communicating ideas.

Review your telling of an event in your draft. What details did you include? Did you make it clear to your readers why this event was important to you? What readers or audience did you have in mind as you wrote this draft? What changes do you need to make so your draft is clearer and more effective in making the points that are important to you? Once you have decided on any changes you will make, write your second draft to share with the class.

EXPLORING YOUR IDEAS

Write in your journal about an experience you had caring for a baby. Choose one specific incident in which you learned something about child care or about yourself, and write about it in your journal. Why does this incident stand out in your mind?

Learning the Art of Bringing Up Baby

SALLY JOHNSON

Sally Johnson's article, which appeared in *The New York Times* (April 3, 1988), describes a program that is helping some people become better parents.

1   Twenty-three-year-old Pam Thomas is the mother of three children, 5 years old, 4 years old, and 4 months old. Her fiancé is in counseling to learn to control his anger. Pam, her fiancé, and the children share a trailer with her father-in-law, who suffers from cirrhosis of the liver.

2   But Ms. Thomas's life has changed in the 18 months since she joined the parent-training program at the Addison County Parent-Child Center. She and her fiancé plan to try joint counseling. She is hoping to get a job as a florist. Perhaps most important, she feels better about herself.

3   "I used to be quiet, but now I speak up when I don't like something," said Ms. Thomas. "I used to holler at the kids a lot and scold them. Now they help me more. I've got my hopes up now."

4   The program that got her hopes up offers parents, particularly teen-age

parents, the opportunity to see how children ought to be reared. Both Federal and state reports have credited the center with everything from lowering the rate of teen-age pregnancy in the county to getting mothers off welfare.

Last month the Department of Education awarded the center an $80,000 grant to write training manuals that will enable others to develop similar programs throughout the country.

The center, which has a staff of 19, enrolls 12 trainees for each six-month program and pays them $1 an hour, plus bonuses for attendance and job performance. They spend three days a week at the center. The days begin with small "homeroom" group meetings in which everyone is encouraged to talk.

"We find that they come in upset from something at home, and this gives them time to talk about it," said Susan Harding, one of the center's two directors. "We teach them that there are appropriate times to talk about personal things and that's not when they're on the job."

The job is an important component of the program. Some trainees work in the office or the kitchen and a few, usually young fathers, work at carpentry or mechanics. Most of the young women spend their days taking care of the 24 babies and toddlers enrolled in the day-care program, learning to be parents.

"We have some clear rules," said Ms. Harding. "It's not O.K. to hit children or yell at them or call them names. A lot of young women come here with no idea that there is an alternative to hitting children."

The trainees are a diverse group. In this session, one is a father and one is a 16-year-old high school dropout who is considered at risk of becoming pregnant. Another is a 39-year-old woman who is hoping to acquire job skills. Some trainees are referred to the program by the state after their children have been taken into protective custody; others walk through the door of their own volition.

There are, however, some common denominators among the participants, says Cheryl Mitchell, the co-director. "Probably 90 percent of the people here were abused as kids," she said. "Their relationship with their peers and their children is shaky. They are generally socially isolated. We also find that drug and alcohol abuse in the family is very common."

The best way to break that cycle, Ms. Mitchell said, appears to be a multifaceted approach that includes assertiveness training, practical experience in caring for children and a comprehensive support system that helps provide basic necessities like food and clothing. In addition, each trainee is assigned a home visitor and a staff supervisor.

"It's often the connection with the supervisor that keeps them coming," said Ms. Harding. "They have someone to encourage them and remind them they're doing well."

The results of the program have been dramatic. Figures compiled by the Vermont Department of Health indicate the teenage pregnancy rate in the county last year was 45.2 out of every 1,000 girls, the lowest in the state, down from 70 in 1979, the year before the center opened.

A report prepared for the Federal Government by a professor at the University of Vermont notes that welfare dependency among families served by the center dropped to 17 percent of the cases studied last year, from 40 percent in 1983. It says the incidence of child abuse was at 2 percent, down from 21 percent and that employment increased to 70 percent from 10 percent.

Then, too, there are the personal tributes. Anne, a 31-year-old mother, said she was "losing my sanity" by staying at home with four boys full-time. She was a trainee last year. This year she is working at the center as a work-study student from a local community college.

"I used to be afraid," she said. "I talk to people more now. The center helps give you a sense of freedom, some time to be alone. It helps give me my sanity." ■

DISCUSSING THE SELECTION

1. What kind of lives were most of the families living before they joined the Addison County Parent-Child Center? In what part of the United States is the center located? Describe the lives of the people who participate

in the program. According to the article, what are their homes like? What are their ages? How many children do they have? How old are the children?

2. What in the article suggests that the families involved had economic problems? How did their economic needs affect their lifestyles?

3. What specific changes were made by becoming part of a group? What psychological changes do you think these people made as they started to interact with each other?

4. Why does the author include the information that most participants in the program had been abused as children? What characteristics do the participants have that relate to their child abuse, according to Johnson?

THINKING CRITICALLY

1. Do you know anyone who ever tried to "break a cycle" that was destructive or humiliating? What is gained from handling such a problem in a group, as opposed to trying to handle it on one's own? Share the experience of the person you know with the class.

2. Do you know any people who are isolated from the mainstream, like the women described in this article? What is being done to help these people connect with the wider world? What do you think these people need that is not now being offered to them?

3. Have you ever been involved in a community program such as the one described in this transcript? What are the important qualities for volunteers or workers in such programs?

4. What do you think is the most important outcome of this program? Explain your answer.

FOCUSING ON THE WRITING

Making Connections Between Ideas

Writers connect their ideas from sentence to sentence and from paragraph to paragraph by using some combination of the following:

Specific words and phrases such as *next, consequently, moreover, so, therefore,* and *then*

Key words or important words that are repeated throughout a piece of writing

Synonyms or words that have the same or close to the same meaning

1. What specific words and phrases does the author use to make connections between ideas? What key words are used throughout the article? What synonyms are used to make connections in the article?

2. What specific words or phrases connect the second paragraph to the first?

3. What similarities do you find between the third paragraph and the concluding paragraph? How do they help a reader to connect the beginning and the end of the article?

4. What information is contained in the introductory paragraph? What do you learn about the participants in this program from this paragraph?

5. What is the purpose of using quotations in the article? Where does Johnson use quotations from program participants? Where does she use quotations from experts? Why is it important to have quotations from both sources?

6. List the facts that are included in the article. What is the purpose for including those facts?

CREATING YOUR TEXT

1. Reread the Johnson article, focusing on the factors that have made the Addison County Parent-Child Center work. Write an essay in which you describe those factors, and explain the reason why each factor made a difference in the success of the center. What have you learned about "the art of bringing up baby" from the success of this center?

2. Some people think that teenage parents should be required to attend a center such as the one described in the Johnson article. Write an essay explaining why you agree or disagree with this proposal. If you think they should be required to attend, what incentives should be provided to the young parents to make sure they attend? How long should they be required to attend? Use your experiences, observations, and readings to support your point of view.

3. Do you think that all high schools should include a course in child care for males and females? In an essay, explain why you agree or disagree with this idea, supporting your idea with your experience, observations, and readings.

4. Imagine that you are a family court judge and you have a case before you in which a parent or parents abused a child. As the judge in the court, you must decide to take the child away from the family and send it into foster care or to require that the parents attend for one year a center such as the one described in the Johnson article. At the end of the year, the family would be reassessed. In an essay, explain how you would decide the case and explain the reasons for your decision. Use your experiences, observations, or readings to support your decision.

REVISING YOUR TEXT

Share your essay with a classmate, discussing the decisions you have made relating to focus and what information to include and what to eliminate. Review the revision questions on page 11 to locate the places in which your draft succeeds and those in which it can be improved. Also, keep the following questions in mind as you review your draft:

Does your essay include your personal experience? Do you connect the personal experience to the general ideas?

Do you include any quotations? Have you included quotations from ordinary people and from the experts? If so, are they effective? If not, would quotations add support or evidence to your essay?

What connections do you make between ideas? Where do you use specific words and phrases, key words, and/or synonyms?

Write your second draft, making any necessary changes, and share it with your class.

EXPLORING YOUR IDEAS

This article describes what a person can gain from volunteering. Write in your journal about any experience you have had in which you volunteered your time to help someone or some organization. What did you gain from this experience? If you have never been a volunteer, imagine that you were required to volunteer your services. What group or organization would you want to help? Explain why.

The Value of Volunteering

CHARLES A. LARSON

Charles Larson, who is now a professor of literature at American University, was a Peace Corps volunteer in the 1960s. His essay about the benefits of being a volunteer appeared in *Newsweek* magazine.

1   The Peace Corps [was] 30 years old in the summer [of 1991]. The 130,000 people who volunteered over the past three decades may have made little dent on American foreign policy. But they have left a mark on individual communities around the world—entire nations, even—that is irreversible. Just to mention two examples, the improved educational standards and increased literacy rates in countries as disparate as Nigeria and Micronesia are due in large part to the work of diligent volunteers during the '60s and '70s.

2   If the Peace Corps never became a powerful force or an international model for politically acceptable aid (neither of which it was intended to be), that's due to the individual volunteers themselves, not the program itself. Each volunteer goes through a process of awakening to the possibilities of self-awareness. Few volunteers I know would disagree: they were the real

beneficiaries of this people-to-people experiment, not the countries that hosted them.

My own particulars were not that extraordinary. When I joined in 1962, at 24, there were fewer than a thousand volunteers. Why did I join them? I feared I would be drafted and end up in Vietnam. When told I was assigned to Nigeria, I had to check a map to learn where the country was. I had no burning sense of altruism, or commitment to the objectives (improved education) for my host country. My most evident quality was that I knew little about myself and even less about others. I was a blank sheet of paper at a moment of crucial self-discovery.

It was a transforming experience. I saw ways of life I would never have seen had I remained within the comfortable domain of my provincial Midwestern upbringing. For the first time, I learned to think of someone besides myself, to consider that there is no single way of observing a problem or answering a troubling question. I discovered that without the mutual tolerance and respect of other peoples' cultures, there is no possibility for harmony in our world.

I'm convinced that what I learned overseas as a Peace Corps volunteer was fairly typical. Yes, there were others who had difficult assignments, but few will deny that their gains were greater than their losses. Would they do it again? You bet, on a moment's notice, as some already have and others plan to do once lives now immersed in families and careers have taken another turn.

Our nation needs the lessons of the Peace Corps today. We talk about the economic morass our country has fallen into, but our moral muddle is much more disturbing. We are a nation of factions, with hardly any two groups agreeing about anything. We have forgotten how to share or how to be understanding of the bottom 20 percent of the population we have largely written out of our lives. Poverty, declining health standards, illiteracy, a deteriorating infrastructure, a general intolerance of anyone different from ourselves—all cry out for serious measures. Yet we are afraid to render even a quick fix for fear of stepping on someone's toes.

We need to get people back together, working with and listening to one another. We need to do this with our young people, at a time when careers haven't been fully launched and when they will still pay attention to another opinion, welcome a differing view. President Kennedy set up the Peace Corps quickly, through executive order, knowing that endless debate would kill the idea by slow suffocation. We need the same kind of forceful action now if we want to change where this country is headed.

We need a two-year national-service plan for every young American—no exemptions, period. That includes the rich and the poor, the educated and the uneducated, even the handicapped. We need to convince each and every individual that there is something that he or she can contribute, that work has value, that an enormous effort will be needed to help turn our nation around.

Most of all, we need teachers—but not only those with university degrees. There are plenty of gifted educators who have never stood in front of a classroom. They can help with literacy programs or teach English to our rising number of immigrants. Others can teach job skills—the value of using one's hands—which include anything from auto mechanics to computer programming. We need health-care workers, nurses' aides—skilled and unskilled—providing care for the elderly and the young. We need preschool centers run by welfare mothers, sharing their frustrations and their joys, but doing something to connect with other people. We need highway and road crews of young men and women, restoring our transportation system before it collapses under the weight of inattention and the lack of funds. We need all of these and more to demonstrate once again that people can make a difference, both individually and collectively. . . . [I]t is necessary for people to assume that sense of action, to give to the nation so that it can give back to us what has been forgotten: tolerance and responsibility. Besides a cure for our moral poverty, we might even help the economy. Or at least learn that every individual has something to offer. ■

DISCUSSING THE SELECTION

1. What is the Peace Corps? What information does Larson include in his essay that tells about the overall goals of the Peace Corps? What

does he include about the personal responsibilities of being in the Peace Corps?

2. According to the Larson essay, what did he gain from his experience? What overall "mark" did the Peace Corps make on the country in which Larson was a volunteer?

3. What problems does Larson describe that are facing our country today? What support does he provide to convince his readers that a two-year national-service plan could solve some of these problems?

4. What specific problems does he think could be improved by a corps of volunteers in this country?

5. Which other specific articles in this book describe ways in which volunteers make a difference in resolving problems in this country?

THINKING CRITICALLY

1. Should people be forced by law to become "volunteers" for two years?

2. Does the government have the obligation to support volunteers if they are required by law to do this service? If so, what services should the government be forced to provide?

3. What should be done to those people who refuse to "volunteer"?

4. What kind of incentives could the government provide that would make more people want to volunteer to help the government?

5. Imagine that you were selecting volunteers for a particular project. Describe your project, and explain what characteristics you would look for in the volunteers you would choose. Explain the reasons for your choices.

FOCUSING ON THE WRITING

1. Larson introduces this essay with a brief history of the Peace Corps. What facts does he include? What is the purpose of this introduction?

2. In this persuasive essay (see page 212 for more information about persuasive writing), Larson has tried to persuade his readers that "we need a two-year national-service plan for every young American—no exemptions, period." What support does he provide to convince his readers that such a program is needed?

3. What support does he provide to prove that "every individual has something to offer"?

4. What support does he provide to convince his readers that the volunteer gains as much as or more than the program or place for which he or she has volunteered?

5. In which part of the essay does he include his personal experience? In which part does he present more general ideas? How does he connect the two?

CREATING YOUR TEXT

1. Using your journal entry as a springboard for ideas, write an essay describing an experience you had as a volunteer for an organization. In your essay, tell your readers about the organization. What was its purpose? What type of work did you do as a volunteer? How did you learn what was expected of you? How long did you work? What did you learn from

your experience? Why would you recommend to your classmates volunteering—or not—for this organization?

2. Some people believe that all young people should be required to serve their country for two years as a volunteer in the armed forces or in a peaceful capacity such as described in the Larson article. Write an essay in which you explain why you think that all young people should or should not be required to serve their country in this way. Use your experiences, observations, or readings to support your point of view.

3. Larson writes,

We are a nation of factions, with hardly any two groups agreeing about anything. We have forgotten how to share or how to be understanding. . . . Poverty, declining health standards, illiteracy, a deteriorating infrastructure, a general intolerance of anyone different from ourselves—all cry out for serious measures.

Write an essay in which you describe your plan to deal with *one* of the above problems. Be specific about what you think should be done to improve the situation that now exists. What steps should be taken to bring about your program? In your conclusion, explain how this project would be positive for you as well as for your community.

REVISING YOUR TEXT

When you have finished your first draft of this essay, share it with a member of your class. Read the essay looking for its strong points and for the areas in which it needs improvement. Then review the revision questions on page 11, while discussing the draft. Also consider the following questions before you begin to work on your second draft:

Is your point of view stated clearly and directly?
Do you provide support for your point of view?
Do you include personal experience to support your ideas?

Do you generalize to illustrate what you have learned from your personal experience?

After reflecting on these questions, write your second draft. Share this with your classmates.

ADDITIONAL PROJECT

Find out what volunteer opportunities exist in your college or neighborhood—in literacy centers, nursing homes, schools, hospitals, and animal shelters, for example. Get information about the requirements for volunteers and the steps one must take to become a volunteer. Share this information with your class. As a class project, write an article for your college newspaper informing the student body about local volunteering opportunities.

EXPLORING YOUR IDEAS

"We like to believe . . . that educational achievement is rewarded with better jobs and higher pay. Unfortunately, there is plenty of evidence that the opposite often is true in the American workplace." Write about what this statement means to you, given your experience and that of people you know.

Merit Gets Them Nowhere

ALBERT SHANKER

Albert Shanker, the president of the American Federation of Teachers and a well-known writer on educational issues, wrote this essay about unequal pay for women. Shanker points out the fact that although women are more educated than ever, they are not paid as much as men with the same qualifications.

Americans are big believers in the importance of education. We like to believe, too, that educational achievement is rewarded with better jobs and higher pay. Unfortunately, there is plenty of evidence that the opposite often is true in the American workplace.

We already know the employers do not reward, and therefore do not encourage, achievement among kids who go directly from high school to work. They don't ask for high school transcripts; they don't favor graduates who have worked hard and performed well; a high school diploma is enough. But it turns out that employers' indifference to achievement does not stop with high school graduates. A recent study from the U.S. Department of Education reports that they are doing exactly the same thing with our highest achieving college graduates: women.

In *Women at Thirtysomething: Paradoxes of Attainment,* Clifford Adelman finds that American women have not only achieved equality of educational opportunity with men, they now also surpass men in academic achievement all along the line. But—and this is the shocker—employers continue to pay women less than men even when they are doing the same jobs and when the men are less qualified. This is evidence that gross inequity toward women persists; it also sends a terrible message to *all* of our students: Working hard and achieving do not pay off.

Adelman bases his conclusions on a national study that followed the school and work experiences of 26,600 members of the high school class of 1972 until they were in their early thirties. Here are some of his findings:

In high school, young women achieved at a higher level than young men. And this is not because they stuck to "easy" subjects. If you compare male and female students who took the same number of courses in mathematics and science, the women, on average, did significantly better than the men.

Parents had bigger ambitions for their sons than for their daughters, and the daughters apparently reflected this in their own ideas about what they would do after high school. Nevertheless, a higher percentage of women from the high school class of 1972 entered college directly from high school than men, and a higher percentage won scholarships.

Once in college, these women were more successful academically than men no matter what field they studied. Women majoring in fields that are traditionally considered male preserves—science, business, and engineering—did especially well in comparison with their male classmates.

Success in college apparently led these women to revise their educational aspirations upward. By the time they received their bachelor's degrees, more young women than men aspired to graduate degrees. And the ones who went on to graduate school were better qualified, too. Forty-four percent of them had grade-point averages of A– or better in comparison with 35 percent of the men.

But the job market did not reward this achievement—far from it. The women suffered more unemployment and under-employment than the men, and their earnings were far lower. In 1985, the average salary for a woman with a bachelor's degree was $18,670; for a man, it was $27,606.

Perhaps it's no surprise to find that many women earned less than men because they had taken low-paying jobs traditionally done by women, like nursing and teaching. But even when Adelman compares men and women who had the same undergraduate backgrounds and the same number of years of job experience—in other words, he didn't include women with children in this comparison—the differences between what they earned was disgraceful. For example, the men who majored in foreign languages earned 54 percent more than the women, and the men who majored in education earned 26 percent more than the women.

There are a few occupations, including chemist, economist, and computer programmer, in which the pay for women, on average, actually surpassed the pay for men. And there are some others in which there was little difference. But for the most part, the pay differences in favor of men were shocking, ranging from 15 percent for pharmacists to 77 percent for architects.

This system of rewarding—or, rather, not rewarding—our hard-working young women is unjust; it's also stupid. Employers talk a lot about the productivity of the United States workforce. They talk about the serious shortage of math and science graduates and how it's going to damage our country's prosperity. And yet, how do they treat well-trained and highly motivated workers? Worse than those that are less qualified.

Adelman says American women are the best educated in the world. They are a tremendous resource, but employers are squandering this resource by failing to recognize it. How long will it be before women ask, "Why should we be chumps? Why should we bother to work hard? It certainly isn't getting us anywhere."

If employers want talented and dedicated workers, they'd better stop talking about it and start rewarding merit. ■

DISCUSSING THE SELECTION

1. Before you discuss this selection in class, for five minutes write as many facts and ideas as you can remember from the Shanker article. What stands out in your mind about this article? What information in it surprised you, and what did you already know?

2. Why do you think most employers do not ask for high school transcripts and instead just ask for the diplomas themselves? Is there a reason for this that Shanker may be overlooking?

3. In paragraph 3, Shanker presents evidence and then makes a conclusion. What is the evidence? What is the conclusion? Do you agree with Shanker's conclusion, or is there any other way this evidence could be interpreted?

4. What fields does Shanker define as traditionally male? What fields as traditionally female? How might these fields have become so defined?

5. In the Cisneros essay on page 34, she explains the way in which her family regarded their sons differently from their daughter. How does this attitude correspond to the one that Shanker presents in this article? How do you explain this attitude in our world today? What can be done to change it?

THINKING CRITICALLY

1. Is there a difference between the way men and women are treated in school? Does this change at different levels of school? Explain your answer with examples from your observations and personal experiences.

2. Is there a difference in the way males and females perform in school? Explain your answer with examples from your observations and personal experiences.

3. In your experience, are men and women treated differently when they go on job interviews? Are they offered different salaries? Explain your answer as in the preceding question.

4. Shanker concludes by stating that women may decide they are chumps and stop working so hard. Is this the only response to this situation? Is the problem that Shanker describes a problem only for women? What can men and women do together to change this situation?

FOCUSING ON THE WRITING

Writing a Summary

Writers often summarize what other writers have written to help them understand what they have read or for later use as notes for studying or reference.

One method for writing a summary is to first write down the name of the author and the title of the selection. Next, find the main idea of the piece of writing. Then, locate the ideas or points that support the main idea. Rewrite all these ideas in your own words so that they will make sense to you at a later date.

1. What is the main point or thesis statement of this article? Where is it located?

2. Make a list of the points Shanker presents to support his thesis statement. Which of these points is based on facts and which, if any, on opinions?

3. Which of these points provides the strongest evidence in proving Shanker's main point? Explain your answer, relying on the evidence provided in the essay.

4. What specific words and phrases does Shanker use to let his readers know when he is using information obtained from Adelman? What examples of paraphrasing occur in the article? From what other sources does Shanker get information for this article? How does he let his reader know this?

5. Using the information you found, write a summary of the Shanker article

in your own words. Compare it with the summaries of other students in your class. What did you focus on that other students did not? Why was this information more important to you?

CREATING YOUR TEXT

1. In the United States today, there is evidence suggesting that educational achievement is not always rewarded with better jobs and higher pay. Write an essay (see page 212 for information about writing a persuasive essay) in which you agree or disagree with this statement, using the evidence gathered from your readings, class discussions, and personal experience.

2. In classrooms, there are differences in the ways that males and females are treated and in the expectations that teachers and schools have for each. Write an essay in which you agree or disagree with the statement, using the evidence gathered from your readings, class discussions, and personal experience.

3. "If employers want talented and dedicated workers, they'd better stop talking about it and start rewarding merit." Write an essay in which you describe step by step (see page 149 for information on writing a process essay) ways in which a corporation can change its policies and begin to treat all its employees more fairly. (You may want to reread the Weber article on page 303 about the changes Du Pont has made in its employment policies.) In your conclusion, explain why this treatment will improve the atmosphere for all workers.

4. Women must do something to ensure that their abilities are rewarded. Write an essay in which you describe step by step what women should do to force employers to make changes in the policies that Shanker describes in this article.

REVISING YOUR TEXT

When you finish your first draft, share it with a classmate. Together, review the revision questions on page 11 and discuss where your draft succeeds and where it needs improvement.

Think about the following questions as you reread your draft:

What audience or readers did you have in mind as you wrote this essay?
What main point did you try to make in your essay? Where did you state your main idea?
Do you connect your paragraphs so that your reader can easily follow what you have written?

After thinking about ways to improve your writing, write your second draft to share with the class.

EXPLORING YOUR IDEAS

Write about what you know about the U.S. bombing of Hiroshima, Japan. When did it take place? In what context did it happen? What happened to the people of Hiroshima? What is your response to this action taken almost fifty years ago? What are relations like today between the United States and Japan? Do you think the two countries feel a long-term effect from World War II?

The Hiroshima Maiden

MARILYN KRYSL

This story from Marilyn Krysl's novel *Atomic Open House* was included in the Summer 1992 issue of the literary anthology *Glimmer Train Stories*. It deals with the aftermath of the August 1945 American bombing of Hiroshima as it was experienced by one girl. Krysl has written five books of poetry and two books of stories. She teaches at the University of Colorado, in Boulder.

It was the low end of afternoon. Judy and Miro and I sat in the grass beside the fishpool. Like animals Judy and I stayed close to her, offering our bodies. When we went to the dime store or the drugstore, we kept her between us. We glared at passersby who stared. Now we looked at our reflection in the water. We'd come from seeing *Pajama Game,* Doris Day singing energetically about romance, sleepwear.

"I am always liking movies," Miro said. "When I am little girl I think I will be actress. I think I will cry so well others cry too. And I think I will be dancing and singing. And kissing many handsome men." She laughed.

"Me too," I said. "Especially the kissing part."

"Robert Mitchum comes," Miro said, "and you fall down, hit by love!"

"Mitchum sweeps you up in his arms . . ." Judy said.

"He kisses you," Miro said, "and you wake up, Snow White!"

"But then the seven dwarves show up," Judy said.

"Robert Mitchum does not like dwarf," Miro said. "He drops you, plop!"

We giggled, and the fish zipped away. A dragonfly sailed across the pool and lit on a lily pad. Miro sat cross-legged, palms up. It was as though she still held that armful of wood, burning.

"Do you think I should wear mask in America?" Miro said.

"Not unless you want to," Judy said. "It's up to you."

"I don't like mask, but in Japan I wear mask. Here I dream mask. I dream my face is scarred, I put on mask. Then I meet handsome movie star. He wants to kiss me. But he cannot kiss me through mask. I take off mask, and my face is beautiful. A miracle! He kisses me with very much passion!"

"Your face will get changed," Judy said. "Pretty soon you'll start your operations."

"Before bomb I go to fortune-teller," Miro said. "I am thirteen, I am hoping to be actress in movies. I ask my fortune. Fortune-teller answers just what I want. She says, *You will be girl men turn to look at.*" Miro studied her face in the water. "You see," she said, "my fortune has come true."

We were still then. I repeated her name in my mind. I said it over, letting it take me across that difficult moment. When Judy spoke it was as though she'd turned the volume down.

"How come you're not mad at Americans?" Judy said.

"Americans are kind," Miro said.

"Nope, they're not," Judy said. "Not all of them. Some Americans are very mean."

"Some mean, some kind," Miro said. "Kind ones invite me to surgery."

"You should be mad at President Truman," Judy said. "He sent down the order."

"How about the man who dropped the bomb," I said. "If you met that man in the B-chan,* you'd be mad."

"He burned you!" Judy said.

---

*B-chan: nickname the Japanese gave to B-52 bombers that frequently flew over Japan.

"He did not burn me on purpose," Miro said. "He thinks he does his job. If Japan soldiers have bomb they have to do their job too."

"They don't have to," I said. "They could say no."

"Say no to emperor? Ha." Miro said.

"Poop on the emperor," Judy said.

"Emperor will not like you say that. He will cut off your head with samurai sword."

Judy giggled.

"If man in B-chan sees my face," Miro said, "he is very unhappy. He feels bad."

"Maybe, maybe not," Judy said. "Maybe he doesn't care. Maybe he's proud of what he did."

"He is proud to fly airplane for his country," Miro said. "I don't think he is proud to burn me. In war men obey. Otherwise . . ."

"Otherwise," I said, "samurai sword."

Miro laughed.

"Some Americans think we had to drop the bomb to stop Japan and end the war," Judy said.

"Maybe Americans are right," Miro said. "Japanese obey emperor. Emperor is very hard to stop. Those who obey emperor are very hard to stop."

"But the emperor's palace was in Tokyo," Judy said. "They didn't drop an atom bomb on Tokyo. They didn't burn the emperor. They burned you."

"Thank you to remind me," Miro said suddenly. "Now I do not forget this."

For a few moments no one said anything.

"I am sometimes very mad," Miro said then. "I think America is crazy and bad. They hurt Japan too much. I am afraid of country that does much hurting. But there is thing that is worse. You see, Japanese like beauty. They do not like ugly person. And I am ugly in special way. They look at me and think *Hiroshima*. I remind them of defeat, and they are ashamed of defeat. They don't want to look at me. They want me to go away.

"In Japan I have operation. Japan doctors do not know how, but I do not know this. They pretend they know how, not to know is shameful." Miro pulled her blouse up and pushed the band of her skirt down. She watched our faces. "They take from stomach to fix face. But they do not have enough medicine. They cut many times. I feel each one, but I want to be pretty again. I cry, but I stay."

"I can't stand this," Judy said.

Ha! I thought. So who's afraid of a hurt girl?

"What do you think?" Miro said. "I look like war. I am ravaged. Not ravishing," she said, pronouncing the word carefully. "Ravaged. I am site of many battles." Slowly she tucked her blouse back in.

"I think doctors know how to sew. But when they sew to face, it does not stay. Still they practice. I am their practice. Shall I count for you how much I cry? I do not know how to say enough numbers. I am foreigner in my own country. Never again do I trust Japan doctor.

"Then Americans come, show me pictures. Faces are better after. What shall I do? Shall I trust American doctors? Can they make me pretty again?

"When I look in mirror I see my made by America face. Shall I come to bad America? Bad America gives me ugly face but only bad America can give me new one. And very much I want new face. Even from bad America. I want new face, so I come." ■

DISCUSSING THE SELECTION

1. Why do the narrator and Judy feel protective toward Miro?

2. Why has Miro come to the United States? "Irony" refers to an expression or situation that turns out the opposite of what one might have expected or hoped for. In what ways is it ironic that Miro has to get help in the United States?

3. How does Miro feel about Americans? How have Americans treated her?

4. How do the narrator and Judy feel about the U.S. action? How does Miro explain it to them?

5. What is Miro's experience with the fortune-teller? In what ways has Miro's dream come true, and in what ways has the prediction backfired on her?

THINKING CRITICALLY

1. Do you know any people who are physically disabled or who have been obviously injured? How have you felt when those people were stared at or pointed to by passersby? Explain to the class the situation, how you felt, and how you responded.

2. Why do you think people stare at the physically or mentally disabled or at people who have been injured?

3. Have you ever been to a fortune-teller? With the class, discuss your experience. Do you think that people can predict the future? Explain your answer.

4. Do you know anyone who has had an experience with war or with armed combat? With your class, discuss this person's experience.

FOCUSING ON THE WRITING

Word Choice

When writers choose words to express their feelings or to describe events, persons, or places, they choose them with care.

Writers look at the *denotations,* or dictionary meanings, of words to assure the accuracy of the word.

They also think about the *connotations,* or associations and suggestions, that a word brings to mind.

Most writers try to avoid *clichés,* or overused expressions and words. They try for a fresh and exciting way of presenting their ideas to keep their readers interested and involved.

1. Writers choose their words carefully to convey a feeling, to evoke an image, and sometimes to establish a point of view indirectly. In the story, Miro states, "I look like war. I am *ravaged*. Not *ravishing*." What is the difference between these two words, and what do they tell the reader about Miro and her feelings of self-esteem?

2. Reread the story looking for other words that are used in different or interesting ways. List them. Find the denotative meanings and any connotative meanings that the words have for you or your peers as readers.

3. In the last paragraph in the story, Krysl presents the irony of the dilemma Miro is facing:

"When I look in mirror I see my made by America face. Shall I come to bad America? Bad America gives me ugly face but only bad America can give me new one. And very much I want new face. Even from bad America. I want new face, so I come."

What is ironic in the situation Miro is facing? What is the irony of Miro's relationship with the United States?

CREATING YOUR TEXT

1. Reread your journal entry, and think about your class discussions concerning this story. Write for five minutes without stopping, putting on your paper any thoughts that come into your head whether they seem related or not to the story you have just read. Just keep writing even if you seem to run out of ideas and simply have to write, "I have nothing to write."

2. Write an essay describing the life of a person you know who was affected by war or experience in combat. Explain the person's background, personal situation, and how he or she was affected by the experience of war. What have you gained in understanding about war from knowing this person? What could others gain from knowing this person?

3. Write a story about a person you know who has a physical or mental disability. Describe the person's disability and how the person's life has been affected by it. How do the person's family and friends assist the person in having a comfortable and fulfilling life? What has your role been in this work? What have you gained from knowing this person? What do you think others would gain from knowing your friend?

4. Recently a federal law was passed that enables people who have physical disabilities to ride public transportation, eat in restaurants, attend theaters, and live more regular lives. Write an essay in which you describe the way in which one institution in your community has been altered to meet disabled people's needs. You may want to write about your school, a local restaurant, a theater, or any other institution with which you are familiar. Be specific about changes that have been made and how these have created a more comfortable atmosphere for disabled people.

REVISING YOUR TEXT

When you have finished writing the first draft of your essay, share it with another class member. Decide which parts of your essay are clear and effective. Decide which parts need improvement. Go over the revision questions on page 12 or 14 to help you evaluate the essay.

In addition, look at your essay thinking about the following questions:

Are the words used effective and interesting?
Did you think about your audience of readers as you decided on the appropriate words to use?
In what order did you present information—chronological, from least important to most important, from most important to least important, and so on? Does that make sense as you read what you have written?

Keeping in mind the suggestions made during the discussion, write your second draft. Share this draft with your class.

ADDITIONAL PROJECT

To find out more about the treatment of the Japanese in the United States during World War II, watch *Come See the Paradise*. Discuss how prejudice and racism are reflected in our treatment of others in this society.

If any family members of students in the class have relatives who served in World War II, invite them to come to visit your class, and discuss this time period with them. You may want to share the Krysl story with them and to discuss how relationships with the Japanese today are affected by the historical background of past experiences. Together, discuss ways in which these relationships can be improved.

EXPANDING YOUR IDEAS

Collaborative Writing Projects

1. To find out more about community services that are available in your area, scan a month's worth of local newspapers (college, community, town, or city papers) looking for articles about services that are working to help the community. These papers are usually available in your local or college library. Decide which of these articles you would like to put together as you create your own class book about neighborhood community services. As a group, write a short paper revealing your source(s) and what you have discovered about your community. In addition, you may find an article so unique or meaningful to you that you may wish to send it to the author of this book for inclusion in the next edition.

2. As a small-group project, contact one of the people mentioned in the articles you have selected in step 1 and find out if he or she is willing to meet with one or two students to discuss the project. If the person is willing, make an appointment to get together. Develop interview questions (see page 254) that will help you understand the steps the person took as part of the community project or program. If the person permits it, use an audiotape as you conduct the interview. If not, take notes. In any case, someone in the group should transcribe the interview. As a group, write about the person focusing on the way in which the person got involved in the needs of the community. After showing it to the person you interviewed, you may submit your finished piece to the school newspaper for publication.

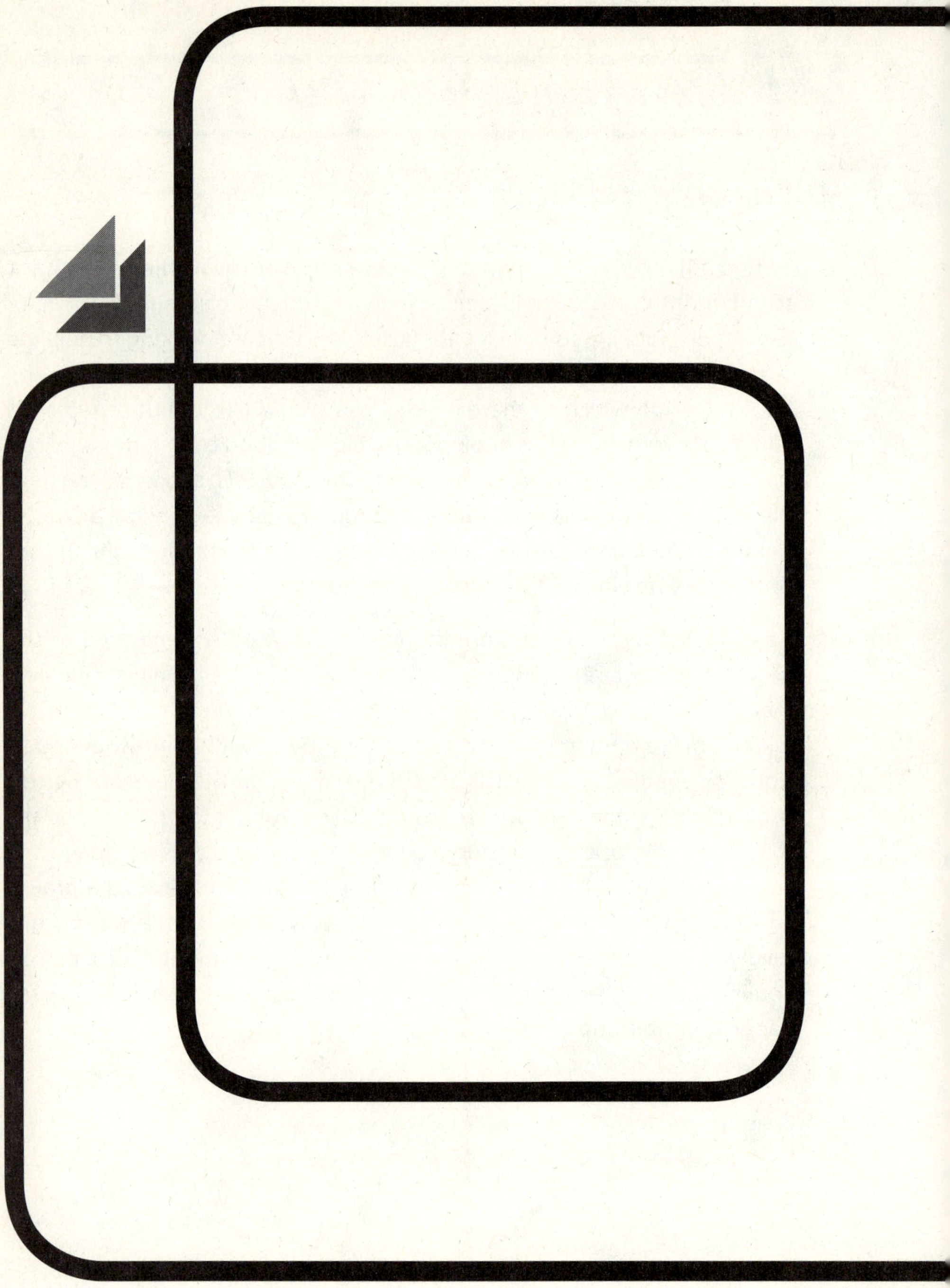

EXPLORING YOUR IDEAS

Write about an experience in which a stranger helped you cope with a difficult time in your life. Then, write about an experience in which a family member or friend helped you cope with a difficult time in your life. Reread what you have written and think about how you felt about each incident. Write about what you learned from each experience.

Moonlight Shadow

BANANA YOSHIMOTO

Now living in Tokyo, Banana Yoshimoto was born in Japan in 1964. She has written two novels, *N.P.* and *Tugumi*, two collections of short stories, and two books of essays. At first, she had to work as a waitress to support herself while she was writing. Her first story, "Moonlight Shadow," won the Nihon University Department of Arts Prize in 1986. This story is included in *Kitchen*, which was published in 1988 and received many awards. Megan Backus translated *Kitchen* into English and her translation helped Yoshimoto to become a well-known writer in the United States.

Wherever he went, Hitoshi always had a little bell with him, attached to the case he kept his bus pass in. Even though it was just a trinket, something I gave him before we were in love, it was destined to remain at his side until the last.

Although we were in separate homerooms, we met serving on the same committee for the sophomore-class field trip. Because we had completely different itineraries, the only time we had together was on the bullet train itself. On the platform after we arrived, we shook hands in a playful show of regret at having to part. I suddenly remembered that I had, in the pocket of my school uniform, a little bell that had fallen off the cat. "Here," I said, "a farewell gift," and handed it to him. "What's this?" he said, laughing, and—although it wasn't the most creative gift—took it from my palm and wrapped it carefully in his handkerchief as if it were something precious. He surprised me: it was not typical behavior for a boy that age.

As it turns out, it was love.

Whether he did it because the gift was from me or because that was how he was raised, not to treat a gift carelessly, it amazed me and made me warm to him.

There was electric charge between our hearts, and its conduit was the sound of the bell. The whole time we spent apart on that class trip, we each had the bell on our minds. Whenever he heard it ring, he would remember me and the time we had spent together; I passed the trip imagining I could hear the bell across the vast sky, imagining the person who had it in his possession. After we got back, we fell deeply in love.

For nearly four years the bell was always with us. Each and every afternoon and evening, in each and every thing we did—our first kiss, our big fights, rain and shine and snow, the first night we spent together, every smile and every tear, listening to music and watching TV—whenever Hitoshi took out that case, which he used as a wallet, we heard its faint, clear tinkling sound. It seemed as though I could hear it even when he wasn't there. You might say it was just a young girl's sentimentality. But I did think I heard it—that's how it felt to me then.

There was one thing that always disturbed me profoundly. Sometimes, no matter how intently I would be staring at him, I would have the feeling that Hitoshi wasn't there. So many times, when he was asleep, I felt the need to put my ear to his heart. No matter how bright his smile, I would have to strain my eyes to see him. His facial expressions, the atmosphere around him, always had a kind of transparency. The whole time I was with him there was that feeling of ephemerality, uncertainty. If that was a premonition of what was to come, what a sorrowful one it was.

A lover should die after a long lifetime. I lost Hitoshi at the age of twenty, and I suffered from it so much that I felt as if my own life had stopped. The night he died, my soul went away to some other place and I couldn't bring it back. It was impossible to see the world as I had before. My brain ebbed and flowed, unstable, and I passed the days in a relentless state of dull oppression. I felt that I was fated to undergo one of those things it's better not to have to experience even once in a lifetime (abortion, prostitution, major illness).

After all, we were still young, and who knows whether it would have been our last love? We had overcome many first hurdles together. We came to know what it is to be deeply tied to someone and we learned to judge for ourselves the weight of many kinds of events—from these things, one by one, we constructed our four years.

Now that it's over, I can shout it out: *The gods are assholes!* I loved Hitoshi—I loved Hitoshi more than life itself.

For two months after Hitoshi died, every morning found me leaning over the railing of the bridge on the river, drinking hot tea. I had begun to go jogging every day at dawn, since I slept very badly, and that point on the bridge was where I rested before the run back home.

Sleeping at night was what I feared most. No—worse than that was the shock of awakening. I dreaded the deep gloom that would fall when I remembered he was gone. My dreams were always about Hitoshi. After my painful, fitful sleep, whether or not I had been able to see him, on awakening I would know it had been only a dream—in reality I would never be with him again. And so I tried not to wake up. Going back to sleep was no answer: depressed to the point of nausea, I would toss around in a cold sweat. Through my curtains I would see the sky getting lighter, blue-white, and I would feel abandoned in the chill and silence of dawn. It was so forlorn and cold, I wished I could be back in the dream. There I would be, wide-eyed, tortured by its lingering memory. It was always then that I truly woke up. Finally, exhausted from lack of sleep, beginning to panic at the prospect of that lonely time—like a bout of insanity—in which I would wait for the first morning light, I decided to take up running.

I bought myself an expensive two-piece sweatsuit, running shoes, and even a small aluminum container in which to carry a hot drink. I thought, ironically, that beginners always over-equip—but still, it was best to look ahead.

I began running just before spring vacation. I would run to the bridge, turn around, and head home, where I would carefully wash out my neck towel and sweaty clothes. While they were in the dryer I would help my mother make breakfast. Then I'd go back to bed for a while. That was my life. In the evenings I'd get together with friends, watch videos, whatever, anything to leave myself as little free time as possible. But the struggle was fruitless. There was only one thing I had any desire to do: I wanted to see Hitoshi. Yet at all costs I had to keep my hands and body and mind moving. Doing that, I hoped, albeit listlessly, would somehow, someday, lead to a breakthrough. There was no guarantee, but I would try to endure, no matter what, until it came. When my dog died, when my bird died, I had gotten through in more or less the same way. But it was different this time. Without a prospect in sight, day after day went by, like losing one's mind bit by bit. I would repeat to myself, like a prayer: It's all right, it's all right, the day will come when you'll pull out of this.

The river, spanned by a white bridge, was wide, and divided our part of the city almost exactly in half. It took me about twenty minutes to reach it. I loved that place—it was there that I used to meet Hitoshi, who had lived on the other side of the river. Even after he died I still loved the place.

On the deserted bridge, with the city misted over by the blue haze of dawn, my eyes absently followed the white embankment that continued on to who knows where. I rested, enveloped in the sound of the current, leisurely drinking hot tea. Standing there in the clear air that tingled with cold, I felt just the tiniest bit close to death myself. It was only in the severe clarity of that horribly lonely place that I could feel at ease. My self-torture stopped when I was there. Without this respite I would never have been able to get through the days. I was pierced by how much I needed it.

That morning I awoke with a start from a vicious nightmare. It was five-thirty. In the dawn of what promised to be a clear day I dressed and went out as usual. It was still dark; not a soul was out. The air was bitingly cold, the streets misty white, the sky a deep navy blue. Rich gradations of red were coming up in the east.

I had to force myself to run. My breath was labored; the notion that running this much on not enough sleep was only tormenting my body passed through my mind, but I ignored it: I can sleep when I get home, I thought in my befuddled brain. The streets were so utterly quiet that I struggled to remain fully conscious.

The sound of the current grew louder as I approached the river; the colors in the sky were changing moment by moment. I was leaning over the railing the way I always did upon reaching the bridge, absently looking at the rows of buildings on the street, which hung in a faint mist, as if submerged in an ocean of blue air. The river was roaring, sweeping along anything and everything in its way on a stream of white foam. The wind it gave off blew cold and seemed to suck the perspiration from my face. A half-moon shone serenely in the still-brisk March sky. My breath came out in puffs of white. I took the cap off my aluminum bottle and poured out some tea, still looking out over the river.

Just then I suddenly heard a voice from behind me pipe up, "What kind of tea is that? Could I have some?" It startled me—so much so that I dropped the bottle in the river. I still had a full cup of steaming tea in one hand.

Imagining god knows what, I turned around, and there stood a young woman with a smile on her face. I knew she was older than me, but for some reason I couldn't guess her age. Maybe about twenty-five . . . She had short hair and very clear, large eyes. She wore a thin white coat, but seemed not to feel the cold in the least. She had popped up before I had a clue that anyone was there behind me.

Then, looking cheerful, she said in a slightly nasal but sweet voice, "It's just like that Brothers Grimm story about the dog, isn't it? Or was that Aesop?" She laughed.

"In that instance," I said coolly, "the dog dropped his bone when he saw his own reflection in the water. Nobody sneaked up behind him."

She said, smiling, "I'd like to buy you a new thermos."

"Thank you," I said, showing her a smile in return. She spoke so calmly that I was not afraid of her, and she wasn't attempting familiarities. She didn't seem crazy, nor did she look like a drunk on her way home at dawn. Her eyes were too knowing and serene; the expression on her face hinted that she had tasted deeply of the sorrows and joys of this world. The air around her seemed somehow charged.

After taking one sip to wet my throat, I offered her the cup. "Here, have the rest. It's Pu-Arh tea."

"Oh, I love that," she said, taking the cup with a slender hand. "I just got here. I came from pretty far away." She looked down at the river. Her eyes had the bright sparkle of a traveler's.

"Sightseeing?" I asked, wondering what could have brought her to this particular place.

"Yes. Soon, on this spot, there'll be something to see that only happens every hundred years. Have you ever heard about it?"

"Something to see?"

"Yes. If all the conditions are right."

"What, exactly?"

"I can't tell you yet. But I promise I will, because you shared your tea with me." She laughed as she said it, and I almost failed to catch that last part. The mood of approaching morning seemed to fill the whole world. The rays of the rising sun spread over the blue sky, illuminating the faintly sparkling layers of air with white light.

It was time to be getting back, so I said, "Well, good-bye." At that she looked me directly in the eye with that same bright expression. "My name is Urara," she said. "What's yours?"

"Satsuki," I answered.

"Let's get together again," said Urara, waving good-bye.

I waved back and started running home. She was an odd one. I had no idea what she was talking about, but somehow I knew that she was someone who did not live like other people. With each step I took I grew more uneasy, and I couldn't help but turn and look back. Urara was still on the bridge. I saw her face in profile as she watched the river. It shocked me—it was not that of the person I had just talked with. I had never seen such a severe expression on anyone.

She noticed me standing there, smiled brightly again, and waved. Flustered, I returned her wave and broke into a run.

In heaven's name, what kind of person was she? I pondered it for quite some time. More and more, that morning in the sunlight, the impression of that mysterious Urara carved itself with baroque filigree into my sleepy brain.

Hitoshi had an extremely eccentric younger brother. His way of thinking, his responses to events, were "curioser and curioser." He lived exactly as if his awareness of things had been formed in some other dimension, after which he was plopped down on this planet to fend for himself. That was my first impression of him, and I stick by it. His name was Hiiragi. He was to turn eighteen this month.

Hiiragi and I had arranged to meet, after he got out of school, in a coffee shop on the fourth floor of a department store. In he came, wearing a sailor-style girl's high school uniform, complete with middy blouse and skirt.

The truth is I was mortified, but he acted so natural that I managed to feign calmness. Sitting down across from me, he asked, breathless, "Were you waiting long?" When I shook my head he smiled brightly. After he had ordered, the waitress stared him up and down and muttered, "Yes, sir," mystified.

He didn't look much like Hitoshi, but sometimes the way his face and fingers moved would remind me so much of his brother that my heart would stop.

"Oh!" I said, purposely giving voice to my surprise, as I always did when he reminded me of Hitoshi. It was part of a ritual between us.

"What is it?" he said, looking at me, cup in hand.

"You . . . you reminded me of him, just then," I said. Then, according to our ritual, he said, "I'll do Hitoshi," and imitated his brother. We both laughed. That was the only way the two of us had to make light of the wounds in our hearts.

I'd lost my boyfriend, but he had lost both brother and girlfriend at once.

His girlfriend, Yumiko, had been a small, pretty girl his own age, and a tennis ace. The four of us were close in age, got along well, and had often hung out together. I would go over to Hitoshi's house and Yumiko would be there with Hiiragi—I couldn't count how many times the four of us stayed up all night, playing games.

The night it happened, Hitoshi was giving Yumiko a ride from his house, where she'd been visiting Hiiragi, to the train station. On the way they got into an accident. It wasn't his fault. Still, the two of them were killed instantly.

"So, you're jogging?" said Hiiragi.

"Yes."

"Then why are you getting so fat?"

"It must be because I lie around all afternoon," I said, laughing. The truth was, I was getting noticeably thinner.

"Sports aren't good for you—it's true," he said. "But I have an idea—they just opened this place near my house that makes incredible tempura on rice. Very fattening. Let's go there now—right now!"

Although Hitoshi and Hiiragi had been very different from each other, they were both just naturally kind in a way that was without affectation or ulterior motives. That's how they were raised. The sort of kindness that makes a person wrap a bell in a handkerchief.

"I'd love to," I said.

The girl's school uniform Hiiragi was wearing had been Yumiko's.

After she died he had started wearing it to school, though he went to one where uniforms were not required. Yumiko had liked to wear the uniform. Both sets of parents had begged him, in tears, not to do it, saying Yumiko wouldn't have liked to see him in a skirt. Hiiragi just laughed and ignored them. When I asked him if he wore it for sentimental reasons, he said that wasn't it. "Things are just things, they can't bring back the dead. It just makes me feel better."

"Are you going to wear it forever?" I asked him.

His face darkened a little. "I don't know."

"Aren't people talking about you? Aren't they saying things about you at school?"

"No, they know that's just how I am. Actually, I'm getting a lot of sympathy. And the girls are crazy about me. It must be because, wearing a skirt, perhaps they think I understand them."

I laughed. "Well, that's good, isn't it?" Outside the glass wall of the coffee shop, crowds of boisterous shoppers came and went. The whole department store that evening was jovial, and gaily illuminated spring clothes were on display.

Now I understood. His sailor outfit—my jogging. They served exactly the same purpose. I wasn't as eccentric as him, so I was satisfied with mere jogging. Because nothing so conventional would do for Hiiragi, he chose the sailor outfit, as a variation. Neither recourse was anything more than a way of trying to lend some life to a shriveled spirit. It was a way to divert our minds, to kill time.

Both Hiiragi and I, in the last two months, had unconsciously assumed facial expressions we had never worn before, expressions that showed how we were battling not to think of what we had lost. If, in a flash, we remembered, we would suddenly be crushed with the knowledge, the knowledge of our loss, and find ourselves standing alone in the darkness.

I got up. "If I'm going to eat dinner out, I have to call home and let them know. What about you? Is it okay for you not to eat at home?"

Hiiragi said, "Oh, yeah, right. My father's away on a business trip."

"So your mother's all alone. You should probably go home."

"It's okay. I'll just have something delivered to her. It's still early, so she won't have started cooking yet. I'll pay for it, and she'll get this surprise dinner—compliments of her son."

"That's a sweet idea," I said.

"It'll cheer her up, don't you think?" Hiiragi smiled artlessly. This young boy, usually so precociously adult, looked his age right then.

One winter day Hitoshi had said, "I have a younger brother. His name is Hiiragi." It was the first time I had heard of him. We were climbing the long stone stairway behind the school, under leaden gray skies that promised snow. His hands in his coat pockets, his breath a cloud of white, Hitoshi had said, "But in a way he's more grown up than I am."

"Grown up?" I laughed.

"How can I say it? . . . he thinks well on his feet. But still, when it comes to the family, he's strangely childlike. Yesterday my father nicked his hand a little on a piece of glass, and my brother freaked out—really, seriously freaked out. You would have thought the sky had fallen. I just now thought of it, his reaction was so out of proportion."

"How old is he?"

"I guess he's . . . what, fifteen?"

"Does he look like you? I'd like to meet him."

"Well, I warn you, he's pretty weird. So much so you'd never take him for my brother. I'm afraid if you meet him you might stop liking me. Yes, he certainly is an odd one," said Hitoshi, smiling a classic elder-brother smile.

"Well, is your little brother so strange that you're going to wait till years from now to introduce me, when you're sure of my unwavering love?"

"No, I was kidding. It'll be all right. I'm sure you'll get on fine. You're a little strange yourself, and Hiiragi likes 'good people.'"

"'Good people?'"

"Right." Hitoshi laughed, still looking straight ahead. At times like that I always felt shy.

The stairs were steep and I hurried up, flustered. The windows of the white school building reflected the darkening dead-of-winter sky. I remembered climbing step by step in my black shoes and knee socks; the swish, swish of the skirt of my school uniform.

Outside, the night was filled with the scent of spring. Hiiragi's sailor-style uniform was hidden under his coat, which was a relief to me. The light given off by the department-store windows shone white on the faces of the bustling crowd. In spite of the sweet smell of spring on the wind, it was still cold. I took my gloves from my pocket.

"The tempura place is near my house, so it's a bit of a walk," said Hiiragi.

"We'll cross the bridge, then, won't we?" I fell silent, remembering the encounter with Urara. Every morning since then I had gone running, but I hadn't seen her again. I was absently thinking about that when Hiiragi suddenly said in a loud voice, "Oh—don't worry, of course I'll drive you back." He had interpreted my silence as worrying about how I'd get home.

"No, no, that's no problem. It's still early," I said, confused, thinking, you . . . you reminded me of him just then, although this time I didn't say it. At that moment he was so like Hitoshi there was no need to ask Hiiragi to do him. A kindness spoken out of reflex, at once impersonal and generous, but by no means bridging the distance established between two people—it always produces in me that sense of transparency, that deeply moving emotion I was being reminded of right then. An unbearable sense of loss.

"The other day," I said as we set off, "one morning when I was jogging, I met a strange person on the bridge. I was just remembering that."

"A strange person? You mean a man?" Hiiragi smiled. "Jogging early in the morning can be dangerous."

"No, it's not that at all. It was a woman. Not an easy person to forget."

"Maybe you ought to see her again."

"Hmm."

It was true; for some reason I wanted terribly to see Urara. That expression on her face—it made my heart stop. She had been gentle and smiling with me, and then, as soon as she was alone again, she . . . if I had to describe it, I'd say the expression on her face was like that of a demon turned into a human who suddenly caught herself feeling emotions and was warning herself that she wasn't permitted to. It was unforgettable. I felt that my own pain and sadness had never even come close to hers. Perhaps there was still much worse in store for me.

We came to a large intersection. Both Hiiragi and I felt a little ill at ease; this was the scene of the accident. Even now cars were coming and going furiously. At the red light Hiiragi and I stopped side by side.

"I wonder if there mightn't be ghosts here." Hiiragi smiled, but his eyes weren't smiling at all.

"I thought you were going to say that," I said, trying to smile back.

The traffic signal changed, and the river of light formed by the cars continued on its way. The signal shone brightly, suspended in the darkness. Hitoshi had died here. A feeling of solemnity slowly came over me. In places where a loved one has died, time stops for eternity. If I stand on the very spot, one says to oneself, like a prayer, might I feel the pain he felt? They say that on a visit to an old castle or whatever, the history of the place, the presence of people who walked there many years ago, can be felt in the body. Before, when I heard things like that, I would think, what are they talking about? But I felt I understood it now.

This intersection, the colors of these buildings, and rows of shops in the darkness were Hitoshi's last sights. And it wasn't all that long ago.

How afraid was he? Did he think of me, if even for a flickering instant? Was the moon climbing high in the sky as it was now?

"It's green." I was staring so absentmindedly at the moon that Hiiragi had to give me a push on the shoulder. The small white light it gave off was so pretty, so cold; it was like a pearl.

"It's amazing how good this is," I said. The tempura on rice we were eating, seated at the counter in this new little shop smelling of fresh wood, was so good it revived my appetite.

"Isn't it?" said Hiiragi.

"Yes. It's delicious. So delicious it makes me grateful I'm alive," I said. So delicious I was moved to praise extravagant enough to make the counter person blush.

"I know. I knew you'd say that. You have excellent taste in food. It really makes me happy that you like it." After saying that all in one breath, with a big smile, Hiiragi went to order the meal for his mother and have it delivered.

With the bowl of food before me, I thought: I'm stubborn, and I'll probably be dragged even deeper into this darkness, but I have no choice. I must keep living this way. But, as soon as possible, I wanted this boy to be always smiling, like he was now, like he always used to, and without the sailor outfit.

It was noon. Suddenly the phone rang.

I had caught cold and was drowsing in bed. I hadn't even been able to go jogging. The ring of the telephone jabbed into my slightly feverish brain again and again. Sleepily I got out of bed. No one seemed to be home, so I had no choice—I went out into the hall and picked up the receiver.

"Yes?"

"Hello. Is Satsuki there?" It was an unfamiliar woman's voice.

"This is she," I said, puzzled.

"It's me," said the person across the phone lines. "Urara."

I was startled. Again she had shocked me. How in the world had she found me?

"Sorry this is so sudden, but I wonder if you're free just now? Can you come out and meet me?"

"Umm . . . sure. But why? How did you get my phone number?" I said, faltering. She seemed to be calling from a phone booth, judging by the sound of traffic in the background. I heard little puffs of laughter.

"I just say to myself, 'I *must* get this phone number,' and it just naturally comes to me," Urara said, as if reciting a spell. She said it in such a matter-of-fact, reasonable way that I thought, oh, I see.

"Meet me on the fifth floor of the department store across from the station, in the section where they sell thermoses." With that she hung up.

Normally there would be no way I'd go out now—the way I feel with this cold, I should stay in bed, I thought after she had hung up. My legs were wobbly and it felt like my fever was getting worse. But still, driven by curiosity to see her again, I started to get ready. In the innermost recess of my heart the light of instinct was twinkling, and I was as free of doubt as if I had heard the command, "Go!"

In retrospect I realize that fate was a ladder on which, at the time, I could not afford to miss a single rung. To skip out on even one scene would have meant never making it to the top, although it would have been by far the easier choice. What motivated me was probably that little light still left in my half-dead heart, glittering in the darkness. Yet without it, perhaps, I might have slept better.

I bundled up in warm clothing and got on my bike. It was a noon enveloped in warm sunlight—it made you think that spring would truly come. A light wind was blowing, soft and gentle on the face. The trees on the street were beginning to sprout their tiny infant leaves. A thin veil of mist hung distantly in the pale blue sky far beyond the city.

Such blossoming delectability did not make my own insides flutter; it left me unmoved. The spring scenery could not enter my heart for love or money. It was merely reflected on the surface, like on a soap bubble. Everyone out on the streets was coming and going, looking happy, the light shining through their hair. Everything was breathing, increasingly sparkling, swathed in the gentle sunlight. The pretty scene was brimming with life, but my soul was pining for the desolate streets of winter and for that river at dawn. I wished my heart would break and get it over with.

There stood Urara, her back to the display of water bottles. Wearing a pink sweater, standing ramrod-straight in the midst of the crowd, this time she looked my age.

"Hi," I called. When I came nearer her eyes widened. "What?" she said. "You have a cold? Oh, I'm sorry. I didn't know when I asked you to come out."

I smiled. "Is it that obvious?"

"Yes, your face is bright red. So . . . let's choose quickly, shall we? Any one you like." She turned to face the display. "So what do you think? Probably a thermos, right? Or for running you might want a lighter one. This one is just like the one you dropped the other day. Or, oh, if it's design you care most about, let's go to where they sell ones made in China."

Her enthusiasm as she said all this made me so happy, even I could feel myself turning bright red.

"Okay, that little white one." Beaming with pleasure, I pointed out a small thermos.

"Mmm. The honored customer is a person of fine discernment," Urara said, and bought it for me.

As we were drinking barley tea in a nearby rooftop garden tea shop, Urara said, "I brought you this, too." She took a small packet from her coat pocket. Then another, and another, again and again. I could only stare.

"Somebody who owns a tea shop gave me this as a parting gift. There are all sorts of herbal teas, barley teas, Chinese teas, too. The names are written on the packages. Something to fill your thermos with. I hope you like them."

". . . Thank you, so much," I said, hesitant, pleased.

"Not at all. It was my fault you dropped yours in the river."

The afternoon was clear and bright. The light illuminating the streets was so vivid it almost made one's heart ache. Clouds moved slowly, dividing the city below into patches of light and shadow. It was a peaceful afternoon. The weather was so tranquil that it almost made me forget I had any problems at all—aside from the fact that my nose was stuffed up and I could taste only a hint of what I was drinking.

"By the way," I said, "how *did* you get my phone number, really?"

She smiled. "I told you. That was the truth. For a long time I've been on my own, moving around from place to place, and I developed this ability to just . . . sense things, calmly, like a wild animal. I don't remember exactly when that started, but . . . So I thought to myself, Satsuki's phone number is . . . ? And when I dialed, I just let my fingers move naturally. I usually get it right."

"Usually?" I smiled.

"Yes, usually. When I'm wrong I just apologize, laugh, and hang up. Still it makes me ashamed of myself." Urara laughed cheerfully.

I wanted to believe she got the number that way rather than by other, more normal methods. That's the effect she had on a person. Somewhere deep in my heart I felt I had known her long ago, and the reunion made me so nostalgic I wanted to weep tears of joy.

"I want to thank you for today. You've made me as happy as a lover," I said.

"All right, then, here's a word from your lover: get over that cold by the day after tomorrow."

"Why? Oh, is it the day after tomorrow? The something to see?"

"Precisely. All right? You mustn't tell anyone else." Urara lowered her voice a little. "The day after tomorrow, come to the place where we met the other day by no later than four fifty-seven A.M. If all goes well you may see something."

"What is this something? What kind of thing? Something invisible?" I couldn't hold back a flood of doubts.

"Yes. But it depends on the weather, and also on you. Because this is a very subtle matter, there are no guarantees. Still, and this is just my intuition, I think there's a profound connection between you and that river. That's why I'm sure you'll be able to see it. The day after tomorrow, at the time I said, in that place, if a number of conditions are met, you *may* be able to see a kind of . . . vision, something that happens only once every hundred years or so. I'm afraid 'may' is the best I can do."

That explanation didn't really clarify much, either. Still, I was deeply thrilled, something I had not felt in a long time.

"Is it a good thing?"

"Yes . . . Not just good, though—priceless. That's up to you."

That's up to me.

Just now, when I'm so weak, with no strength to defend myself . . .

"Yes," I said, "I'll be there."

The connection between me and the river. Even with my heart beating wildly, my mind shouted out an impromptu *yes!* The border between my country and Hitoshi's—that's what the river was to me. When I thought of the bridge, it was always with Hitoshi standing there, waiting for me to come. I was always late; he was always there before me. When we said good-bye, it was there that we parted, he going to one side of the river, me to the other. The last time was that way, too.

"So," I had said, "you're going over to Takahashi's house after this?" I was still happy then and had a healthy plumpness that I've lost now. This was our last conversation.

"Yes, after I stop off at home first. We haven't gotten all the guys together in a long time."

"Give them my regards. But I know what you all talk about when it's just guys."

"Anything wrong with that?" He laughed.

We had done nothing but have fun that whole day and, a little tipsy, we walked along laughing and joking. The bitingly cold night road was splendidly colored by the starry sky overhead, and I was lighthearted. The wind stung my cheeks, the stars twinkled. Our hands, joined in my pocket, palms touching, felt very warm and soft.

Then, "Oh," he said, as if suddenly remembering something. "But I swear, I'd never say anything bad about you!" He was so touchingly funny as he said it that I had to bury my face in my muffler to stifle my laughter. To have loved each other this much for over four years, I thought, isn't it marvelous. That me seems ten years younger than I feel now. The faint sound of the river reached our ears; the moment of our parting was approaching.

The bridge. That bridge was where we left each other, never to meet again. The river roared, and the cold wind was like a slap in the face. Amid its vivid thundering, under the sky full of stars, we exchanged a short kiss, and thinking how much fun that winter vacation had been, we parted, smiling. The tinkle of the bell disappeared into the night. Hitoshi and I both cherished that sound.

We had horrible fights and we both had our little outside flings. We suffered from the changing balance between love and desire. Children that we were, we hurt each other many times over. So it isn't that we were always as happy as we were that day; our times together were often painful. Still, it was a good four years, and that day was an unusually perfect one for us, so much so as to make us fearful it would end. Of that day in which everything was just too beautiful in the transparent winter air, what I remember most is the sight, when I turned back to look, of Hitoshi's black jacket melting into the darkness.

That scene is one I cried about over and over again. Or rather, whenever I recalled it, the tears would flow. I would dream of myself crossing the bridge, chasing after him and calling out, "You mustn't go!" In the dream, Hitoshi would smile and say, "I didn't die after all, because you stopped me."

Sometimes the memory would come to me in the middle of the day, and I would manage not to break down in public—but what good did it do me? I felt he had gone somewhere endlessly far from me, and my stoicism only made the feeling worse.

When I parted with Urara, that "something" I *might* be able to see at the river was, for me, half joke, half hope. Urara, beaming, disappeared up the street.

Maybe she's just telling me some weird kind of lie, I thought, but I wouldn't even mind if, bright and early, I ran there, chest pounding, only to make a fool of myself. She had shown my heart a rainbow. The thing was . . . she had reminded me that I could get excited over something unknown, and a tiny window opened in my heart. Even if nothing happened—even if it turned out to be just the two of us watching the sparkling glints off the cold, flowing river—it would feel good. It would be enough for me.

That was what I was thinking as I walked along, holding my thermos. On the way to get my bike where I'd left it at the station, I spotted Hiiragi.

There he was, in the middle of the street, wearing his regular clothes. He must be skipping school, I thought, which made me smile.

It wasn't that I was hesitant to run up to him and call his name—it was just that because of my fever I couldn't muster the energy, so all I did was walk toward him without changing my pace. Just then he set off in the direction I was going anyway, so quite naturally I followed him up the street. He was a fast walker, and I, unwilling to go faster, soon fell behind.

I watched Hiiragi. In his own clothes, he was good-looking enough to turn people's heads. Wearing a black sweater, he was walking along like he always did—tall, long-limbed, calm, cool, and light on his feet. No wonder, I thought as I watched him from behind, the girls couldn't get enough of him. Yumiko had died, and he was wearing her uniform in her memory. It just didn't happen that often, losing one's brother and girlfriend at once. It was the epitome of unusual. Maybe I, too, were I a carefree high school girl, would long to be the one to restore him to life and would fall in love with him. Girls that age find nothing more attractive.

If I just called out his name he would turn and smile at me. I knew that. But still, somehow I had a bad feeling about calling to him as he walked alone up the street; I felt there was nothing anyone could do for him. Or maybe it was just that I was terribly tired. Nothing could enter directly into my heart. All I wanted was to get through this as quickly as possible, to see the day when memories would be just memories. But the more I wanted that, the further away it seemed. Thinking of the future only made me shudder.

Then Hiiragi suddenly stopped, and I automatically stopped, too. Now you really are trailing him, I said to myself, smiling. I took a step toward him and was about to call out—then I realized what he was looking at and froze in my tracks.

He was staring into the window of a tennis shop. How well I understood the blank look on his face as he peered into that window. He seemed to be feeling nothing at all. But in that very lack of expression, the profundity of what he was doing was transmitted nonetheless. It's like unconscious conditioning, I thought, like a baby duck trailing after some moving object, taking it for its mother. Though the baby duck is unaware of it, it's very touching for the observer.

That's how I felt, watching Hiiragi.

In the spring light he stood among the crowd, staring, staring detachedly into that window. The sight of all that tennis equipment must have had a powerful effect on him. It did the same thing for Hiiragi that being with him did for me: thanks to the trace of Hitoshi in him, his very presence calmed me. I thought how sad that was.

I myself saw one of Yumiko's tennis matches. The first time I met her I thought she was cute, all right, but she struck me as a bit average, rather overly cheerful, not too deep, and I couldn't imagine what Hiiragi saw in her that bewitched him so. With Yumiko, Hiiragi was in a dream. On the surface he was the same old Hiiragi, but something in her quieted his spirit. In real strength, she was his match.

"What is it about her?" I asked Hitoshi one time.

"Apparently it's tennis," he said, smiling.

"Tennis?"

"Yes. According to Hiiragi, she's incredible."

It was summer. The sun beat down mercilessly on the high school tennis court. Hitoshi, Hiiragi, and I had gone to watch Yumiko play in the finals. The shadows were deep and dark under the blazing sun; our throats were dry. Everything was dazzlingly bright.

And no doubt about it, she was incredible. She was a different person, not the little girl who ran after me laughing, calling, "Satsuki, Satsuki." I was amazed when I saw her play. Hitoshi seemed surprised, too. Hiiragi said with pride, "See what I mean? Incredible, isn't she?"

She played a take-no-prisoners game of tennis, propelled by the full force of her intensity and powers of concentration. Then I knew how strong she really was. Her face was all determination. It was a face capable of murder. Still, after the deciding shot, the instant she'd won, she turned to Hiiragi with her old baby-faced smile. It was impressive.

The four of us had a lot of fun together, and I liked her very much. She'd say to me, "Satsuki, let's the four of us always hang out together, don't you two ever break up." Teasing, I would smile and say, "Well, it won't be us." She would laugh and say, "Well, it won't be us either!"

And then it happened. It's too horrible.

I doubted if he was recalling her at this moment like I was. Boys don't go out of their way to feel pain. But still, his eyes, his whole person, were saying one thing only. He himself would never speak it. To say it would mean to suffer from it. To suffer terribly. That thing was, "I want her to come back."

More than words, it was a prayer. I couldn't bear it. Was that, then, how I looked by the river at dawn? And is that why Urara had spoken to me? Me, too. I, too, wanted to see him. I wanted him. Hitoshi. To come back. At the very least, I wanted to say a proper good-bye.

I knew I wouldn't tell Hiiragi what I'd seen today. I resolved to speak up cheerfully the next time, but for now I left without calling to him.

With all that activity, my fever went up. It makes sense, I thought; it simply follows that if one goes running around town in the condition I was in, delirious, this would be the result.

My mother laughed and asked me if it might not be like a teething fever. Weakly, I laughed back. But in a sense I think it was. Perhaps my unproductive thoughts had spread like poison throughout my body.

That night, as usual, I awoke from a dream of Hitoshi. I dreamed that in spite of my fever I had run to the river and Hitoshi was there. He said to me, smiling, "You've got a cold; what are you doing?" That was the lowest point yet. When I opened my eyes it was dawn, time to get up and get dressed. But it was cold, so very cold, and in spite of the fact that my whole body felt flushed, my hands and feet were like ice. I had the chills; I shuddered, my whole body in pain.

I opened my eyes, trembling in the half-darkness. I felt I was battling something absurdly enormous. Then, from deep within, I began to wonder if I mightn't lose.

It hurt to have lost Hitoshi. It hurt too much.

When we were in each other's arms, I knew something that was beyond words. It was the mystery of being close to someone who is not family. My heart dropped out, and I was feeling what people fear the most; I touched the deepest despair a person can know. I was lonely. Hideously lonely. This was the worst. If I could get through this, morning would come, and I knew without a doubt that I would have fun again, laugh out loud. If only the sun would rise. If only morning would come.

Whenever it had been like this before, I had set my teeth and stood up to it; but now, lacking the strength to go to the river, I could only suffer. Time inched along, as if I were walking on shards of glass. I felt that if I could only get to the river, Hitoshi really would be there. I felt insane. I was sick at heart.

    I sluggishly got up and went to the kitchen for some tea. My throat was parched. Because of my fever, the whole house looked surreally warped, distorted; the kitchen was ice-cold and dark. Everyone was asleep. Delirious, I made tea and went back to my room.

    The tea seemed to help. It soothed my dry throat and my breathing became natural again. I sat up in bed and parted the curtains.

    From my room I had a good view of the front gate and yard. The trees and flowers rustled, trembling in the blue morning air—they seemed painted in flat colors, like a diorama in a museum. It was pretty. These days I was well aware of how the blue air of dawn makes everything seem purified. As I sat there peering out the window, I saw the shadow of a person coming up the sidewalk in front of my house.

    I wondered if it was a dream and blinked my eyes. It was Urara. Dressed in blue, grinning broadly, she looked at me and came toward me. At the gate she mouthed, "May I come in?" I nodded. She crossed the yard and reached my window. I opened it, my heart pounding.

    "Sure is cold out," she said. An icy wind came in through the window, freezing my feverish cheeks. The pure, clean air tasted delicious.

    "What's up?" I asked. I must have been beaming like a happy little kid.

    "I'm on my way home. Your cold is looking worse, you know. Here, I'll give you some vitamin C candy." Taking the candy from her pocket, she handed it to me, smiling artlessly.

    "You're always so good to me," I said in a hoarse voice.

    "You look like your temperature is very high. You must feel rotten."

    "Yes," I said. "I couldn't go running this morning." For some reason I felt like crying.

    "With a cold"—she spoke evenly, lowering her eyes a little—"now is the hardest time. Maybe even harder than dying. But this is probably as bad as it can get. You might come to fear the next time you get a cold; it will be as bad as this, but if you just hold steady, it won't be. For the rest of your life. That's how it works. You could take the negative view and live in fear: Will it happen again? But it won't hurt so much if you just accept it as a part of life." With that she looked up at me, smiling.

I remained silent, my eyes wide. Was she only talking about having a cold? Just what was she saying? The blue of the dawn, my fever, everything was spinning, and the boundary between dream and waking blurred. While her words were making their way into my heart, I was staring absently at her bangs, which were fluttering in the wind.

"Well, see you tomorrow." With a smile, Urara gently shut the window from the outside. She skipped lightly out the gate.

Floating in a dream, I watched her walk away. That she had come to me at the end of a long night of misery made me want to cry tears of joy. I wanted to tell her: "How happy I am that you came to me like an apparition in that bluish mist. Now everything around me will be a little bit better when I wake up." At last I was able to fall asleep.

When I awoke I knew that my cold was at least a little better. I slept so soundly that it was evening before I woke up. I got out of bed, took a shower, put on a fresh change of clothes, started drying my hair. My fever was down and I felt quite well, except for the sensation of my body having been through the mill.

I wondered, under the hot wind of the hair dryer, if Urara had really come to see me. Maybe it was just a dream—her words resounded in my brain as if it had been. And had she really only been talking about having a cold?

My face in the mirror had a touch of dark shadow on it, making me wonder—was this a harbinger of other terrible nights to come, like the aftershocks following an earthquake? I was so tired that I couldn't bear to think about it. I was truly exhausted. But still... more than anything, I wanted to evade those thoughts, even if I had to do it on my hands and knees.

For one thing, I was breathing more easily than I had been even yesterday. I was sick to death at the prospect of more suffocatingly lonely nights. The idea that they would be repeated, that that was just how life was, made me shudder with horror. Still, having tasted for myself that moment when I suddenly could breathe easy again made my heart beat faster.

I found I was able to smile a little. The knowledge of how quickly my fever had dissipated made me a little giddy. Just then there was an unexpected knock at my bedroom door. I thought it was my mother and said, "Come in." When the door opened, I was amazed to see Hiiragi.

"Your mother says she kept calling you, but you didn't answer," he said.

"I was drying my hair, I guess I couldn't hear." I was embarrassed to be caught in the intimacy of my room with just-washed, unstyled hair, but he said, nonplussed, "When I phoned, your mother said you had a cold, like a terrible teething fever, so I thought I'd come and see how you're doing."

I remembered that he'd been here with Hitoshi, like the day of the festival and that time after the baseball game. So, just like old times, he grabbed a cushion and flopped down. It was only I who had forgotten how well we knew each other.

"I brought you a get-well present." Hiiragi laughed, indicating a large paper bag. At this point I couldn't tell him I was actually just about over it. I even forced a cough. He had come all this way because he thought I was sick. "It's a chicken filet sandwich from Kentucky Fried, which I know you love, and some sherbet. Cokes, too. And, I brought enough for myself, so let's eat."

He was treating me like I was made of brittle glass. My mother must have said something to him. I was embarrassed. Still, it wasn't as if I were so much better I could say flat out, "I'm completely well!"

In the brightly lit room, warmed by my little heater, the two of us calmly ate what he had brought. The food was delicious, and I realized how very, very hungry I was. It occurred to me I always enjoyed what I ate when I was with him. How wonderful that is, I thought.

"Satsuki."

"What?" In a reverie, realizing he had said my name, I looked up.

"You've got to stop torturing yourself, all alone, getting thinner and thinner—you even got a fever from it. When you feel like that, call me up. We'll get together, go do something. Every time I see you you look more frail, but you pretend everything's all right. That's a waste of energy. I know you and Hitoshi were so happy together that now you could die of sadness. It's only natural."

He had never said anything like that. It was odd—that was the first time I had seen him express such emotion: sympathy as open and unguarded as a child's. Because I had thought his style too cool for that, it was totally unexpected, this purehearted concern. But then I remembered Hitoshi saying how Hiiragi, usually old beyond his years, reverted to a childlike state where the family was concerned. I had to smile—I felt I understood now what Hitoshi had meant.

"I know I'm still a kid, and when I take off the sailor outfit I feel so alone I could cry, but we're all brothers and sisters when we're in trouble, aren't we? I care about you so much, I just want to crawl into the same bed with you."

He said it with such an utterly sincere face, and it was so obvious his intentions were honorable, I had to smile in spite of myself. Then I said to him, deeply moved, "I'll do as you say. I really will, I'll call you, I mean it. Thank you. Really, truly, thank you."

After Hiiragi left I went back to sleep. Thanks to the cold medicine I took, I slept through a long, peaceful, dreamless night. It was the divine, anticipatory sleep I remember having slept as a child on Christmas Eve. When I awoke, I would go to Urara waiting at the river, and I would see the "something."

It was before dawn. Although my health was not quite back to normal, I got dressed and went running. It was the kind of frozen morning in which moon shadows seem to be pasted on the sky. The sound of my footsteps resonated in the silent blue air and faded away into the emptiness of the streets.

Urara was standing by the bridge. When I got there her hands were in her pockets and her muffler covered her mouth, but her sparkling eyes showed she was smiling brightly. "Good morning," she said.

The last few stars in the blue porcelain sky winked, a dim white, as if about to go out. The scene was thrillingly beautiful. The river roared furiously; the air was very clear.

"So blue it feels like it could melt right into your body," said Urara, gesturing at the sky.

The faint outline of the rustling trees trembled in the wind; gently, the heavens began to move. The moon shone through the half-dark.

"It's time." Urara's voice was tense. "Ready? What's going to happen next is, the dimension we're in—time, space, all that stuff—is going to move, shift a little. You and I, although we'll be standing side by side, probably won't be able to see each other, and we won't be seeing the same things . . . across the river. Whatever you do, you mustn't say anything, and you mustn't cross the bridge. Got it?"

I nodded. "Got it."

Then we fell silent. The only sound the roaring of the river, side by side Urara and I fixed our eyes on the far bank. My heart was pounding. I realized my legs were trembling. Dawn crept up little by little. The sky changed to a light blue. The birds began to sing.

I had a feeling that I heard something faint, far away. I looked to one side and was startled—Urara wasn't there anymore. The river, myself, the sky—then, blended with the sounds of the wind and the river, I heard what I'd longed for.

A bell. There was no question, it was Hitoshi's. The sound came, faintly tinkling, from a spot where no one was standing. I closed my eyes, making sure of the sound. Then I opened them, and when I looked across the river I felt crazier than I had in the whole last two months. I just barely managed to keep from crying out.

There was Hitoshi.

Across the river, if this wasn't a dream, and I wasn't crazy, the figure facing me was Hitoshi. Separated from him by the water, my chest welling up, I focused my eyes on that form, the very image of the memory I kept in my heart.

Through the blue haze, he was looking in my direction. He had that worried expression he always had when I acted recklessly. His hands in his pockets, his eyes found mine. The years I had spent in his arms seemed both very near and very far away. We simply gazed at each other. Only the fading moon saw the too-violent current, the too-distant chasm between us. My hair, the collar of Hitoshi's dear, familiar shirt fluttered in the wind off the river as softly as in a dream.

Hitoshi, do you want to talk to me? I want to talk to you. I want to run to your side, take you in my arms, and rejoice in being together again. But, but—the tears flowed—fate has decided that you and I be so clearly divided like this, facing each other across the river, and I don't have a say in it.

My tears fell like rain; all I could do was stare at him. Hitoshi looked sadly back at me. I wished time could stop—but with the first rays of the rising sun everything slowly began to fade away. Before my eyes, Hitoshi grew faint. When I began to panic, he smiled and waved his hand. Again and again, he waved his hand. He was disappearing into the blue void. I, too, waved. Dear, much-missed Hitoshi—I tried to burn the line of his dear shoulders, his dear arms, all of him, into my brain. The faint colors of his form, even the heat of the tears running down my cheeks: I desperately struggled to memorize it all. The arching lines described by his arm remained, like an afterimage, suspended in the air. His form was slowly growing fainter, disappearing. I stared at it through my tears.

By the time I could no longer see anything at all, everything had returned to normal: morning by the river. I looked to one side; there stood Urara. Still facing straight ahead, a heartbreaking sadness in her eyes, she asked me, "Did you see it?"

"Yes," I said, wiping away my tears.

"Was it everything you had hoped?" This time she turned to face me, smiling. Relief diffused through my heart. "It was," I said, smiling back at her. The two of us stood there in the sunshine for some time, as morning came.

The doughnut shop had just opened. Urara, her eyes a little sleepy, said over a hot cup of coffee, "I came to this place because I, too, lost my lover to an early death. I came hoping to say a last good-bye."

"Were you able to?" I asked.

"Yes." Urara smiled a little. "It really does happen only once every hundred years or so, and then only if a number of chance factors happen to line up right. The time and the place are not definitely set. People who know about it call it 'The Weaver Festival Phenomenon.' It can only take place near a large river. Some people can't see it at all. The residual thoughts of a person who has died meet the sadness of someone left behind, and the vision is produced. This was my first experience of it, too. . . . I think you were very lucky today."

"Every hundred years . . ." My mind raced at the thought of the probabilities involved in my having been able to see it.

"When I arrived here to take a preliminary look at the site, there you were. My animal instincts told me that you had lost someone yourself. That's why I invited you." The morning sun shone through her hair. Urara, smiling, was still as a statue while she spoke.

What kind of person was she, really? Where had she come from and where would she go from here? And who had she seen across the river? I couldn't ask her.

"Parting and death are both terribly painful. But to keep nursing the memory of a love so great you can't believe you'll ever love again is a useless drain on a woman's energies." Urara spoke through a mouthful of doughnut, as if making casual chitchat.

"So I think it's for the best that we were able to say a proper, final good-bye today." Her eyes became terribly sad.

". . . Yes," I said. "So do I." Urara's eyes narrowed gently as she sat in the sunlight.

Hitoshi waving good-bye. It was a painful sight, like a ray of light piercing my heart.

Whether it had been for the best was not something I as yet fully understood. I only knew that, right now, sitting in the strong sunlight, its lingering memory in my breast was very painful. It hurt so much I could barely breathe.

Still . . . still, looking at the smiling Urara before me, amid the smell of weak coffee, the feeling was strong within me of having been very near the "something." I heard the windows rattle in the wind. Like Hitoshi when we parted, no matter how much I could lay bare my heart, no matter how much I strained my eyes, that "something" would remain transitory. That was certain. That "something" shone in the gloom with the strength of the sun itself; at a great speed, I was coming through. In a downpour of blessings, I prayed, as though it were a hymn: Let me become stronger.

"Where will you go now?" I asked as we walked out of the doughnut shop.

Smiling, she took my hand. "We'll meet again someday. I'll never forget your phone number."

With that, she melted into the wave of people crowding the morning streets. I watched her go and thought, I, too, will not forget. How very much you have given me.

"I saw something the other day," said Hiiragi.

I had gone to meet him to give him a birthday present during the lunch break at his high school, my alma mater. I had been waiting on a bench by the school grounds, watching the students come and go, when he came running up to me. He was no longer wearing the sailor outfit. He sat down next to me.

"You saw what?" I asked.

"Yumiko," he said. My heart skipped a beat. Students in white gym suits ran past us, kicking up dust.

"The morning of . . . was it the day before yesterday? . . ." he continued. "It may have been a dream. I was sort of half-asleep when suddenly the door opened and Yumiko walked in. It was all so normal I forgot she was dead and I said, 'Yumiko?' She smiled, put her finger to her lips, and said, 'Shhhhh.'

She went to my closet, carefully took out the sailor outfit, and bundled it up in her arms. Then, her lips silently forming 'Bye-bye,' she waved good-bye. I didn't know what to do—I fell back asleep, thinking it must have been a dream. But the sailor outfit is gone. I looked everywhere for it. Then I just suddenly burst out crying."

"Hmm," I said. Could it be that it could happen somewhere other than the river? It was the right day, the right morning. With Urara gone I had no way of knowing for sure. But he was so calm about it. There was more to Hiiragi than met the eye. Perhaps he had the power to draw an event to himself that should only have occurred at the river.

"Do you think I've lost my mind?" he asked, jokingly.

In the faint spring afternoon sunshine, the lunch hour hubbub coming from the school building carried on the wind. I laughed, gave him his present, a record, and said, "I recommend jogging when you feel like that."

Hiiragi laughed, too. Sitting there in the light, he laughed and laughed.

Hitoshi:

I'll never be able to be here again. As the minutes slide by, I move on. The flow of time is something I cannot stop. I haven't a choice. I go.

One caravan has stopped, another starts up. There are people I have yet to meet, others I'll never see again. People who are gone before you know it, people who are just passing through. Even as we exchange hellos, they seem to grow transparent. I must keep living with the flowing river before my eyes.

I earnestly pray that a trace of my girl-child self will always be with you.

For waving good-bye, I thank you. ■

DISCUSSING THE SELECTION

1. What does the title of this story mean? Support your answer with evidence from the story.

2. What is the significance of the bell? What does the bell indicate about Satsuki? What does the bell indicate about Hitoshi? What evidence in the story supports your ideas?

3. What specific evidence in the story indicates that Satsuki is suffering from grief? How does she cope with her grief? How does Hiiragi cope with his grief?

4. What are some of the differences between the two brothers, Hitoshi and Hiiragi? Why does Satsuki remain friendly with Hiiragi? Why does he remain friendly with her?

5. When does Urara appear in the story? What occurs to indicate that Urara is unusual in her abilities and knowledge?

THINKING CRITICALLY

1. How does the reader know that Satsuki trusts Urara? Why does she trust her? What is Urara's role in this story?

2. What do you find out about Hiiragi from this story? Why does he dress in a girl's uniform for part of the story? Why does he stop doing this? What is his role in the story?

3. What is the difference in the roles that Urara and Hiiragi play in helping Satsuki heal from her loss? What other stories do you know in which someone helps the main character to fulfill a goal or a dream? Which of these stories would you recommend to other readers in your class? Explain why you think your classmates might enjoy these stories.

4. Have you ever had an experience in which you wanted to say something to someone who was no longer in your life? How did you cope with it? Explain your situation to the class and tell how the situation was finally resolved.

5. In what ways was this story sad? In what ways was it positive? What is your overall feeling about this story?

FOCUSING ON THE WRITING

1. Do we know the inner thoughts and feelings of any of the characters in this story? What type of narrator is found in "Moonlight Shadow"?

2. Reread the story focusing on the river. When in the story does the river appear? In what ways is the river significant to Satsuki's experience? What are some symbolic meanings of the river in life? What other stories do you know in which a river was significant? Compare the way those writers used the river in their stories with the way Yoshimoto used the river in this story.

3. In the story, Satsuki thinks:

   Maybe she's just telling me some weird kind of lie, I thought, but I wouldn't even mind if, bright and early, I ran there, chest pounding, only to make a fool of myself. She had shown my heart a rainbow.

   "Shown my heart a rainbow" is a poetic way of expressing Satsuki's feelings. What does it mean? What does the rainbow symbolize?

4. Compare the writing in this story with the Ames story on page 167 and the Shreve story on page 189. These stories also deal with loss. What specific differences do you notice in the writing—place and character descriptions, ways the characters talk, vocabulary and word choice, emotional tone, and the beginning and ending of the stories. Which writer's style do you prefer and why?

5. Yoshimoto writes the following statement in the "Afterword" section of *Kitchen*, the book from which this story was excerpted:

   For a very long time there was something I wanted to say in a novel, and I wanted, no matter what it took, to continue writing until I got the saying of it out of my system. This book is what resulted from that history of persistence.

   As a writer, think about what you want to say that only you can say. In your journal, write about what you would like to say and use the writing experiences in this book to help you do it.

CREATING YOUR TEXT

1. Rewrite the story, "Moonlight Shadow," from the point of view of one of the other characters in the story, revealing that person's thoughts and feelings in detail.

2. Think about a time when you were able to help someone overcome a difficult obstacle. Write an essay in which you describe the problem, your response, and the result. What did you learn about yourself from this experience?

3. The behavior of the characters in "Moonlight Shadow" is influenced by the culture and experiences of living in Japan. Write an essay describing a person you know whose behavior is affected by cultural, ethnic, or religious background. Describe a particular event and how that person responded to it because of his or her background. What have you learned from knowing and observing that person?

4. Hiiragi's friendship with Satsuki helps her heal from her loss. Write about an incident in which a younger person has helped you deal with a problem. Describe the person and explain how his or her point of view enabled you to see your experience differently.

5. When in life should people be active and when should they be passive in dealing with difficult problems? Explain your ideas, describing specific events in your life, observations, or readings that have developed your present understanding.

REVISING YOUR TEXT

Review the first draft of your writing by going over the revision questions on page 12 for an essay and on page 14 if you have written a story.

Notice "how" you included stories in your essays. Think about the following questions as you reread what you have written:

Do you describe your characters in detail? What specifically do you want your reader to know about your characters? If your characters talk, do they each have distinct and individual voices?

What details do you include about the settings in which your stories occur to give your reader a sense of place?

Do you include a beginning, middle, and end to each event so your reader can follow your ideas and understand why you have chosen to tell these stories?

Do your stories fit in with the theme of the particular question you have chosen to answer?

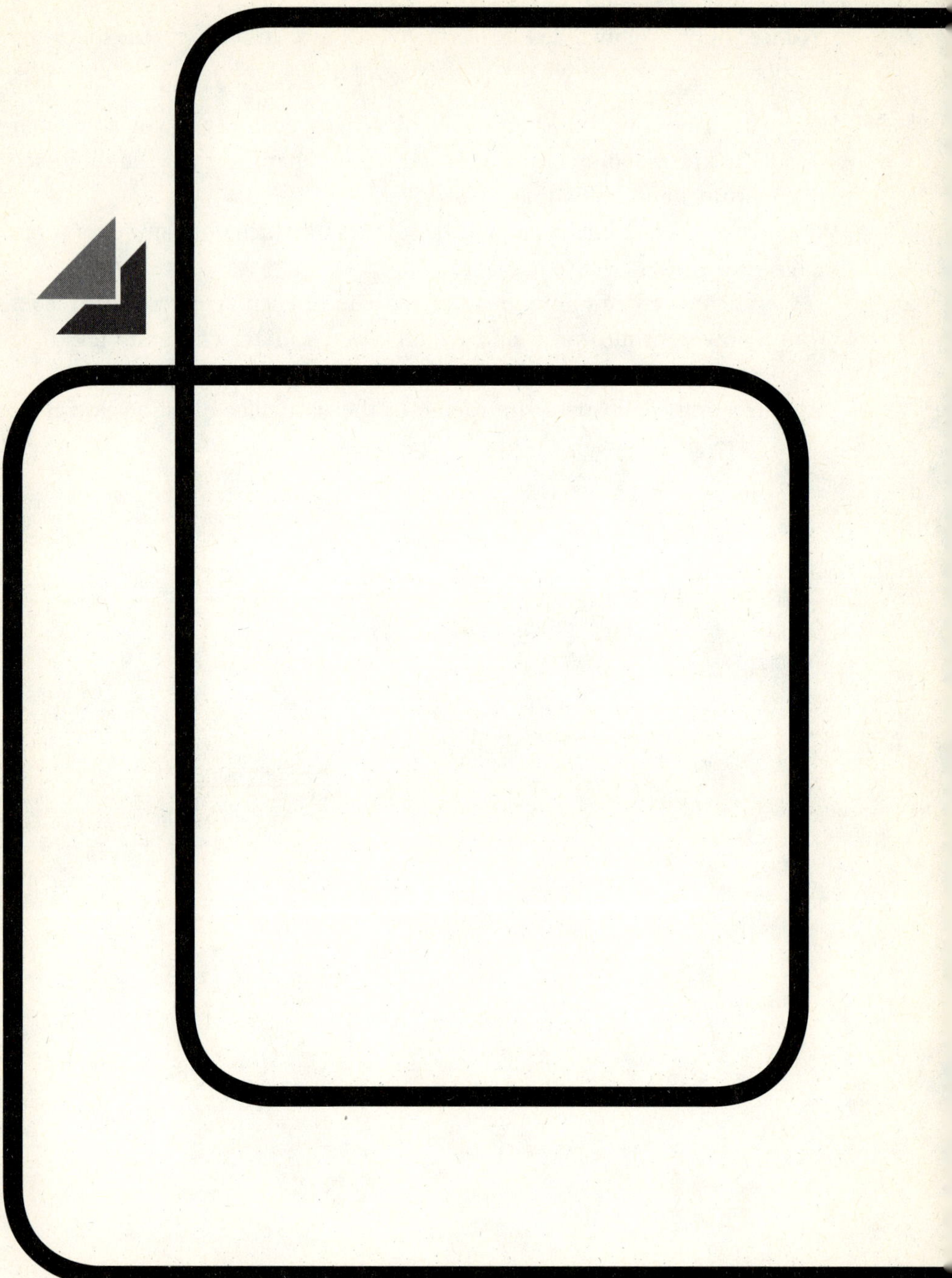

Appendix I

Focus on Editing

Most writers prefer to write out their ideas in a rough first draft. They, then read over what they have written, focusing on how clearly they have expressed themselves. After they have identified the areas that need more work, they write a second draft making any needed changes. Finally, writers proofread or edit their draft to finish the final paper.

Editing is the stage in the writing process that involves careful proofreading for correct format, punctuation, grammar, spelling, consistency of voice, and best possible word choice. The writer's goal is to create a text that is as correct and clear as possible so readers will understand the ideas presented.

The numbered questions in this appendix correspond with the editing questions on page 15. If you have difficulties with a specific question, read the explanation following the question before editing your paper.

1. Is each paragraph indented?

When you write essays for college papers and for personal letters, indent the first word in each new paragraph five spaces or one "tab" on the word processor or typewriter. If you are writing by hand, indent approximately that amount of space, so your readers know where each new paragraph begins.

When you type business letters or reports, you do not need to indent each paragraph, but you do have to add an extra line of space between the paragraphs.

2. Does each sentence begin with a capital letter? Did you capitalize all the words that need capitalizing?

Each new sentence must begin with a capital letter. This rule enables readers to know immediately where ideas begin and end. In addition, the following words should be capitalized:

Days of the week
Months of the year
Holidays and holy days
Geographical names including names of
  planets
  continents
  countries
  states
  counties and provinces
  sections of the country (e.g., the South)
  cities, towns, and villages
  streets, roads, and highways
  bodies of water (e.g., the Pacific Ocean)
  parks (e.g., Yosemite National Park)
  mountains, deserts, and landforms (e.g., the Grand Canyon)
Names of deities (e.g., God, the Lord, Allah, Zeus)
Names of sacred books (e.g., the Bible, the Koran)
People's names

Titles when they are part of a name:

> Aunt Rose is coming to dinner. **not** My aunt is coming to dinner.
> When Dad talks, I listen. **not** When my dad talks, I listen.

Brand or product names (e.g., Kleenex, Reebok shoes)
Names of books, plays, newspapers, magazines, songs, articles, movies, works of art, and stories
Names of nationalities, races, and religions
Names of organizations and teams
Official titles (e.g., President Bill Clinton)
The following abbreviations: U.S., M.D., Ph.D., R.R.
Official documents (e.g., the Bill of Rights)
Special events (e.g., Desert Storm)
Political parties (e.g., the Republican Party)
Periods in history (e.g., the Renaissance)

3. Does each sentence end with one of the following punctuation marks: period, question mark, or exclamation mark?

A **period** (.) is used to indicate the end of a sentence that is a statement. A **question mark** (?) is used at the end of a direct question, e.g., What can I do to make a difference? Use a period at the end of an indirect quotation, e.g., I wasn't sure what I could do to make a difference. An **exclamation point** (!) is used to express strong feeling. It should be used rarely and only to make an important point. Keep in mind, however, that every complete sentence, even if is very short, must end with a period, question mark, or exclamation mark.

4. Is each sentence complete with a subject and verb?

A complete sentence always has a subject and verb.

> *She races.*
> *He runs.*

Sentences can have more than one subject and verb.

Beth and *Roger compete* in races every year.
Beth exercises and *practices* every day.
Beth and *Roger exercise* and *practice* every day.

When writing directions or commands, the verb can be understood to be *you* or *the reader*.

[*You*] Be sure to wear comfortable shoes.

Two related sentences can be joined together by a comma and a coordinating or connecting word such as *and, but, or, for, yet, so,* or *nor*.

She ran fast, *and* she won the race.
Roger also ran fast, *but* he only came in third.

One sentence can be joined to another idea by a subordinating word such as *because, since, when, as, after, before, while, if, although, though,* or *unless*.

Roger felt happy *because* he was one of the top five runners.
Beth won the race *although* she wasn't wearing her favorite shoes.

Notice that "Roger felt happy" is a complete sentence, but "because he was one of the top five runners" is not complete by itself. "Beth won the race" is a complete sentence, but "although she wasn't wearing her favorite shoes" is not complete by itself. The subordinating word creates a fragment that needs to be connected to a complete sentence.

Notice that these sentences can be reversed.

Because he was one of the top five runners, Roger felt happy.
Although she wasn't wearing her favorite shoes, Beth won the race.

5. Does each verb agree with its subject? Does each verb have a final *-s* or *-ed* when necessary?

The present tense of the verb that follows *he, she, it,* or a singular noun requires a final *s*.

He practices before he goes to school in the morning.
She buys new running shoes every two months.

Notice that usually when there is an *s* on the subject, there is no *s* on the verb.

> *Runners* practice a lot.
> *Their shoes* wear out quickly.

There is no *-s* ending on the verbs that directly follow *to, does, did, can, could, will, would, may, might, should, ought to, must,* and *shall.*

> He *does run* for charity whenever possible.
> She *might try* out for the Olympics in 1996.

Use the *-ed* ending for the simple past tense of the verb.

> He *practiced* every day even when he had other work.
> She *bought* her new shoes in the same store.

Use the *-ed* ending on the verb that comes after the following words: *has, have, had, am, is, are, was, were, be, being.* (*Am, is, are, was, were* are also followed by verbs ending in *-ing* when they show a continuous, long term or future activity, e.g., I am taking a gymnastics class this semester. I am going to run in the marathon next November.)

> Roger *has practiced* for more than five years.
> They *have exercised* together since they met in college.
> They *had entered* races together until they graduated.
> I *am excited* each time I watch them run together.
> They *were honored* when they graduated from college.
> They *would like to be respected* for their achievements.

There is no *-ed* ending on the verbs that directly follow *to, did, can, could, will, would, may, might, should, ought to, must,* and *shall.*

6. Are there any fragments?

Fragments are incomplete sentences. They are not acceptable in academic writing, although they sometimes are used by professional writers to make a special effect. Fragments often occur when writers begin sentences with subordinating words *because, since, when, as, after, before, while, if, although, even though, though, unless,* or *whereas.*

Since she was in school.

Fragments can be corrected by dropping the subordinating word or by connecting the fragment to a complete sentence.

> She was in school.
> Since she was in school, she couldn't practice that often.

Fragments also often occur with *-ing* verbs.

> *Running* around the track many times.
> Her breath *coming* in hard bursts.
> Roger *being* the next one to take over in the relay race.

Fragments using *-ing* verbs can be corrected by connecting the fragment to another sentence. They can also be corrected by making the verb form complete or changing it.

> Running around the track many times, she was feeling strong.
> Her breath *was coming* in hard bursts.
> Her breath *came* in hard bursts.
> Roger *was* the next one to take over in the relay race.

Fragments also occur with *who, which,* and *that.*

> The coach *who* blew the whistle. She didn't see my hand signal.
> The track *which* was uneven. It slowed the runners down.
> The new shoes *that* I bought. They hurt my feet.

These fragments can be corrected by omitting the word or by connecting the fragment to the next sentence.

> The coach blew the whistle.
> The track was uneven.
> I bought new shoes.
> The coach who blew the whistle didn't see my hand signal.
> The track which was uneven slowed the runners down.
> The new shoes that I bought hurt my feet.

Be careful to use *who* for people and *which* for things.

7. Are there any run-on sentences or comma splices?

A run-on sentence or comma splice occurs when there are two or more complete sentences that are joined only by a comma or have no punctuation between them. As was mentioned with fragments, run-ons are not acceptable for academic writing, but some professional writers use them for a special effect.

> They felt good about running they liked winning.

> Beth and Roger were running in many races, they were finishing in the top five in most of them.

Run-ons can be corrected by putting a period at the end of the first sentence and then capitalizing the first word of the next sentence.

> They felt good about running. They liked winning.

Or a **semicolon** (;) can be used in place of the comma if the two sentences have a close connection.

> They felt good about running; they liked winning.

A coordinator such as *and, but, or, for, so, yet,* or *nor* with the **comma** (,) can also be used to correct run-ons.

> Beth and Roger were running in many races, *and* they were finishing in the top five in most of them.

A subordinator such as *because, since, when, as, after, before, while, if, although, though, unless,* or *whereas* can be used in place of the comma.

> When Beth and Roger were running in many races, they were finishing in the top five in most of them.

TRY A VARIETY OF WAYS TO CORRECT YOUR RUN-ONS.

8. Do your pronouns agree with the nouns to which they refer?

Pronouns should agree with the nouns in the sentence to which they refer.

> Roger always eats carbohydrates before *he* runs. *He* finds that *they* give him energy.

Beth and Leslie are in the same women's running club. *They* warm up together before races. *They* bring *their* food to the track and eat together. They often eat pasta because *it* gives them endurance for the race.

Be careful when you use words such as *everyone, everything, everybody, someone, something, somebody,* and *anyone, anything,* and *anybody*. These words must be followed with the singular pronoun of *he* or *she*.

The coach made sure that *everyone* was in *his* and *her* correct place before the race began.

9. Is your voice consistent?

Writers use *I* when they want to make a personal statement. They use *you* when giving directions. *We* is used to refer to people in general. *They* is plural and is used to refer to more than one person. *One* is singular and is less personal than *I*. Try not to shift from one to another.

10. Are all the words spelled correctly?

Keep a list of the words that you have problems spelling, and check your final draft against this list before you hand it in. Use the dictionary or spell check to make sure that all words are spelled correctly.

Keep in mind the following spelling rules.

- *I* before *e* except after *c* or when sounded like *a* as in *neighbor* and *weigh*.

friend	receive	vein
piece	conceive	sleigh
believe	perceive	reign

  Some exceptions to this rule are: *their, weird,* and *foreign*.

- When a verb ends in *-y*, keep the *y* when you add *-ing*, but when you add *s* or *ed*, change the *y* to *i*.

study	stud*ying*	stud*ies*	stud*ied*
cry	cr*ying*	cr*ies*	cr*ied*
carry	carr*ying*	carr*ies*	carr*ied*

- To make a noun that ends in *y* plural, change the *y* to *i* and add *-es*.
  festiv*y*   festiv*ies*
  inquir*y*   inquir*ies*

  If the noun ends in *-ey*, make if plural by adding *-s*.
  monk*ey*   monk*eys*
  attorn*ey*   attorn*eys*

- Be careful to include the final *-d* in the following words: *used to, supposed to,* and *accustomed to*.

11. Did you choose the best words to convey your meaning? Did you eliminate biased or sexist language?

Reread your essay making sure that all words are correctly and appropriately used. Use the dictionary or ask your friends, teacher, or tutor for help if you are unsure about a particular word.

Be careful to avoid biased language that might offend or be impolite. Use Native Americans, not Indians. Use African Americans or blacks, not AfroAmericans or negroes. Use Latino or Latina, in most cases, instead of Hispanic (this varies in particular areas, so check what is the proper usage in your locale). Use Asian American or Asian, not Oriental. Use European Americans or whites, not Anglos or WASPS.

Be fair when you describe people. If you describe a group as "a doctor, a dentist, a woman professor, and a black lawyer," you are suggesting that all people are white men unless they are specially described. Instead write, "a doctor, a dentist, a professor, and a lawyer."

Avoid sexist language. In general, use chairperson, not chairman. Use flight attendant, not stewardess. Use mechanic, not repairman. Use fire fighter, not fireman. Do not assume all doctors are men and all nurses are women. Do not use expressions such as "man and wife;" instead, write "husband and wife."

Be careful not to write "A police officer should keep *his* gun in a safe, locked place." Instead, "Police officer*s* should keep *their* gun*s* in safe, locked places." OR eliminate the pronoun by writing, "The police should keep guns in safe, locked places." Do not write, "A secretary should store *her* frequently used addresses on the computer." Instead, "Secretaries should store *their* frequently used addresses on the computer." OR eliminate the pronoun by writing "Secretaries should store frequently used addresses on the computer."

12. Did you overuse words? Could some of these words be replaced with a synonym or a pronoun?

When you proofread your writing, notice if you have used particular words over and over again. If so, use your dictionary or thesaurus (in book or computer form) to try to replace overly used words and phrases with synonyms.

You can also use pronouns to avoid frequently repeating the same words.

ORIGINAL PARAGRAPH:
Runners try to wear comfortable running shoes when they run in a race. Runners prefer to wear familiar running shoes so they will not be uncomfortable when they run.

REVISED PARAGRAPH:
Racers try to wear comfortable running shoes when they compete. Runners prefer to wear these familiar shoes so they will not have discomfort during their race.

Appendix II

Organizations and Activities to Make a Difference

We make a difference by our actions—personally, interpersonally, and globally. This appendix is included to give you some suggestions of procedures and organizations that can assist you in finding out more about your individual areas of interest.

The appendix is divided into the following strategies of action—Gathering Information, Writing to Legislators, Becoming an Aware Consumer, Becoming a Volunteer, and Participating in Society and Organizations. At the end of the description of each strategy is a short list of resources. As you become more involved, your list will grow and become more personalized to fit your interests.

GATHERING INFORMATION

Most of us begin by having an interest or idea about a problem in our society that we think is important and that warrants action. Once the problem area has been identified, we need to get more information about the problem and find out what is already being done about it.

Writing a letter is a good way to obtain information. Although your letter will be personal, a sample letter is included on page 421 to give you an idea of the form to use for a formal letter. Remember to include an SASE (stamped, self-addressed envelope) so the organization can write back to you.

Suggested Resources

These are just a few general organizations to get you started. Your local or city telephone book should help you find others that are located in your area.

Health Organizations

Alcoholics Anonymous
P.O. Box 459
Grand Central Station
New York, NY 10163

American Association of Blood Banks
1117 N. 19th Street, Suite 600
Arlington, VA 22209

American Cancer Society
National Headquarters
1599 Clifton Rd., NE
Atlanta, GA 30329

American Council for Drug Education
204 Monroe Street, Suite 110
Rockville, MD 20850

American Diabetes Association
1660 Duke Street
Alexandria, VA 22314

American Foundation for AIDS Research
5900 Wilshire Blvd.
2nd floor E.
Los Angeles, CA 90036

American Heart Association
7320 Greenville Avenue
Dallas, TX 75231

American Lung Association
1740 Broadway
New York, NY 10019

Children's Wish Foundation, Intl.
32 Perimeter Center E., NE
Suite 100
Atlanta, GA 30346

Gay Men's Health Crisis
P.O. Box 274
132 West 24th Street
New York, NY 10011

Sample Information Request Letter

Your address, Number and Street
Town, State, Zip Code

Date

National Safety Council
444 N. Michigan Avenue
Chicago, Illinois 60611

To Whom It May Concern:

I would like more information about your organization. I am interested in learning about being a safer driver and about the problems of teenagers and drunk driving. If you have any free booklets on these subjects, I would appreciate receiving them. Please let me know if you are sponsoring any activities in my area in the near future.

I have included an SASE for your response. Thank you for your attention to this matter.

Sincerely,

[signature]

NAME (typed or printed carefully)

Guide Dog Foundation for the Blind, Inc.
371 East Jericho Turnpike
Smithtown, NY 11787-2976

March of Dimes Birth Defects Foundation
1275 Mamaroneck Avenue
White Plains, NY 10605

National Handicapped Sports and Recreation Association
1145 19th Street, NW, Suite 717
Washington, DC 20036

Ronald McDonald House
3101 Berger Avenue
San Diego, CA 92123

Human Rights

American Civil Liberties Union
132 W. 43rd Street
New York, NY 10035

Americans United for Life
343 Dearborn St., Suite 1804
Chicago, IL 60604

Amnesty International, USA
322 Eighth Avenue
New York, NY 10001

The Center to Prevent Handgun Violence
1225 Eye Street, NW, Suite 1100
Washington, DC 20005

Congress of Racial Equality
1457 Flatbush Avenue
Brooklyn, NY 11210

Disability Rights Center
2500 Q Street, NW, Suite 121
Washington, DC 20007

National Abortion Federation
1436 U Street, NW, Suite 103
Washington, DC 20009

National Right to Life Committee
419 Seventh Avenue, NW
Suite 500
Washington, DC 20004

National Student Campaign Against Hunger and Homelessness
29 Temple Place
Boston, MA 02111

Animal Rights

Alliance for Animals
P.O. Box 909
Boston, MA 02103

American Association of Zoological Parks and Aquariums
Rt. 88, Ogelbay Park
Wheeling, WV 26003

American Humane Association
9725 E. Hampden Avenue
Denver, CO 80231

Cousteau Society
930 West 21st Street
Norfolk, VA 23517

The World Wildlife Fund
1250 24th Street, NW
Washington, DC 20037

The Environment

The American Camping Association
5000 State Rd., 67 North
Martinsville, IN 46151-7902

Americans for the Environment
1400 16th Street, NW, 2nd floor
Washington, DC 20036

Organizations and Activities to Make a Difference   423

Americans for Safe Food
1501 16th Street, NW
Washington, DC 20036

Center for Hazardous Material
   Research
320 William Pitt Way
University of Pittsburgh Applied
   Research Center
Pittsburgh, PA 15238

Clean Water Action
1320 18th Street, NW
Washington, DC 20036

Environmental Protection Agency
401 M. Street, NW
Washington, DC 20460

Goddard Space Center
NASA
Office of Public Affairs
Greenbelt, MD 20771

Greenpeace
1611 Connecticut Avenue, NW
Washington, DC 20009

Keep America Beautiful, Inc.
9 W. Broad Street
Stamford, CT 06902

National Council of Churches ECO
   Justice
Working Group
c/o United Methodist General
Board of Church and Society
100 Maryland Avenue, NE
Washington, DC 20002

National Recreation and Parks
   Association
3101 Park Center Drive
Alexandria, VA 22302

The Sierra Club
730 Polk Street
San Francisco, CA 94109

WRITING TO LEGISLATORS

Writing can make a difference in our world when we let our elected officials know what issues are important to us. Individuals and groups can send letters asking questions about issues, stating opinions, and/or asking for support on specific legislation.

When you write, be sure to explain the reasons for your opinions. Remember that your legislators may not know particular events that happened in your hometown and how these should impact on the way that they vote. Tell your legislators how you would like to see your tax dollars spent. Feel free to ask questions in your letter and include your name and address so you can get a response.

The appropriate form of address for members of the House of Representatives is: The Honorable (full name of representative), House of Representatives, Washington, DC 20515.

For members of the Senate, the form is: The Honorable (full name of senator), United States Senate, Washington, DC 20510.

To write to the President, Vice President, or First Lady, the address is: The White House, 1600 Pennsylvania Avenue, Washington, DC 20500.

For state officials, you can write to: (full name of state official), state capitol of your state, city, state, and zip code.

An example of a letter appears on page 425.

Suggested Resources

Contact The League of Women Voters, tel. (202) 429-1965 for information about registering to vote, learning more about issues, and learning about your rights.

Contact National Association of Realtors, tel. (202) 383-1000. Ask for a free copy of *The U.S. Congress Handbook,* which lists the names and addresses of all political representatives and gives tips for writing a member of Congress.

Contact People for the American Way, tel. (202) 467-4999 to obtain *Congressional Directory* for $7.95. This provides the names, addresses, political affiliations, and committee memberships of every member of Congress.

Contact Public Citizen, (202) 833-3000, for information about Public Citizen's Clean Up Congress Campaign, an organization founded by Ralph Nader to oversee the actions of Congress and to ensure the public good.

A book, *Dear Mr. President,* by Marc Davenport, published by Carol Publishing Company, New York, in 1991 includes 100 form letters about a variety of environmental and other issues. It also includes a complete index of legislative addresses. Readers can copy these letters to send to the appropriate persons, but the real purpose of these models is to give citizens a starting point for writing their own letters.

BECOMING AN AWARE CONSUMER

Every time we shop, we register our opinions about companies whose products we choose for their efficiency, price, packaging, and availability. As consumers, we have the power to decide which products to buy and which

Organizations and Activities to Make a Difference

Sample Letter to a Representative

Date

The Honorable (Your Representative's Name)
House of Representatives
Washington, DC 20515

Dear Representative (Name):

I would like you to support bill (bill number, if you know it)—the Family Leave Bill. I believe in legislation to support the welfare of the family and especially of children. My sister has a newborn baby, and the company where she works required her to go back to work one week after the child was born. I am aware how difficult it is for her to work and still take care of her baby. It was hard for her to get good child care for an infant, but she could not afford to lose her job. I think this bill is important, and I would like you to support it.

What is your position on this issue?

Sincerely,
(Your name and address)

---

to avoid. As part of this process, we should ask ourselves some of the following questions when we make shopping decisions:

- Is the product recyclable? If so, do I recycle soda and beer cans and bottles, plastic containers and newspapers?
- Is there excessive packaging? Can I buy this with less packaging and therefore less waste?

- Can I buy this in bulk quantity?
- Is this product hazardous to use (especially important if you have children)? If so, is there a nonhazardous substitute for cleaners, pesticides, paints, solvents, etc.?
- Do I need to buy a disposable item that will be thrown away, or is there a substitute that can be used over and over?
- Do I need to use plastic, or will paper, cloth, or glass work as well?
- Do I bring used paper or plastic bags when I shop? Or do I carry a canvas bag that is reusable?
- If I use plastic bags, do I try to use biodegradable ones?
- Do I buy phosphate free/biodegradable detergents and soaps?
- Do I avoid aerosol antiperspirants, hair sprays, and other aerosol sprays when possible?
- Are animals used for testing this product?
- When something breaks, can it be repaired rather than replaced?
- If this product is not used often, can I rent or borrow it rather than purchase it?
- Do I buy lower wattage light bulbs when possible?

Suggested Resources

Read *Shopping for a Better World,* available from The Council on Economic Priorities, 30 Irving Place, New York, NY 10003, (800) 729-4237, for $7.49, including shipping and handling. Bring it with you when you go shopping.

110 Things You Can Do For a Healthy Environment, Seventh Generation, (800) 456-1177, $2.00.

Toxics Stepping Lightly on the Earth: Everyone's Guide to Toxics in the Home, Greenpeace, Box 3720, Washington, DC 20007, (202) 462-8817.

"The Earth's Future Is in Your Shopping Cart," c/o National Consumers League, Suite 516, 815 15th Street, NW, Washington, DC, 20005, Attn: Shopping Guide.

To find out which companies test on animals and which do not, send for *Cruelty-Free Shoppers' Guide,* PETA, Box 42516, Washington, DC 20015, (301) 770-7444, $2.00.

BECOMING A VOLUNTEER

Working for a cause that we believe in is a powerful way to make our feelings known and to connect with other people who may benefit from our abilities and our willingness to help.

Many organizations need volunteers to continue their work. Some of the organizations you contacted to gather information might need someone of your interests and abilities to work with them. In addition, the following list of organizations are often in need of volunteers. The organization's national address or telephone number, given below, should be able to provide information about the addresses and telephone numbers of local chapters in your area.

ACTION
202-634-9108
ACTION is the Federal Domestic Volunteer Agency with more than 400,000 volunteers serving in community programs all over the United States.

Coalition for Literacy
P.O. Box 81826
Lincoln, NE 68501
(800) 228-8813—The National Contact Hotline
This number helps to link volunteers, students, businesses, and community groups with local literacy programs.

Literacy Volunteers of America (LVA)
5795 Widewaters Parkway
Syracuse, NY 13214
(315) 445-8000

Peace Corps (See Larson, page 351 for more information)
P-301
Washington, DC 20526
(800) 424-8580

National Volunteer Hotline
425 2nd Street, NW
Washington, DC 20001
(800) HELP-664

Covenant House
346 W. 17th Street
New York, NY 10011-5002
(800) 999-9999

Senior Companion Program
202-634-9108
Matches volunteers with homebound elderly to provide friendship and care.

Salvation Army
National Headquarters
799 Bloomfield Avenue
Verona, NJ 07044
201-239-0606

Student Conservation Association
P.O. Box 550
Charlestown, NH 03603
603-543-1700
Seeks volunteers for public parks and lands.

United States Jaycees
918-584-2481

Volunteers of America, Inc.
(800) 654-2297

Volunteer—The National Center
703-276-0542
A referral and information service for those wanting to volunteer in their community.

PARTICIPATING IN SOCIETY AND ORGANIZATIONS

The most fundamental way to participate in society is to vote. It is not difficult to get your voter's registration card, but you need to do this in advance of Election Day. Ask for voting information from your college, the League of Women Voters, or by calling your local legislator's office.

Recycle whenever you can. In most communities today, you can recycle paper, newspaper, magazines, typing paper, and corrugated cardboard. You can recycle many plastics; check for the recycling symbol on containers. Tires, motor oil, scrap metal, and glass also should be recycled. Cut six-pack holders into smaller pieces so they will not end up snagging fish or other marine life. Dispose of balloons by cutting them or putting them in the garbage, but not by letting them float in the air. Deflated balloons can injure wildlife.

Plant trees—the American Forestry Association has launched a nationwide campaign to plant 100,000,000 trees to combat global warming. Contact Tree People, (818) 769-4014 or the American Forestry Association (202) 659-5170 for more information.

Join the organizations that matter to you. As a member, you will receive information, meet other people with similar interests, and can join in taking action to support the causes in which you believe.

Each of us can make a difference in this world.

Acknowledgments

ALVAREZ, JULIA "Daughter of Invention," from HOW THE GARCIA GIRLS LOST THEIR ACCENTS. Copyright © Julia Alvarez 1991. Published by Plume, an imprint of New American Library, a division of Penguin Books USA, Inc. First published in hardcover by Algonquin Books of Chapel Hill. Reprinted by permission of Susan Bergholz Literary Services, New York.

AMES, JONATHAN "I Wanted to Know Why," from I PASS LIKE NIGHT by Jonathan Ames. Copyright © 1989 by Jonathan Ames. By permission of William Morrow & Company, Inc.

BARRY, LINDA "The Sanctuary of School," Education Life, *New York Times*, January 5, 1992. Copyright © 1992 by the New York Times Company. Reprinted by permission.

BATES, KAREN GRIGSBY "They've Gotta Have Us." © Karen Grigsby Bates, 1991. All rights reserved. Reprinted with permission of The New York Times Magazine.

CANDELARIA, NASH "El Patron" from THE DAY THE CISCO KID SHOT JOHN WAYNE. Copyright © 1988.

CISNEROS, SANDRA "Only daughter," by Sandra Cisneros. Copyright © by Sandra Cisneros 1990. First published in *Glamour*, November 1990. Reprinted by permission by Susan Bergholz Literary Service, New York.

GARRETT, GEORGE "The Right Thing To Do at the Time," first published in Alan Cheuse and Caroline Marshall, eds., THE SOUND OF WRITING (Anchor Books, Doubleday, 1991). Reprinted by permission.

GROGAN, DAVID & SUGDEN, JANE "Cinderellas in Toe Shoes," *People Weekly* © 1991 Time Inc.

HINDS, MICHAEL deCOURCY "Coats for the Homeless Is Shelter, Too," *Philadelphia Journal, New York Times,* March 2, 1992. Copyright © 1992 by The New York Times Company. Reprinted by permission.

HUGHES, LANGSTON "Thank You, M'am." Reprinted by permission of Harold Ober Associates Incoporated. Copyright © 1958 by Langston Hughes. Copyright renewed 1986 by George Houston Bass.

JOHNSON, SALLY "Learning the Art of Bring Up Baby,"*New York Times*, April 2, 1988. Copyright © 1988 by The New York Times Company. Reprinted by permission.

KLASS, PERRI "Mothers with AIDS: A Love Story," by Perri Klass. Copyright 1990 by Perri Klass. First published in *The New York Times Magazine.* Reprinted by permission of the author.

KRAMER, LINDA "The Physician Who Healed Himself First." Joe Treen and Linda Kramer/*People Weekly* © 1991 Time Inc.

KRYSL, MARILYN "The Hiroshima Maiden," from *Glimmer Train Stories,* Summer 1992, Issue 3, pp 67–71. Reprinted by permission.

LARSON, CHARLES R. "The Value of Volunteering," *Newsweek,* July 22, 1991. Reprinted by permission of the author.

LEVIN, SUANNA "Running Toward Victory." "Breaking the Silence" by Aliza Moldofsky. Reprinted by permission of MS. MAGAZINE, © 1991.

LING, AMY "Amy Tan." Reprinted by permission of the publisher from Ling, Amy, BETWEEN WORLDS: WOMEN WRITERS OF CHINESE ANCESTRY. (New York: Teachers College Press, © by Teachers College, Columbia University.) All rights reserved pp. 136–138.

MALCOLM, ANDREW H. "Two Intitutions Solve Common Problem," *New York Times,* February 11, 1992. Copyright © 1992 by The New York Times Company. Reprinted by permission.

MEIER, DANIEL "One Man's Kids," New York Times Magazine, November 1, 1987. Copyright © by The New York Times Company. Reprinted by permission.

NORDAN, LEWIS "Owls." Copyright © 1991 by Lewis Nordan. From MUSIC OF THE SWAMP by Lewis Nordan. Reprinted from THE MUSIC OF THE SWAMP by permission of Algonquin Books of Chapel Hill, a division of Workman Publishing Co., New York, NY.

PATTERSON, LINDSAY "My Father, Dr. Pat," *New York Times,* August 30, 1980. Copyright © 1980 by The New York Times Company. Reprinted by permission.

POWELL, COLIN "The Unwritten American Bargain." Reprinted, with permission, from the *American School Board Journal,* February 1991. Copyright 1991, the National School Boards Association. All rights reserved.

QUINDLEN, ANNA "Getting Involved." From LIVING OUT LOUD by Anna Quindlen. Copyright © 1987 by Anna Quindlen. Reprinted by permission of Random House, Inc.

Acknowledgments

RÍOS, ALBERTO ALVARO "West Real," by Alberto Alvaros Ríos originally appeared in *Ploughshares,* Vol. 18, No. 1, Spring 1992.

ROBBINS, WILLIAM "Acts of Charity Spring from Rock of Honesty," *New York Times,* December 16, 1990. Copyright © 1991 by the New York Times Company. Reprinted by permission.

RODRIGUEZ, RICHARD "Reading to Know." From HUNGER OF MEMORY by Richard Rodriguez. Copyright © 1982 by Richard Rodriguez. Reprinted by permission of David R. Godine, Publisher.

ROHTER, LARRY "The Poor Man's Superman: Scourge of Landlords," *New York Times,* August 15, 1988. Copyright © 1988 by The New York Times Company. Reprinted by permission.

SHANKER, ALBERT "Merit Gets Them Nowhere." Reprinted with permission of the American Federation of Teachers.

SHEEHAN, SHARON "Another Kind of Sex Ed," *Newsweek,* July 1992.

STONE, ELIZABETH "Family Stories: Why They Matter." From BLACK SHEEP AND KISSING COUSINS by Elizabeth Stone. Copyright © 1988 by Elizabeth Stone. Reprinted by permission of Time Books, a division of Random House, Inc.

TAN, AMY "Mother Tongue." Copyright © 1990 by Amy Tan. First published in *The Threepenny Review.* Reprinted by permission of the author.

TERRY, WALLACE "It's Such a Pleasure to Learn." Reprinted by permission of the author and the author's agents, Scott Meredith Literary Agency, Inc., 845 Third Avenue, New York, NY 10022.

"The Voice of the Land Is in Our Language."

WEBER, JOSEPH "Meet Dupont's 'In-House Conscience.'" Reprinted from June 24, 1991 issue of *Business Week* by special permission, copyright © 1991 by McGraw-Hill, Inc.

WEESE, DOUGLAS M. "Iron Man," *Horizon Air,* March 1992, pp. 18–19. Reprinted by permission.

YOSHIMOTO, BANANA "Moonlight Shadow." From the book KITCHEN by Banada Yoshimoto. Copyright © 1988 by Banada Toshimoto, translation copyright © 1992 by Megan Bakus. Used with the permission of Grove/Atlantic Monthly Press. Paperback available from Washington Square Press, 1230 Avenue of the Americas, New York, NY 10020.

The publishers have made every effort to locate the owners of all selections of copyrighted works and to obtain permission to reprint them. Any errors or omissions are unintentional and corrections will be made in future printings if necessary.

Index

"Acts of Charity Spring From Rock of Honesty," 146–148
"Aliza: Breaking Silence," 281–283
Alvarez, Julia, 90–96
Ames, Jonathan, 167–170
"Amy Tan," 47–49
Analyzing, 313
"Annie John," 216–219
"Another Kind of Sex Ed," 182–184
Audience awareness, 278

Barry, Lynda, 202–205
Bates, Karen Grigsby, 107–110
Biography, writing and reading, 10
Brainstorming, 4–5

Candelaria, Nash, 269–276
Cause and effect, 87
Chronological order, 206
"Cinderellas in Toe Shoes," 338–340
Cisneros, Sarah, 34–37
Closing paragraph, 31

Clustering, 5–6
"Coat for the Homeless Is Shelter, Too," 324–326
Comparison-and-contrast essay, 186
Conclusion, 31
Connections between ideas, 348

"Daughter of Invention," 90–96
Deductive reasoning, 38–39
Definition essay, 163–164
Description, 119, 228, 328, 341–342
Dialogue writing, 156–157
Drafting, 8–9
Draper, Robert, 114–117

Editing, 9–10
"El Patrón," 269–276
Event, description of, 341–342
Explanation, 163–164

Facts vs. opinions, 179
"Family Stories," 20–22

Figures of speech, 236
First person, 50
Freewriting, 6–7

Garrett, George, 288–292
General to specific, 38–39
"Getting Involved," 159–162
Grogan, David, 338–340

Hinds, Michael deCourcy, 324–326
"Hiroshima Maiden, The," 365–368
Hughes, Langston, 152–155

Ideas, connecting, 348
Importance order, 307
Induction, 284
Interviewing, 254
Introductory paragraph, 23–24
Inventing, 4–8
"Iron Man," 84–86
"It's Such a Pleasure to Learn," 248–252
"I Wanted to Know Why," 167–170

Johnson, Sally, 344–346
Journalistic thinking, 7
Journalistic writing, 81
Journal keeping, 7–8

Kincaid, Jamaica, 216–219
Klass, Perri, 174–177
Kramer, Linda, 223–226
Krysl, Marilyn, 365–368

Larson, Charles A., 351–353
"Learning the Art of Bringing Up Baby," 344–346
Levin, Susanna, 78–80
Ling, Amy, 47–49
Lipsky, David, 123–136
"Locker Room, The," 189–191

"Meet Du Pont's 'In-House Conscience,'" 303–306
Meier, Daniel, 100–103

"Merit Gets Them Nowhere," 358–360
Moldofsky, Aliza, 281–283
"Moonlight Shadow," 375–401
"Mothers with AIDS: A Love Story," 174–177
"Mother Tongue," 53–59
"My Daughter Smokes," 26–29
"My Father, 'Dr. Pat,'" 41–43

"Narration," 69–70
Narrators, types of, 97–98
New York Times, 331–333
Nordan, Lewis, 64–68

Object description, 328
"One Man's Kids," 100–103
"Only Daughter," 34–37
Opinions vs. facts, 179
Order, chronological, 206
Order of importance, 307
"Owls," 64–68

"Pan Asian Repertory Theatre's Tisa Chang," 297–299
Patterson, Lindsay, 41–43
Person, description of a, 228
Persons, first, second and third, 50–51
Persuasion essay, 212–213
"Physician Who Healed Himself First, The," 223–226
Place, description of, 119
Point of view, 97–98
"Poor Man's Superman, Scourge of Landlords, The," 262–265
Powell, Colin L., 209–211
Process essay, 149–150

Quindlen, Anna, 159–162

"Reading to Know," 239–243
Reading and writing as interconnected, 8
Revising, 9
"Right Thing to Do at the Time, The," 288–292

Index

Ríos, Alberto Alvaro, 231–234
Robbins, William, 146–148
Rodriguez, Richard, 239–243
Rohter, Larry, 262–265
"Running Toward Victory," 78–80

"Sanctuary of School, The," 202–205
Second person, 50
Sentence variety, 335
Shanker, Albert, 359–360
Sheehan, Sharon A., 182–184
Showing versus telling, 104
Shreve, Susan Richards, 189–191
Siegal, Fern, 297–299
Specific to general, 284
Step-by-step process essay, 149–150
Stone, Elizabeth, 20–22
Sugden, Jane, 338–340
Summary writing, 362

Tan, Amy, 53–59
Terry, Wallace, 248–252
"Thank You, M'am," 152–155
Thesis statement, 60–61
"They've Gotta Have Us," 107–110
Third person, 50–51

"This Lady Came Down from the Mountains," 114–117
"Three Thousand Dollars," 123–136
Tone, 293
"Two Institutions Solve Common Problem," 331–333

"Unwritten American Bargain, The," 209–211

"Value of Volunteering, The," 351–353
"Voice of the Land Is in Our Language, The," 310–312

Walker, Alice, 26–29
Weber, Joseph, 303–306
Weese, Douglas M., 84–86
"West Real," 231–234
Word choice, 369
Writing biography, 10
Writing process, 4–10
Writing and reading as interconnected, 8

Yoshimoto, Banana, 375–401